The Minister's C
Disorders and T

The Minister's Guide to Psychological Disorders and Treatments, 2nd edition, is a thorough yet succinct guide to everything a minister might need to know about the most common psychological disorders and the most useful mental health treatments. Written in straightforward and accessible language, this is the minister's one-stop guide to understanding common mental health problems, helping parishioners who struggle with them, and thinking strategically about whether to refer, and if so, to whom. This thoroughly updated edition is fully aligned with the latest edition of the *Diagnostic and Statistical Manual of Mental Disorders* (*DSM-5*) and the latest evidence regarding evidence-based psychological treatments. The second edition also contains a new chapter on ministerial triage as well as additions to the *DSM-5* such as autism spectrum disorder and somatic symptom disorders. Written with deep empathy for the demands of contemporary pastoring, this guide is destined to become an indispensable reference work for busy clergy in all ministry roles and settings.

W. Brad Johnson, PhD, is professor of psychology in the department of leadership, ethics, and law at the United States Naval Academy and a faculty associate in the Graduate School of Education at Johns Hopkins University. He is a clinical psychologist and former lieutenant commander in the Navy's Medical Service Corps.

William L. Johnson, PhD, was professor emeritus of the department of psychology at Whitworth University while maintaining an active private practice in psychology. For much of his career, he was a church elder and busy consultant to a generation of pastors.

The Minister's Guide to Psychological Disorders and Treatments

Second Edition

W. Brad Johnson and
William L. Johnson

Routledge
Taylor & Francis Group

NEW YORK AND LONDON

First published 2014
by Routledge
711 Third Avenue, New York, NY 10017

and by Routledge
27 Church Road, Hove, East Sussex BN3 2FA

Routledge is an imprint of the Taylor & Francis Group, an informa business

Library of Congress Cataloging-in-Publication Data

Johnson, W. Brad.
[Pastor's guide to psychological disorders and treatments]
   The minister's guide to psychological disorders and treatments /
by W. Brad Johnson and William L. Johnson. — Second Edition.
      pages cm
   Rev. ed. of: The pastor's guide to psychological disorders and
treatments. c2000.
   Includes bibliographical references and index.
   1. Pastoral psychology.   2. Psychiatry and religion.   I. Title.
   BV4012.J645 2014
   253.5′2—dc23
   2013048262

ISBN: 978-0-415-71244-6 (hbk)
ISBN: 978-0-415-71245-3 (pbk)
ISBN: 978-1-315-88405-9 (ebk)

Typeset in Minion
by Apex CoVantage, LLC

Lovingly dedicated to Rachel H. Johnson,
an extraordinary woman

Contents

Foreword

Fourteen years ago, I was asked by my friends Brad and Bill Johnson to write a foreword for the original edition of this book. I was then a pastor, and now, after 29 years of pastoral ministry, I sit on a seminary faculty. I was delighted to discover upon arrival at this seminary that the first edition of *The Pastor's Guide to Psychological Disorders and Treatments* was a required textbook in the Introduction to Pastoral Counseling course. With continued changes in the world of psychology and with the publishing of the *DSM-5*, there is need for this new edition.

Three years ago, Bill Johnson went to be with the Lord after a courageous and unrelenting battle with Parkinson's disease. I don't know if I ever watched such deep suffering with such transforming grace. I deeply miss Bill's earthly presence. I had the joy of serving in a congregation where Bill was an elder. While he made an indelible mark for many as a professor of psychology as well as in private practice, for me he was a spiritual mentor and guide. On this earth, he taught me more about being a pastor than any of my many professors. I have met no one that understood the dimensions of faith and psychology so well. In life and in death, he was the Lord's. Brad Johnson has updated their previous joint work, with Bill's fingerprints likely remaining on every page. Brad is a remarkable soul in his own right, and in many ways a treasure in the Christian community as well as in his work at the United States Naval Academy. By knowing this family, "the lines have fallen for me in pleasant places."

This is a vital and important book for the pastor. We often enter pastoral ministry with pictures of pulpits and visions of renewal in our hearts. What is often a surprise is the enormity of the pastoral needs all around us. Sometimes the presenting issue is simple and straightforward. More often it is complex and beyond our ability to discern. The field of psychology is vast and specialized. Our seminary training in pastoral areas is usually limited, and we feel ill equipped for the demands of the crisis before us. For such pastors, this book is a tremendous resource. It places the psychological information into the context of the pastor's role in shepherding a church community. The authors offer guidelines for assessing when a referral to another mental health professional is necessary. The Johnsons nimbly integrate faith and therapy together. In my years in ministry, I have not seen such a comprehensive resource for pastoral care actually aimed at pastors. This is a book that should reside on every pastor's shelf. May this book allow others to find healing through your shepherding of their souls!

Jim Singleton, ThD
Associate Professor of Pastoral Leadership and Evangelism
Gordon-Conwell Theological Seminary

1   Why a Minister's Guide?

Ministry may be one of the most difficult jobs in the world. Pastor Paul Tripp recently called the minister's life—with its unrelenting personal and spiritual demands—a *dangerous calling*.[1] Ministers are called to be active and wise pastoral shepherds to a wide range of flawed and fallen human beings. To make matters worse, pastors themselves are mortal, imperfect, and naturally limited in their capacity to understand and help with every problem and situation presented by parishioners. In addition to preaching, teaching, evangelizing, and generally administering the local church, pastors are likely to spend a great deal of time counseling men, women, and families who come to them with the widest possible array of personal problems. At times, psychological disorders undermine parishioner health and happiness.

Only recently have seminaries begun to consistently teach professional pastoral care skills to seminarians; this may amount to a single course in pastoral counseling.[2] The extent to which these seminary courses address specific varieties of emotional and behavioral problems—including prevalent mental disorders—varies widely. Imagine the freshly minted parish minister standing before his or her congregation on Sunday morning. Among the faces staring back, the minister recognizes a couple who has just admitted their schizophrenic son to a psychiatric hospital, a new mother suffering unremitting depression following the birth of her daughter, a middle-aged woman anxiously ruminating about unexplained physical symptoms, and a recent widower who the minister knows is contemplating suicide. How comfortable will the minister feel helping these parishioners? In our experience, some ministers find themselves particularly gifted when

1

it comes to counseling; some even discover counseling—including the ability to recognize, discuss, and help a parishioner find help for a psychological disorder—to be the component of ministry they most enjoy. But others do not feel at all called to this task; these pastors fear or even loathe the demands of counseling parishioners.

Here is the rub: Regardless of how much a minister does or does not enjoy helping church members with emotional problems, survey data suggest that when people experience distress, 40 percent go to their clergyperson first.[3] As a result, the average pastor reports spending between 10 percent and 46 percent of his or her time counseling. Unlike healthcare professionals, clergy cannot simply refer—at least not at first—a suffering parishioner. The minister may be the first and perhaps only person some congregants suffering psychological disorders will allow into their private lives.[4] So, despite the fact that some ministers have little formal training in correctly identifying and confidently discussing emotional and behavioral problems with parishioners, nearly one-half of parishioners will first turn to their pastor when distressed.

The pastoral care tradition in Christian ministries is always associated with the image of the shepherd.[5] For clergy called to the profession of ministry, pastoral care involves the responsibility for caring for the whole community, including those with all manner of emotional distress, problem behavior, and even acute mental illness. Just as the lost lamb tugs at the minister's heart, so do the sheep that are suffering. We think there might be no coincidence about the fact that the pioneer and founder of clinical pastoral education (CPE), Anton Boisen, lived his entire life battling schizophrenia.[6] Suffering his first bout of psychosis as a very young man, Boisen went on to open the first unit of CPE at Worcester State Hospital, a psychiatric facility. Following Boisen's lead, effective pastors must develop wisdom and practical competence in understanding the complicated interaction of spiritual health, heredity, biochemistry, and environmental factors in creating psychological disorder.

This is a guide to the varieties of *mental illness*: a collective term for a group of disorders that affect how a person thinks, feels, and behaves.[6] Nearly one-third of the population in most Western countries meet sufficient criteria for diagnosis with a mental disorder.[7] Further, in any 12-month period, more than one-fourth of the U.S. population, roughly 60 million adults, suffers from mental or addictive disorders.[8] Less than one-third ever receives professional help. This would suggest that ministers and family physicians would be called upon to help individuals and families with a wide range of sometimes quite serious problems. These may include difficult psychiatric syndromes such as depression, trauma-related syndromes, panic, phobias, drug or alcohol dependence, psychotic disorders, or chronic personality disorders, as well as comparatively less serious concerns such as marital or sexual problems, low moods, problems with children, job-related difficulties, grief, and stress-related conditions. Although many ministers might be undaunted by this list and may have specialized training in pastoral counseling, most are unlikely to feel qualified to treat serious emotional or psychiatric problems. In our experience, there is often a wide range of skill level and confidence among pastors when it comes to determining which problems to address in counseling and which to refer to a mental health professional. Consider the following three case vignettes:

Marlyce, a 32-year-old divorced mother of two, presents for her first pastoral counseling appointment. Marlyce is new to your church, and you know very little about her or her background. In this first counseling session, Marlyce is dressed quite provocatively and insists on sitting close to you during the session. She then begins to describe a lengthy history of sexual abuse and chronic symptoms of depression and suicidal thinking. She has been treated with antidepressant medication for several years, and episodes of suicidal behavior have resulted in at least four psychiatric hospitalizations. In your office, she is tearful and has frequent outbursts of angry screaming when describing her abuse and "all the men" who have "used" her over the course of her life. Marlyce ends the session by stating that you'll probably turn out like "all the rest" and that she feels like hurting herself. She abruptly leaves without scheduling another appointment to see you.

Steven is a 51-year-old married construction worker. He has been a solid member of the church for three decades and has always been a stable family man. Steven began coming to you six months ago for "guidance" about feelings of despair and hopelessness, which he had never before experienced. He has worked diligently in pastoral counseling sessions with you on exploring the root of his depressed mood. He has had no major life changes and appears to have much to look forward to. A recent physical exam showed him to be healthy. He has become even more active in scripture study, prayer, and fellowship opportunities through the church. In spite of this, he begins to appear increasingly disheveled, he sleeps only three to four hours per night, and his wife complains to you that Steven is "barely eating." For the first time in his life, Steven is completely disinterested in sex.

Anthony Jones and his parents call and request an "emergency" appointment with you on Saturday afternoon. Anthony is 16-year-old and the youngest of three Jones children. When the Joneses arrive, it is apparent that a significant crisis has occurred. Anthony sits as far away from his parents as possible and glares at the ground. He has a swollen lower lip. His mother appears horrified and shaken while his father is obviously quite angry. You immediately hear that Anthony's parents discovered a significant amount of methamphetamine in Anthony's bedroom earlier that day. They note that their son had been increasingly secretive and withdrawn during the past year. His grades had slipped, and he had begun affiliating with a group of friends with whom his parents are quite uncomfortable. Anthony admits grudgingly that the amphetamine is his, that he "needs it," and that he "will never live with them again," pointing at his parents. At this, Mrs. Jones becomes hysterical. You then learn that Mr. Jones became so enraged with his son that he punched him in the mouth after discovering the drugs in his room.

How would you proceed with these parishioners? What are the primary concerns in each case? Do they suffer from formal psychological disorders? Would it be wise to engage any of them in an ongoing pastoral counseling relationship? Do their presenting symptoms suggest the need for referral to a mental health specialist? What type of professional is indicated? What treatments are likely to be offered? Because of widely varied seminary and postseminary experiences with mental health services and counseling skills, responses to these questions may be remarkably varied among members of the clergy. Rest assured, however, that each of these cases would prove quite challenging to most mental health professionals as well!

Over the course of our careers, each of us has had the pleasure of working closely with a number of excellent pastors in several different denominations. As psychologists and active church members, we often found ourselves called on by our own pastors, and others in the community, to help with difficult personal problems among church members. Most often, these pastors were providing excellent ministerial care in the sense of tremendous caring, steadfast support, and facilitation of referrals for problems that appeared more serious. However, there were often questions about how to refer parishioners, what signs and symptoms indicated significant pathology, which problems were manageable via counseling, prayer, and pastoral support, and which problems might necessitate more intensive mental health treatment. Pastors wondered about the type of psychiatric disorder indicated by certain symptoms and to which type of professional various members should be referred. They had excellent questions about the type of training indicated by specific professional degrees and which psychological treatments were most likely to be effective for certain problems. They also experienced ethical and legal quandaries about referring church members and wondered what to do when parishioners had bad experiences with mental health professionals. Finally, there were "crisis" calls regarding how to proceed and who to contact when a member was suicidal or involved in an episode of domestic violence.

We decided to write this guide for our friends. It is for ministers who work hard at meeting their flocks where they are, in the midst of human frailty and an often insane world, and for ministers with some training in pastoral care, but seldom an expertise in psychology or psychiatry. This book is designed to be a quick and easy reference source for parish clergy, institutional chaplains, and well-trained laity interested in the essential concerns posed by common psychological (psychiatric) disorders (we use the terms "psychiatric" and "psychological" interchangeably). We begin by summarizing the most common forms of mental health treatment; we emphasize those treatments that are considered most effective. We also describe commonly used psychological tests and the most common psychiatric medications. Next, four chapters are devoted to a careful summary of the major psychological disorders. We discuss how to select a mental health professional and what kinds of expertise may be indicated by certain degrees and credentials. The most important ethical guidelines and practice standards for mental health professionals are outlined. Finally, a brief chapter is devoted to *pastoral triage*—the art of quickly determining the nature and severity of a parishioner's mental health condition and when indicated, making a helpful referral.

As Howard Clinebell and other luminaries in the field of pastoral care have often observed, it is imperative that clergy respect the real limits posed by their time, training, and competence.[4] A well-timed, empathic referral to a trusted mental health professional is both a caregiving gift to an impaired parishioner and a hallmark of self-awareness and respect for the limits of one's competence in this area. We hope this guide assists ministers with identifying the various psychiatric disorder categories and appreciating the sometimes hazy contours between serious and less serious conditions so that they will be empowered to make more precise and therefore effective referrals.

We have written this guide in hope of offering ministers a useful and fruitful resource as they attempt to help children, adults, and families in their churches. We hope it comes to be a tattered and much-referenced guidebook for those who counsel as part of their ministries. Most of all, we hope this guide will serve God's kingdom as pastors find the right services for parishioners in need.

Notes

1. Tripp, P. D. (2012). *Dangerous calling: Confronting the unique challenges of pastoral ministry.* Wheaton, IL: Crossway.
2. Roberts, S. B. (Ed.). (2012). *Professional spiritual and pastoral care: A practical clergy and chaplain's handbook.* Woodstock, VT: SkyLight Paths Publishing.
3. Benner, D. (2003). *Strategic pastoral counseling: A short-term structured model* (2nd ed.). Grand Rapids, MI: Baker Book House.
4. Clinebell, H. (2011). *Basic types of pastoral care and counseling* (Rev. ed.). Nashville, TN: Abingdon Press.
5. Patton, J. (2005). *Pastoral care: An essential guide.* Nashville, TN: Abingdon Press.
6. Lowery, M. J. G. (2012). Behavioral health. In S. B. Roberts (Ed.), *Professional spiritual and pastoral care: A practical clergy and chaplain's handbook* (pp. 267–281). Woodstock, VT: SkyLight Paths Publishing.
7. Sherer, R. (2002). Mental health care in the developing world. *Psychiatric Times, 19*(1), 1–5.
8. Kessler, R. C., Chiu, W. T., Demler, O., Merikangas, K. R., & Walters, E. E. (2005). Prevalence, severity, and comorbidity of 12-month *DSM-IV* disorders in the National Comorbidity Survey replication. *Archives of General Psychiatry, 62*(6), 617–627.

2   Types of Mental Health Treatment

In this chapter, we attempt a most ambitious task—to briefly and succinctly summarize the major mental health treatments. We begin by defining the essential characteristics of counseling and psychotherapy. We then explore the important issue of treatment "efficacy" (i.e., does therapy actually work?). We consider the necessity of referring parishioners to "Christian" or religious providers. We then summarize the essentials of psychological testing, including suicide risk assessment. The bulk of this chapter is devoted to summarizing each of the major types of mental health intervention. Specifically, we present the basics of individual, marital, family, and group therapy, psychiatric medication, inpatient hospitalization, drug and alcohol treatment, eating disorder programs, hypnosis, and electroconvulsive therapy. We conclude with a brief warning about "fads" in mental health treatment.

What Are Counseling and Psychotherapy?

Counseling and psychotherapy are often interchangeable terms that describe the process of helping another person make some psychological or behavioral change—typically from a less adaptive state to a more adaptive state. Often described as "talk therapy," counseling and psychotherapy incorporate exploration of thoughts, feelings, and behavior for the purpose of helping the client solve problems or achieve a higher level of functioning. In the mental health field, counseling is generally considered less formal and may be conducted by a nondoctoral-level practitioner. *Counseling* may address less psychiatrically acute conditions such as adjustment problems, career choices, common phase-of-life challenges, and relationship issues, while *psychotherapy* is generally thought to focus on more serious personality or psychiatric disorders—often disorders of longer duration or associated with greater life impairment. In our experience, these distinctions are not very useful. In this chapter, we use the term "psychotherapy" to encompass all approaches to helping people that are rooted in verbal interaction and a good working relationship. At times, skilled practitioners will engage in systematic treatment of serious pathology, while at other times they will simply help a client explore life options or process a stressful event. We refer to all of these approaches as psychotherapy.

In psychotherapy, a mental health professional (MHP) applies specific interventions designed to promote new understandings, behaviors, and emotions on the part of the client. The fact that these interventions are deliberately planned and systematically guided by both theory and (ideally) research evidence, makes them psychotherapy and not some less formal approach to helping. All psychotherapy is rooted in a relationship between the MHP and client. A good therapy relationship is characterized by listening, receptiveness, warmth, empathy, and a lack of negative evaluation on the part of the therapist. Undergirding all effective psychotherapy is an assumption by the therapist that people have the capacity for change. That is, clients can learn more adaptive ways of perceiving, evaluating, and responding to themselves, others, and the world around them.

Psychotherapy first emerged only a century ago with the development of psychoanalysis in the late 1800s. Prior to this, approaches to helping people overcome psychiatric disorders ranged from the barbaric to the bizarre. For example, beginning in the Stone Age, *trephining*—the practice of drilling holes in the skull to release evil spirits—was used to reduce abnormal behavior. During the Middle Ages and into the Renaissance, the primary interventions for psychiatric disturbance included exorcism and bloodletting. As late as the 1800s, staff at insane asylums would spin psychotic patients in chairs, dip them in ice baths, induce insulin shock, or lock them in cages to control aberrant behavior. Today, psychotherapy is typically practiced in the MHP's office and is centered on verbal exchange regarding the client's symptoms and concerns.

Mental health professionals may focus on a wide range of interventions that are selected in light of the specific client's strengths, deficits, and symptoms. In psychotherapy, the therapist may attempt to (1) change maladaptive behavior patterns; (2) improve interpersonal skills; (3) resolve conflicts among various motives; (4) modify irrational or dysfunctional beliefs about self, others, and the world; (5) reduce problematic and self-defeating emotional responses; (6) enhance an integrated or cohesive sense of identity;

and (7) facilitate mood change. Psychotherapy appointments are usually scheduled on a weekly basis. This allows for steady progress on the problem as well as adequate time between sessions for the client to work on issues discussed in the session, complete homework, or experiment with new behaviors and ways of thinking. Psychotherapy may or may not be reimbursed by insurance companies and, if coverage is available, it is often incomplete.

Psychotherapy is not magic. Some parishioners will make no gains or show only modest improvement after therapy. This is because psychiatric problems are often long-standing and extremely complicated. Some disorders begin in early childhood, become fixed patterns by adolescence, and are sustained in adulthood by disturbing or chaotic relationships and environments. For example, people with personality disorders (see Chapter 5) are especially resistant to change. Nonetheless, skillful psychotherapy can be helpful to most people suffering from a wide range of concerns and symptoms. For some, it may be the only real hope of achieving long-lasting change.

Although research in the field of psychotherapy suggests that young, attractive, verbal, and intelligent clients are most likely to make gains in therapy, in our experience, *motivation for change* is probably the most important determinant of outcome. In fact, we concur heartily with Albert Ellis, one of the greatest original psychotherapists. He argued strongly that for people to really improve in therapy, they had better be willing to work their rear ends off (our paraphrase) not only during the therapy sessions, but also between sessions and after therapy is finished in order to sustain therapy gains.[1] Psychotherapy research has confirmed that client motivation and a less severe and chronic mental illness are two of the best predictors of a positive psychotherapy outcome.[2]

Does Psychotherapy Really Work?

When you refer a troubled parishioner for psychotherapy, is he or she likely to actually improve? As previously noted, this may depend to a large extent on the client's motivation for change. Treatment outcome is also likely to depend on such critical factors as the therapist's technical skill and natural interpersonal gifts, the quality of the therapeutic relationship, accurate identification of the target problem, and the extent to which the treatment approach "matches" the client's problem. In 1952, Hans Eysenck, a respected German psychologist who practiced in Great Britain, published an article that sparked a great deal of debate and research on the effectiveness of psychotherapy. Eysenck concluded that over half of all persons with psychiatric distress get better on their own—with no treatment at all.

He called this *spontaneous remission.*[3] Although some people *do* get better without professional help, it turned out that Eysenck grossly overestimated the number of impaired people who spontaneously improve. Today, hundreds of research studies on the effectiveness of psychotherapy have demonstrated unambiguously that those who have therapy improve more and improve more rapidly than those who do not have therapy.[4] For example, an analysis of over 475 psychotherapy studies found that the typical psychotherapy client is better off and less distressed than 80 percent of those who remain untreated.[5] In addition, there was only minimal difference in outcome between different types of psychotherapy (most approaches to helping people change seemed to work well). So the chances that a parishioner in distress will benefit from competent psychotherapy are quite strong. Furthermore, most of the improvement is likely to occur early in psychotherapy (most treatment gains occur during the first six months of any type of psychotherapy).

Today, there is evidence that effective approaches to psychotherapy share several *common factors* or *active ingredients.*[6] Effective mental health treatment must somehow address troublesome and dysfunctional thoughts, emotions, and behaviors. To achieve that outcome, effective therapies typically include the following curative ingredients:

- *Self-control:* As clients learn to influence and control their own maladaptive thoughts, physical responses, and behavioral habits, they often experience greater mastery and less distress.[7]
- *Practicing new skills:* When clients deliberately and consistently implement new cognitive, emotional, and behavioral strategies, sustained change is more likely.
- *Insight:* As clients engage in self-exploration and introspection—guided and reinforced by the therapist—they may shift perspective and change behavior.[8]
- *Expectation of a positive outcome:* The extent to which both the therapist and the client believe in the likely efficacy of treatment will powerfully determine eventual success.

In addition, there are several psychotherapy *process variables* that consistently predict positive therapy outcomes. These include the following:

- *Therapist personal qualities:* Warmth, acceptance, and nonjudgmental positive regard.
- *Therapeutic alliance:* A strong and respectful client–therapist relationship.

- *Clear informed consent:* The therapist explains why a treatment approach is indicated, exactly how it will work, and expectations for the client's full participation.

Not only is psychotherapy likely to produce significant reductions in distress, but it is also evaluated quite positively by clients themselves. In 1995, *Consumer Reports* published a highly influential survey study of the magazine's readership regarding satisfaction with and effectiveness of psychotherapy.[9] Among the 4,100 respondents who had undergone professional mental health treatment, 85 percent believed they had improved significantly as a result of their mental health treatment and most were also quite satisfied with their MHP. Those who continued longer in therapy reported the most gain, and there were no differences among psychiatrists, psychologists, or social workers when it came to satisfaction. Readers were less satisfied with counselors and family physicians than the other provider types.

Overall, findings from psychotherapy outcome research seem to support cautious optimism regarding the effectiveness and efficacy of psychotherapy. As a general rule, parishioners who are distressed or show evidence of any of the disorders covered in this guide are likely to improve with psychotherapy delivered by a competent MHP. They are also likely to be reasonably satisfied with their care. Having said this, we recommend that you carefully read Chapter 7. There is a wide range of practitioners available to clients in most metropolitan areas. Although most are likely to be quite competent, others may be poorly suited to the profession, poorly trained, or incompetent to practice with the sorts of clients and client problems of concern to you. It is critical that you carefully screen those MHPs to whom you plan to refer. Elicit recommendations from other clergy until you have a list of consistently recommended and highly respected MHPs to whom you may refer parishioners.

Should Therapy (and the Therapist) Be Christian?

Pastor Jones lives in a community with very few Christian mental health practitioners. What is worse, the two Christian MHPs with whom Pastor Jones is familiar do not seem very competent. The few parishioners she has referred have reported little benefit from the therapy and have not remained in therapy long. Pastor Jones has heard from parishioners and friends that Dr. Hogan, an experienced psychologist (though not a Christian), is an exceptionally talented and seasoned psychotherapist. Although he does not share the faith of his religious clients, he is very sensitive to religious concerns and collaborates effectively with clergy.

Should Pastor Jones refer parishioners to Dr. Hogan? Our recommendation would be *yes*. Although it would certainly be ideal for pastors to have a number of competent Christian MHPs to whom to refer parishioners in distress, this is often not the case. If a qualified MHP is respectful of clients' faith and willing to see religious commitment as a strength in psychotherapy, then we see no reason why the MHP *must* be Christian or even religious for that matter.

We encourage you not to limit your referral list exclusively to Christian providers for the following reasons: (1) There may not be Christian MHPs in your community, or those who are Christian may not have a reputation for excellence (or even basic competence); (2) We believe God can use secular MHPs to the glory of His Kingdom in much the same way that He can use secular physicians and dentists. Although it is certainly true that the work of psychotherapy often intersects with the personal spiritual side of a parishioner at deep levels, kind and respectful secular MHPs can be expected to help parishioners with their presenting problems; (3) Very few parishioners are referred to MHPs for spiritual concerns. Rather, they suffer primarily from psychiatric distress, which should be treated by competent MHPs. Whether these MHPs have a similar faith or theological savvy is probably less important in most cases of emotional disturbance; (4) We would strongly prefer a competent MHP to one that advertises himself or herself as a Christian, but is less effective. We have found that God uses the gifts of such excellent professionals to bring relief to His people.

If you are fortunate enough to have a good Christian MHP to whom you refer parishioners, you may wonder what is distinct or unique about Christian counseling and what to expect when the MHP indicates that he or she practices a Christian approach. Although there is certainly wide variability among individual MHPs, there are at least three distinct components to competent Christian counseling that you should expect to find.[10] First, Christian therapy is *psychologically sound*. Christian psychotherapists should be up to date with the latest research in their field and use cutting-edge and scientifically sound therapy techniques when these are appropriate with their clients and not at odds with clients' faith.[11] Second, Christian counseling should be *scripturally congruent*. This means that the therapist carefully evaluates therapy techniques via the grid of a mature faith commitment. Third, Christian counseling is *Holy Spirit directed,* meaning that the Christian MHP recognizes that the outcome of counseling rests on God's power.

Keep in mind that although many parishioners may prefer a mental health professional of the same faith, others may be less concerned about this issue and some may even reject the notion of seeing a Christian provider. As long as the MHP shares—or is genuinely respectful of—a client's core values, then specific client–therapist congruence with respect to religious affiliation or doctrinal belief may not be essential to a good psychotherapy outcome.[12]

Psychological Assessment and Testing

Psychological Assessment

The initial contact between a parishioner and a mental health professional will typically set in motion a process called *assessment*. During the assessment phase of treatment, the MHP attempts to more clearly understand the nature and extent of the problem for which assistance is sought. The goal of assessment is to identify the main dimensions of the client's problem, develop a diagnosis, and predict the client's likely response to various treatment options. The process of assessment is sometimes quite brief and may be completed during the initial portion of the first session. At other times, it may be lengthy and involve the administration of multiple assessment instruments—especially when the client has many problems or when the source of his or her symptoms is unclear.

Although each type of MHP may approach assessment somewhat differently, assessment is an essential component of competent practice and, for most professionals, an ethical requirement. Why is assessment so important? Consider the following cases:

> A counselor begins "anger management" therapy for a young man who has recently developed sudden mood swings and outbursts of anger and tearfulness that are uncharacteristic. The treatment is ineffective, and only after his death from a brain hematoma does she learn about a recent head injury he suffered at work. Or consider the psychologist who discharges a 68-year-old man from the hospital emergency room because the man appears happy and claims the police were mistaken in assuming he was walking in traffic in an attempt to kill himself. After this man's successful suicide the next day, the psychologist learns the patient had recently lost his spouse of 40 years and had no other social support. Finally, imagine the pastoral counselor who immediately provides "biblical counseling" to a woman with depressive symptoms. When her symptoms do not improve, the woman feels even more depressed, assuming she has now failed spiritually as well. After she is hospitalized for severe depression and suicidal thoughts, it becomes evident that the woman has a long family history of biological depression. She improves rapidly when given the appropriate antidepressant medication.

Each of these cases offers an example of why careful assessment of each client is so important to most mental health practitioners. Appropriate treatment of a client cannot occur without a solid *clinical assessment*. This should include the causes and nature of the client's symptoms, environmental stresses and resources, personality traits, strengths and weaknesses, and the client's insight about the problem.[13] Ideally, treatment will not proceed without a clear diagnosis of the client's problem.

Although some ministers and parishioners might have valid concerns about the stigmatizing effects of diagnostic "labeling," we believe the benefits to an accurate and assessment-based diagnosis outweigh the risks. An accurate clinical diagnosis will allow a client to better understand the clinical syndrome causing havoc in his or her life. It will also facilitate accurate treatment selection and case management. In fact, numerous malpractice lawsuits have been brought against MHPs who provided ineffective or even harmful treatment because of a lack of assessment or inaccurate diagnosis of the client's problem.

Although assessment and diagnosis are both ongoing processes, the MHP will be most concerned with these activities early in his on her relationship with a parishioner. Crucial decisions will stem directly from early assessment. These decisions may include which treatment(s), if any, will be prescribed, whether hospitalization is required, which medications, if any, should be offered, and whether various family members should be included in therapy along with the parishioner. During the initial assessment, the MHP will typically want to hear about the main problem or complaint, formulate an initial diagnosis, gain some sense of the person's history and development, develop a picture of his or her context (including stressors and supports), assess the person's primary personality features (especially any signs of a personality disorder; see Chapter 5), and develop hypotheses about how the person is likely to behave in the future.

Although many sources of information may be pursued during an assessment, the MHP will typically conduct a face-to-face interview with the parishioner to glean most of the aforementioned information. Crucial to formulating an accurate diagnosis and evaluating the history and symptoms of the person seeking treatment, interviews may be informal and free-flowing or highly structured. *Structured interviews* require adherence to a series of standardized questions in specific sequence; such structure improves the reliability and validity of the diagnosis process. In addition, the parishioner may be referred for a physical examination (particularly when the primary symptoms could have a biological basis). The MHP may also engage in observation of the parishioner's behavior in his or her routine environment. For example, observing a child with behavioral problems at home or at school can be quite helpful in shedding light on the causes and reinforcements of his or her problem behavior. Assessment may also involve administration of standardized psychological instruments. *Psychological testing* is conducted by psychologists as a routine part of the assessment process.

Psychological Testing

Psychologists use scientific approaches to developing standardized psychological tests.[14] These tests allow the psychologist to obtain a sample of the parishioner's behavior in response to a set of questions or other stimuli. The person's responses can then be compared with others in his or her age and gender group, which also allows comparison of the person's score(s) to others with or without mental health problems. Tests may provide important data regarding a parishioner's personality characteristics, motivations, values, experience of specific symptoms (e.g., depression), intellectual ability, relationship skills, and so forth. Good psychological tests are carefully developed and standardized to give both reliable (consistent) and valid (accurate) results, in contrast to the popular tests one may find in magazines or on the Internet. The content of these tests is usually protected by the companies that develop and publish them. Psychologists use tests in much the same way that physicians use laboratory findings—to gain better information about the nature of a client's problem in order to select and deliver the most effective treatment. The following list highlights the major psychological tests for the assessment of intelligence, personality and psychopathology, and specific symptom distress.

Commonly Used Psychological Tests

Intelligence

Stanford-Binet Intelligence Scale—5th edition (SB5)
Wechsler Adult Intelligence Scale—4th edition (WAIS-IV)
Wechsler Intelligence Scale for Children—4th edition (WISC-IV)

Personality and Psychopathology

16 Personality Factor Inventory—5th edition (16PF)
Child Behavior Checklist (CBC)
Millon Clinical Multiaxial Inventory—3rd edition (MCMI-III)
Minnesota Multiphasic Personality Inventory—2nd edition (MMPI-2)
Rorschach Inkblot Test
Sentence Completion Test

Taylor-Johnson Temperament Analysis (T-JTA)
Thematic Apperception Test (TAT)

Specific Symptom Distress

Beck Depression Inventory—2nd edition (BDI-II)
Outcome Questionnaire (OQ-45)
Symptom Checklist 90 (SCL-90)

Intelligence tests are carefully developed and standardized measures of the various facets of intellectual ability. They typically have multiple subtests designed to tap the different manifestations of intelligence such as memory, language, comprehension, reasoning, and processing speed. These tests must be administered and interpreted by a psychologist and usually require two or three hours to complete. The result is a standard score that compares a person's raw scores with those of his or her peers. Most tests render an *intelligence quotient* or *IQ* score—the mean IQ score in all populations for which the test is normed is 100. Not only do intelligence tests give an accurate reading of a client's overall intellectual ability, but also they provide specific feedback regarding relative intellectual strength and weakness. For instance, most intelligence tests yield subscores for verbal intelligence (use and comprehension of language) and performance intelligence (spatial reasoning). Intelligence tests are also critical in detecting learning disabilities and neurological (brain) injuries or deficits.

Tests of personality and psychopathology attempt to measure personality characteristics and the extent to which a person shows evidence of one or more psychiatric disturbances. Personality tests are generally divided into *objective* and *projective* tests. Objective personality inventories are structured questionnaires, which the person completes independently; he or she must choose between response alternatives. The results are carefully quantified and compared with standard norms as well as groups from selected clinical populations (e.g., depressed patients, anxious patients, traumatized patients). The most popular of the personality inventories is the *Minnesota Multiphasic Personality Inventory* (MMPI-2). It is the most frequently used personality inventory in the world. A psychologist with experience interpreting the MMPI-2 will be able to draw conclusions about the person's approach to assessment (open or defensive) and the extent to which his or her responses are similar or dissimilar to normal and clinically disturbed groups. Other personality inventories such as the *Millon Clinical Multiaxial Inventory* (MCMI-III) and *16 Personality Factor Inventory* (16PF) are also useful for specific assessment purposes.

Projective personality tests are unstructured because they rely on pictures, incomplete sentences, inkblots, or other ambiguous stimuli to elicit responses. The most famous projective technique is the *Rorschach Inkblot Test,* which requires the person to tell the examiner what he or she sees in the various inkblot stimuli. Responses are then pooled and scored. Conclusions are made about the person's personality structure, thinking style, primary concerns, and evidence of disturbance. Other commonly used projective tests include the *Thematic Apperception Test* (TAT), in which the person makes up stories to go with pictures, and the *Sentence Completion Test,* which requires the person to finish incomplete sentences. The downside of projective techniques is their unstructured nature and the fact that different examiners sometimes arrive at very different conclusions using the same test results (unreliability). Projectives should be used only to augment findings from other sources such as clinical interviews and objective tests.

Some psychological tests are designed to tap the parishioner's functioning in a specific symptom area (or several areas). For example, the *Beck Depression Inventory* (BDI-II) is a pure measure of depression. In responding to this test, the client will help the examiner understand to what degree he or she experiences symptoms of depression. The score will become one factor in determining whether a diagnosis of depression is appropriate. The *Symptom Checklist 90* (SCL-90) and *Outcome Questionnaire* (OQ-45) are brief objective tests that tap several different symptom areas and provide the examiner with clues as to which symptoms are currently most problematic.

Most standardized psychological tests may be purchased and administered only by licensed psychologists or other MHPs with specific graduate training in the psychometric properties of tests and test interpretation. To find information on any psychological test, we recommend consulting either *Tests in Print* (TIP)[15] or the *Mental Measurements Yearbook* (MMY).[16]

Suicide Risk Assessment

Assessment of suicide risk is among the most vexing and difficult tasks faced by MHPs. Professionals often must decide whether to have suicidal clients admitted to a psychiatric hospital or to send them home. They must decide whether to call the police, and even warn others about the client's condition, or whether to maintain confidentiality and attempt to provide outpatient treatment alone. Not only are the consequences of incorrect clinical decisions in this area potentially grave, matters are made worse by the fact that the decision to attempt suicide is often complex and influenced by many factors. Therefore, even the most seasoned and conservative MHPs may at times "miss" indicators of suicidal thinking in clients. And of course, some people suffering psychological problems kill themselves without giving their therapists any warning at all.

In evaluating a client's risk of suicide, MHPs will use multiple sources of data including psychological test results, the client's behavioral and verbal presentation, information about his or her history (especially previous episodes of suicidal behavior or impulsive acting out), an analysis of the client's environment, and input from significant others in the client's life.[17] The most common predictors of suicide are summarized in the following list.

Common Predictors of Suicide Risk

1. *Demographics:* Older white males are most likely to commit suicide, followed by young inner-city black men. Women are 1.5 to 3 times more likely than men to attempt suicide while men are about 3 times more likely than women to complete suicide.
2. *Depression:* Depressed people are much more likely than others to kill themselves.
3. *Alcoholism and drug use:* Both are highly correlated with suicide.
4. *Suicidal thoughts, talk, and preparation:* Those who actually kill themselves *are* likely to have contemplated it for some time, talked with someone about it, and even made plans.
5. *Previous suicide attempts:* A substantial proportion of those who kill themselves have attempted at least once before.
6. *Lethality of method:* Overall, men choose more lethal methods; lethality predicts successful completion.
7. *Isolation and loss of support:* Those with little social support and those who have recently lost a loved one or ended a relationship are at higher risk for suicide.
8. *Hopelessness:* This is one of the strongest predictors of suicide. Clinicians are most alarmed by clients who appear to have lost all hope for change or improvement.
9. *Modeling:* A family—or close acquaintance—history of suicide predicts higher risk.
10. *Life stress:* Recent economic, employment, or relational stress as well as recent exposure to a trauma are all risk factors for suicide.
11. *Impulsivity:* Those with a history of impulsive behaviors (e.g., violence or substance abuse) are at increased risk of impulsive suicidal behavior.

It is important that ministers remain alert to signs of suicidal thinking and behavior among parishioners. If a pastor has referred a parishioner for evaluation of suicide risk, it is essential that he or she follow through to ensure that the parishioner makes contact with the provider. After this has occurred, it is important that the pastor contact the MHP to report new indications of suicide risk should they become evident. Of course, this is most helpful if the parishioner has signed a release allowing the MHP to talk with the pastor. Keep in mind that MHPs are acutely concerned about suicide risk among their clients. They have clear moral, ethical, and professional responsibilities to place the life and welfare of their clients above all else. Most MHPs will be highly attuned to suicide risk factors.

Individual Psychotherapy

At the start of this chapter, we defined and discussed counseling and psychotherapy. In this section, we briefly describe the major approaches MHPs might use to treat individual clients in psychotherapy. Unlike marital, family, or group psychotherapy, these interventions are focused on an individual client. The MHP will attempt to help the parishioner make some discernible change in line with his or her therapy goals. Changes might include reduction or elimination of distressing symptoms, development of new understandings of self or others, improvement in specific skills (e.g., assertiveness or interpersonal skills), and increased flexibility and adaptability. The therapist typically provides an environment in which the client can practice new ways of feeling and acting. Of course, the MHP brings much more than skills and techniques to the therapy enterprise. His or her personality (including empathy, warmth, and kindness) is a critical ingredient in creating a strong *therapeutic relationship* (sometimes called a good working alliance).

Although there are hundreds of "types" of psychotherapy, in reality, most of these can be easily reduced to a handful of original and distinct "schools" of psychotherapy.[18] In the subsections that follow, we summarize the four most common types of individual psychotherapy. These are *psychodynamic, behavioral, cognitive-behavioral,* and *humanistic* psychotherapies. Although each of these approaches to therapy can be tailored to the beliefs and concerns of religious clients, some may be more problematic for parishioners than others. For an excellent Christian examination of each approach, we recommend Jones and Butman's book, *Modern Psychotherapies: A Comprehensive Christian Appraisal.*[19] Keep in mind that when parishioners suffer from serious psychological disorders such as major depression, bipolar disorder, or schizophrenia, it will often be imperative that they receive psychotherapy in combination with an appropriate and sufficient dose of psychotropic medication. In this case, the psychotherapist or counselor must work collaboratively with a prescribing physician.

Psychodynamic (Psychoanalytic) Psychotherapy

Psychodynamic therapy and *psychoanalysis* are related forms of psychotherapy that emphasize techniques rooted in the writings and practice of Sigmund Freud. We briefly describe both traditional psychoanalysis and the more recent version of this approach known as psychodynamic psychotherapy.

Psychoanalysis is based on Freud's view that people are often unaware of the factors that determine their emotions and behavior. These *unconscious* factors produce psychiatric symptoms, personality problems, occupational trouble, and relational difficulties. Psychoanalysis is a long-term and intensive procedure for helping a client uncover repressed memories, thoughts, and fears (frequently developed during childhood) and understand the role these factors play in causing the client's current problems. In traditional psychoanalysis, the client is often asked to attend hour-long sessions several times per week for several years. The therapist, called an *analyst,* asks the client to lie on a couch. The analyst sits behind the client to reduce distraction.

The primary techniques of psychoanalysis include the following: (1) *free association*—the client must say whatever comes to mind, regardless of how personal, painful, or even irrelevant it may seem; (2) *analysis of dreams*—the client is asked to remember and report content from dreams, allowing the analyst to interpret the unconscious or hidden meanings and conflicts evident in the dream content; (3) *analysis of resistance*—the analyst points out and interprets a client's unwillingness or inability to talk about certain thoughts, motives, or experiences (missing sessions is usually considered evidence of resistance); and (4) *analysis of transference*—because a client often reacts to the analyst in the same manner that he or she has reacted to significant others, the analyst may point out and interpret elements of the therapy relationship as a means of helping the client understand how he or she behaves in relationships in general.

Psychoanalysis is rarely practiced by therapists today. Experience and research have shown it to be long, very expensive, and less effective than many other forms of therapy. In fact, we can think of no client problem for which we would recommend psychoanalysis as the preferred treatment. Not only is this approach unnecessarily long and expensive, traditional psychoanalysts tend to be fairly inflexible in their approaches—using only psychoanalytic techniques. Some parishioners (with plenty of time and financial resources) may find psychoanalysis interesting and personally helpful as a means of learning more about themselves and their motives. Nonetheless, this would not be an appropriate referral for the typical parishioner seeking relief from distress.

Psychodynamic psychotherapy is the contemporary alternative to psychoanalysis.[20] Although it uses many of the same principles and understandings pioneered by Freud and other psychoanalysts, sessions tend to be weekly, the client and therapist sit face-to-face, the therapist is more verbal (compared with the silence of the psychoanalyst), and the treatment process is more interactive. Instead of several years, psychodynamic therapy may range from a few sessions to a year or more, but 20 sessions are not uncommon. Psychodynamic therapists do not focus so much on hidden drives and unconscious conflicts but tend to help clients correct distorted views of their interpersonal relationships through interaction with the therapist. Exploration of important early experiences may still be part of treatment, but this occurs in a much more active and abbreviated fashion.

Short-term approaches to psychodynamic psychotherapy may be useful for some parishioners—particularly those with strong verbal skills and a great deal of intellectual curiosity. They may be less helpful for parishioners in acute distress (depression or anxiety) and more useful for those with recurrent relationship problems. Although highly skilled psychodynamic therapists may help parishioners increase self-understanding and modify unhealthy patterns of responding to others, it is important that treatment be clearly problem-focused and not unnecessarily long.

Behavior Therapy

Behavior therapy came to prominence in the mental health field in the 1960s; it is rooted in the work of prominent learning theorists such as Ivan Pavlov and B. F. Skinner. Behaviorists use change techniques based on research with animals and humans, and use such established learning principles as reinforcement (positive and negative), punishment (aversive control), extinction (weakening a behavior through nonreinforcement), and counterconditioning (substituting one behavior for another). Very few MHPs are likely to be "pure" behavior therapists. Most will use behavioral techniques when the parishioner's presenting problems include specific behaviors that are either excessive (e.g., phobic reactions, compulsive behaviors, excessive drinking) or lacking (e.g., attentiveness, social interaction, self-care), or both. Behavior therapies are quite pragmatic because they focus on the elimination of problematic behaviors and strengthening of new, more adaptive responses. In contrast to the psychodynamic therapies, behavioral approaches do not emphasize such things as the parishioner's personal history or inner conflicts. Behavior therapists use both the presentation and removal of rewards as well as aversive consequences to achieve their therapeutic goals—which are typically concrete and easy to measure.

Behavior therapists tend to use some very specific and well-researched interventions with their clients.[21] *Extinction,* one of the most common approaches to modifying behavior, involves removing whatever reinforcements are maintaining a problematic behavior. For example, a child who is acting out at school may immediately be reinforced by the attention he or she receives from teachers and peers. The behavior therapist may work with the teacher to cease giving the child any attention when he or she acts out, focusing on children who are behaving appropriately instead. Attention will be redirected at the child only when his or her behavior has become appropriate again. One of the most common behavioral techniques, based on the principle of extinction, is *flooding.* In flooding, the client is encouraged to face his or her real-life anxiety-arousing situation, usually with the therapist in a coaching role, and is highly encouraged not to avoid or attempt to escape the situation (the client's previous maladaptive response). Thus, the agoraphobic client (see Chapter 3) is taken to a busy mall and remains there with the therapist until his or her anxiety subsides, thereby learning a new response to the mall. An alternative to flooding is *imaginal flooding,* in which the client faces his or her feared situation using only imagery. Using imagery, a man so fearful of germs that he washes his hands 30 times a day may be asked to imagine (in vivid detail) falling into the hole of an outhouse. Although intensely anxious, he is pushed to stay with the image until his panic subsides and is replaced by a less anxious or more relaxed response.

Systematic desensitization is another behavioral technique for modifying phobic behavior (reinforced by the relief of escaping or avoiding the feared object or situation). The client is taught to systematically relax himself or herself. After creating an "anxiety hierarchy" with the therapist (a list of feared situations from least to most anxiety-provoking), the client is guided to face (in life or imagination) the least fear-inducing situation while in a state of relaxation. This continues gradually until the person can remain relaxed while imagining or actually facing the most anxiety-producing object or situation on his or her list. In effect, the behavior therapist is replacing anxiety or avoidance with relaxation.

Aversion therapy involves modification of behavior using punishment. Obviously, aversive techniques should be used only after other alternatives have been tried. In one example, an extremely self-injuring autistic child may bang her head repeatedly against a wall—producing head injury and possibly brain damage. A brief electric shock delivered immediately after the child begins banging her head may effectively eliminate the behavior permanently after only a few trials. In another example, an alcoholic man may be placed on the drug Antabuse, which will cause him to become violently ill the moment he ingests alcohol.

Behavior therapists are more inclined to use *positive reinforcement* to shape desired behavior, especially with children or clients in institutions. An adult can also be taught to effectively apply reinforcements to himself or herself for desirable behavior (e.g., watching a favorite television show only if he or she has exercised). *Modeling* involves teaching clients new skills by intentionally demonstrating them and then asking clients to imitate them—usually while the therapist reinforces their behavior and helps with fine-tuning. So a parishioner fearful of talking to women (as potential dates) may learn some important social and communication skills by watching his therapist demonstrate them in the session.

Behavior therapy has the advantage of precise treatment goals (specific changes in problematic behaviors), scientifically supported treatment techniques, relative brevity, and reduced expense compared with many other therapy modalities. Behavior therapy may be especially helpful for anxiety-based problems in adults and behavior problems in children. Disorders as wide-ranging as phobias, tantrums, bed-wetting, and panic attacks are all likely candidates for behavioral techniques.

Cognitive-Behavior Therapy

Cognitive-behavior therapies (CBTs) are among the most frequently employed by MHPs today. This group of therapies emphasizes both the behavioral interventions discussed previously and the powerful effects of *thoughts* and *beliefs* on behavior and emotion. Therapy in a cognitive-behavioral framework involves collaborative agreement between client and therapist on the problems to be addressed, followed by application of a range of techniques designed to change distorted or false core beliefs. These may be beliefs about events, oneself, or other people. Cognitive-behavior therapies are generally problem-focused, brief, and quite effective for problems from anxiety to anger to depression. These techniques are generally well researched and frequently used by most MHPs at least some of the time.

Albert Ellis and Aaron Beck, the originators of CBT, each developed distinct approaches to a range of psychological problems. *Rational-emotive behavior therapy* (REBT) was developed by Ellis. REBT therapists believe that people are not disturbed by troubling or stressful events (A's), but by their irrational and self-defeating beliefs (B's) about the events in their lives.[1,22] These irrational beliefs lead to negative and maladaptive emotional and behavioral consequences (C's). So the parishioner who becomes angry with his wife following a disagreement is not angry and violent because of his wife's behavior, but because of what he tells himself *about* her behavior (e.g., "She is *damnable* for not supporting me," or "She absolutely *must* agree with me!" or "I *can't stand it* when she does that"). Irrational beliefs such as these are the target of therapy as the therapist disputes their validity, shows the client how counterproductive they are, and helps the client find helpful and rational alternatives (e.g., "I really wish she'd agree with me, but I see that sometimes she does not"). Common irrational beliefs include "I *must* be loved and approved of by those who are important to me" and "I *must* be completely successful and perfect in everything I do."

When therapists are using *cognitive therapy* as developed by Beck, they are apt to focus on the *logical errors* clients make in their day-to-day perception of events as well as *automatic negative thoughts* about events. Errors include the tendency for people to selectively focus on the negative in a situation while ignoring the positive, overgeneralizing in a self-defeating way (e.g., "The fact that I failed to complete one of my scheduled tasks today proves I am worthless"), magnifying the significance of undesirable events (e.g., "The fact that he ended our relationship means I'll never love again"), and engaging in absolutistic thinking (e.g., "The fact that she didn't call proves she hates me"). In contrast to the persuasive and confrontational style used in REBT, cognitive therapists focus more on having clients gather information (in the sense of an experiment) in order to demonstrate that their thinking was largely in error and that their assessments about themselves and events were erroneous.

CBTs are quite popular with MHPs. Many practitioners to whom you refer will employ these approaches. They are generally effective with a range of emotional and behavioral problems, and have been especially useful for treating depression and anxiety disorders. Special versions of CBT have even been developed and demonstrated to be effective for severe personality disorders (see Chapter 5). For instance, *dialectical behavior therapy* (DBT) can be quite effective in the treatment of *borderline personality disorder*— even when these clients are quite fragmented and suicidal.[23]

Humanistic/Client-Centered Therapies

Humanistic psychotherapists, sometimes known as *client-centered* psychotherapists, emphasize helping a client grow and self-actualize as opposed to helping him or her overcome symptoms or disorders. Humanists tend to view human beings as essentially "good" and simply in need of encouragement to fulfill innate potential. Influential humanistic psychotherapists included Carl Rogers, Rollo May, and Abraham Maslow. Rogers is best known for his view of the importance of the *self-concept* and the importance of clients developing congruence between their "real" selves (their actual view of themselves) and their "ideal" selves (who they would like to be).[24] Maslow is famous for the idea of *self-actualization*—the notion that when basic needs are met and people are supported and encouraged, they can achieve their full potential. Unless the typical person is excessively stressed, discounted, or otherwise blocked from doing so, he or she will generally tend to choose pathways toward personal growth and self-actualization.

In contrast to behaviorists or psychoanalysts, MHPs with a client-centered or humanistic therapy orientation will tend to be *nondirective* in the sense that they intentionally listen to clients more and intervene less often. The notion here is that with certain "necessary and sufficient conditions for change" (these include *warmth*, *empathy*, and *unconditional positive regard* from the therapist), clients will naturally become more self-accepting (achieve greater self-congruence between their real and ideal selves) and begin to make decisions that maximize their potential. Expect client-centered MHPs to be gentle and caring with clients but not especially focused on targeting specific symptoms or even making a precise diagnosis. This may be an especially useful modality for parishioners whose primary struggle is with loss, poor self-esteem, or shame resulting from harsh self-criticism.

Eclectic Psychotherapy

The MHPs to whom you refer parishioners will rarely be rigidly or dogmatically wedded to a single therapy approach. More often, they will be at least somewhat *eclectic*—meaning they tend to use techniques from more than one school of therapy depending upon the unique client and problem. In our view, this is quite desirable for a couple of reasons. First, no single approach to therapy is likely to work with every client. Excellent psychotherapists are willing to carefully tailor their approaches based on empirical research about the best treatment for a certain disorder and based on their clinical assessment of each client. Second, eclecticism reflects a willingness to place the client's improvement before dogmatic adherence to a single treatment approach. Of course, knowing an approach to therapy well is a professional strength for an MHP. We simply recommend looking for excellent training *and* flexibility. As a minister, you may wish to familiarize yourself with the major approaches to psychotherapy practiced today. The best text on this topic is Wedding and Corsini's *Current Psychotherapies*.[18]

Marital Therapy

When parishioners approach the pastor with a personal concern or request for counseling, quite often the problem will relate directly or indirectly to marital dissatisfaction or distress. In fact, counseling for couples who are married, planning marriage, or considering termination of marriage may be one of the most frequent counseling activities for all ministers. The need for skilled treatment of distressed couples may also be one of the more common reasons for referral to an MHP specializing in couples work.

Although most MHPs can practice marital or *couples* therapy, we highly recommend looking carefully for one or more specialists in this area. Marriage and family therapists, social workers, psychologists, and psychiatrists may all have reasonable competence and even expertise in this area; however, many will not. It is important to learn whether the practitioner has both training and considerable experience with couples. As a minister, it is especially important that you remain attuned to recommendations and feedback from parishioners regarding which marriage therapists in the community are most respected and effective. Which MHPs seem to most consistently keep couples working together? Which therapists are known for using the couple's spiritual commitments and faith resources in therapy? Which ones are known for not "siding" with either spouse, but encouraging both partners to take an active role in creating change? We recommend that you find MHPs with clear expertise in marital therapy, an excellent reputation for getting good results, and a therapy model that emphasizes activity-based homework assignments (e.g., practice with communication), development of needed skills (e.g., assertiveness or active listening), attention to sexual health and fulfillment, and an emphasis on both accountability and forgiveness. Perhaps the most salient focus in couples work will be the couples' processes of communication, in particular, their capacity to engage in *active listening*. Skilled marriage and couples MHPs will also help the couple to interrupt repetitive negative interaction cycles, create new patterns of interaction, and restore a sense of bonding or intimacy. On average, professional couples counseling may range from 1–3 sessions (short-term) to 12–24 sessions (long-term).

Not surprisingly, research has shown that couples who are happily married, or who have strong potential for remaining married, can be differentiated from couples with a poor probability of successfully staying together. For example, University of Washington psychologist John Gottman's research on thousands of couples has shown consistently that factors such as criticism, contempt, defensiveness, and communication avoidance are strong predictors of divorce.[25] Alternatively, couples that remain calm, speak nondefensively, validate one another, and continue to work at improving their marriages, are considerably more likely to stay together.

Marital therapy will typically address meeting each partner's needs in the relationship; active, clear, and respectful communication; forgiveness; enhanced sensitivity to one's partner's perspective; taking responsibility for one's own contribution to marital dysfunction; frustration tolerance; and modification of unreasonable expectations. Not surprisingly, a couple's commitment to the marriage is one of the strongest predictors of treatment success. Of course, many spouses will not state (or necessarily even be aware of) their level of commitment early in the marriage, and this may surface only during therapy. Although most marital therapy sessions will involve both spouses, the therapist may at times hold individual meetings with each spouse as a means of collecting background information and allowing for safe disclosure of things such as fear of harm, level of actual commitment to the marriage, and so forth. Finally, structured marital separations may at times be incorporated into therapy as a reasonable way of protecting one spouse, to allow the couple to explore volatile emotions or very painful events, or as a method of building commitment to begin the relationship anew.

Family Therapy

Roughly 60 years ago, some MHPs began offering approaches to treatment that involved the whole family. They recognized that family relationships and interaction patterns played a significant part in the health of individual family members. In fact, they discovered that although clients could be effectively treated in hospitals and other settings, their emotional disturbances and psychiatric problems reappeared when they were discharged and returned to their families.[26] Therefore, these MHPs began treating the entire family—involving all members of the family in therapy sessions. Family therapy may even include grandparents, noncustodial parents, stepparents, stepsiblings, and half siblings.

Family therapy is most often initiated when the family member with the "problem," often called the *identified patient,* is brought in for treatment. This is often a child or adolescent who is acting out or has become depressed. Mental health practitioners who practice family therapy are alert to the possibility that symptoms in one family member merely reflect the disturbance of the larger family system. In family therapy, the MHP treats the entire family and, as in the case of marital therapy, must remain impartial and committed to the health of all family members. When specific family members also require individual therapy, they are usually encouraged to see a separate MHP.

Although there are many types of family therapy, *structural family therapy* is one of the most common and most promising approaches.[27] This approach assumes that the family system is a more powerful determinant of psychological disorder than individual personality styles or conflicts. Family therapists are likely to attempt "structural" change; that is, change in the way the family is organized. This often involves eliminating problematic subsystems and shoring up poor boundaries. For example, a mother and her teenage son may form an unhealthy subsystem or alliance (because of the mother's poor boundaries) that harms the marital relationship, distances the father, and allows the son to behave as a mini-parent. The family therapist would move to confront this system problem, prescribe changes to the structure, and perhaps even have the family members act out day-to-day interactions for the purpose of illustrating structural problems and correcting them.

Family therapy is often a very useful modality—particularly when a child or adolescent appears to be acting out in a way that signals a larger system problem in the home. Although some MHPs are well trained and experienced in this treatment form, marriage and family counselors, psychologists, and social workers are probably most likely to have training in this therapy modality. As in the case of marital therapy, ask colleagues and trusted MHPs about professionals in your community with expertise in family therapy. Behavioral and structural approaches to family therapy have proven most effective with a range of presenting problems.

Group Therapy

Like individual therapy, group therapy is intended to help people learn skills, develop self-understanding, and reduce problematic behaviors or symptoms. First developed during World War II as a cost-effective approach to helping many people at once, group therapy has grown in popularity such that most communities currently have a range of ongoing group therapy opportunities for parishioners. Most groups have between 6 and 12 members and 1 or 2 leaders. Again, a range of MHPs may offer groups of various kinds. Four major types of group experiences may be helpful to your parishioners: *long-term groups, time-limited groups, focused groups,* and *self-help groups.*

Long-term therapy groups are the most traditional, yet least common approach to group therapy. Group members typically commit to attend weekly sessions for a substantial period of time (e.g., several months to several years). Members often continue in the group longer than their initial commitment, and members may come and go while the core group continues. The aim of these psychotherapy groups is typically interpersonal interaction with an emphasis on members receiving support, feedback, and, when needed, confrontation from other members. Developing a better understanding of one's own psyche and interpersonal style is usually the goal. The therapists are usually nondirective, letting the group members "work" on issues while they occasionally offer feedback and facilitate the discussion. Long-term groups may be especially useful for more verbal parishioners with chronic relational or interpersonal problems.

Time-limited groups are similar to the traditional group format just described, with the exception that the therapist contracts to work with the group members for a more abbreviated period of time (e.g., two to six months). Group members are usually selected for the group on the basis of their potential match with the other members and the primary problems of interest to the group. They are encouraged to stay with the group for the duration and to "terminate" (work through saying goodbye to the members) when the group ends. These groups have a distinct beginning, middle, and end. They usually do not add members once the group has begun. The length of the group will depend on the purpose of the group and the characteristics of its members. For example, a leader may create a two-month group for new managers for the purpose of providing intensive interpersonal feedback or a six-month group for extremely introverted and low social skill clients who have never had sustained relationships.

Focused therapy groups tend to be both time-limited and directed at a specific topic or problem area. For example, MHPs may offer groups for clients with depression, those recovering from divorce, or parents of children with attention-deficit/hyperactivity disorder (ADHD). Groups may also focus on specific skill development. For example, it is not uncommon to find groups on anger management, assertiveness training, communication skills, stress management, and weight loss. There are groups focusing exclusively on men's issues or women's issues. Focused groups offer an excellent resource for short-term and problem-specific assistance. Clients benefit not only from the group focus and therapist's expertise, but perhaps even more so from the encouragement, support, and example of other group members who share their own difficulties and work through them.

Finally, ministers may consider referring parishioners to a relevant *self-help group*. Self-help groups abound in most communities and range from Alcoholics Anonymous to Parents Without Partners to Widow to Widow (for bereaved women). Millions of Americans will use self-help groups during their lifetimes, and self-help group involvement has burgeoned during the last half-century. Self-help groups are designed for people with a symptom, disorder, situation, or experience in common who meet together to fulfill needs, overcome difficulties, or cope with a crisis.

Self-help groups are typically organized and run at the local level and are supported only by donations from participants. Information disclosed by participants remains "anonymous" or confidential. They have the benefit of informality and low cost to members. The main goals of a self-help group are providing mutual support, education, and a safe space for personal change. Although each group may have a designated leader, this person will rarely have professional mental health training but will have experience with the problem of concern to the group members. For example,

Alcoholics Anonymous (AA) is run exclusively by recovering alcoholic men and women who typically rotate leadership responsibilities.

Self-help groups are extremely diverse in makeup, focus, and effectiveness. As a minister, it is recommended that you become acquainted with the leadership of those self-help groups of greatest interest to you as referral targets. In some communities, there are groups or meetings tailored to Christians or other religious groups, and it is common for churches to sponsor their own self-help groups. These groups are ideal for parishioners with limited financial resources, those who are more needy or dependent in personality style, and those with very focused difficulties (e.g., alcoholism, drug use, grief from death of a loved one or divorce, weight problems). The only real problem we see with self-help groups is the potential that they will be the only source of help offered to a person with a serious psychiatric (or even physical) problem. For example, a severely alcohol-dependent person should not be referred to AA until *after* he or she has been carefully evaluated by a physician and possibly hospitalized for the dangerous process of detoxification from alcohol. Similarly, referring a seriously depressed and bereaved widow or widower to a self-help group for grief may be unwise until after a mental health professional determines that risk for suicide is not significant.

Psychiatric Medications

Seventy years ago, medication was seldom used to treat psychiatric disorders. At that time, a medication for the treatment of psychotic disorders—*Thorazine* (chlorpromazine)—was synthesized and used with chronically psychotic patients. The results were stunning.[28] Thorazine radically altered the care of schizophrenic patients. Instead of simply warehousing these patients in hospitals, this antipsychotic medication radically reduced their symptoms and made it possible for thousands of patients to be released from hospitals and treated as outpatients.

Today, psychiatric medications have become an integral part of the comprehensive care of persons with psychiatric disorders. Although they are frequently used in cases of more severe disorders (e.g., severe depression, bipolar disorder, panic disorder, schizophrenia), they may also be used to alleviate symptoms following a difficult event or to increase a parishioner's ability to function in specific circumstances. Far from magical cures, medications act by controlling symptoms by altering brain functioning—typically by influencing levels of chemical neurotransmitters. They correct or compensate for some biochemical malfunction in the body and help lessen the burden of a psychiatric disorder without necessarily curing it. Medications make it possible to treat people in less restrictive settings. In other words, they do not have to be hospitalized or bedridden, but can continue functioning in a reasonably successful way while working at successfully managing their disorders. In addition, psychiatric medications often make other kinds of treatment (e.g., psychotherapy) more effective. For example, a parishioner with a severe biologically based depressive disorder may be so impaired that he or she is unable to concentrate or even find the energy to get out of bed. Antidepressant medication may allow this person sufficient relief from depressive symptoms to participate in psychotherapy and continue successful employment.

As noted in Chapter 7, only physicians with MD or DO degrees may prescribe medication. Ideally, psychiatric medicine will be managed by a psychiatrist (physicians with considerable experience and training in psychiatric medications). This is particularly important when the parishioner has a serious psychiatric disorder or when his or her age, other medical problems, or other medications make prescribing more complicated. It is not uncommon for people undergoing psychiatric treatment to be placed on more than one type of medication in order to optimize therapeutic value and control side effects. It is essential that parishioners not attempt to self-medicate or alter their dosages without consulting their physicians. Physicians are prepared to take into account many variables likely to affect the way medications work in particular clients. These variables include the type of mental disorder, body weight, diet, physical conditions, habits such as drinking and smoking, and level of compliance with prescribed medications.[28]

The length of time a parishioner may be placed on medications depends on a range of factors including the specific disorder, symptom severity, and characteristics of the client (e.g., age, genetic predisposition to the disorder). Once placed on a psychiatric medication, a person generally stays on it for several months to several years to ensure stability. It can be quite harmful to prematurely withdraw a client from medication only to have him or her suffer a return of symptoms. Medications do not produce the same effects in all persons. Body chemistry, age, sex, size, and physical health all influence the medication's effect. Different psychiatric medications also take different amounts of time to reach maximum effectiveness. For example, antidepressant medications often require several weeks before significant reductions in problem symptoms occur, while some antianxiety medications take effect quite rapidly.

In this section, we briefly describe five categories of *psychotropic* (psychiatric) medications. We cover *antidepressant, antianxiety, mood stabilizing, antipsychotic,* and *stimulant* medications. We also provide short tables summarizing the most common medications prescribed in each category. These tables include both the trade name (most familiar to parishioners) and the generic name of each medication. These medications have been approved by the FDA as a result of research studies that demonstrate their efficacy with certain psychiatric disorders. For detailed information regarding any prescription medication, we recommend that parishioners consult the most recent edition of the *Physician's Desk Reference.*[29]

Antidepressant Medications

Antidepressant medications are a booming business for the world's pharmaceutical companies. They will certainly be among the most commonly prescribed medications for parishioners. Antidepressants should generally not be prescribed unless the parishioner's depression is rather severe (in the judgment of the MHP) or unless it has persisted without improvement for some time (several months or more), and interferes with normal occupational and relational functioning. Although research has shown that depressed persons who receive a combination of psychotherapy and antidepressant medication improve most rapidly, some parishioners may prefer not to use antidepressants unless psychotherapy alone proves ineffective. Others may elect to try medications alone.

In most cases, antidepressants will be prescribed for major depressive disorder (see Chapter 3). A person may be experiencing some combination of the following symptoms: depressed or irritable mood, loss of interest in previously enjoyed activities, sleep disturbance, appetite change, feelings of guilt or worthlessness, loss of energy, loss of concentration, agitation or retardation (slowed movements), and thoughts of death or suicide. Although antidepressants will usually be used for parishioners with depressive symptoms, they are often used for serious anxiety disorders as well.

Antidepressant medications will generally not take effect immediately; most require between one and three weeks to show significant benefit (if any). Some depressive symptoms may diminish early in treatment while others require more time. In general, no improvement after five or six weeks would signal the need for the physician to try a different dosage, a different medication, or discontinuation of medication altogether. Patients are usually started on low to moderate doses that are increased as it becomes clear the person tolerates the medicine satisfactorily. Antidepressants do not create a euphoric state but merely improve mood and lower anxiety. They will not have much effect on the mood of a nondepressed person and do not have addictive properties. Strong research evidence indicates that antidepressant medications are very useful in cases of severe depression, but in the case of mild or moderate depression, the efficacy of these drugs is no better than the effect of a placebo.[30]

There are several distinct types of antidepressant medication, and each type produces specific side effects, which parishioners should discuss carefully with their physicians. *Side effects* are any drug effects other than those intended as part of the therapeutic action of the drug. The following section describes the major types of antidepressants.

Selective Serotonin Reuptake Inhibitors

Today, selective serotonin reuptake inhibitors (SSRIs) are the most popular and widely prescribed of the antidepressant medications. The most recognized SSRI antidepressants are Prozac, Paxil, and Zoloft. The SSRIs act to reduce depression by blocking the brain's reuptake of serotonin (a common neurotransmitter in the brain thought to play a role in depression), thereby increasing the amount of available serotonin. These medications are extremely popular because of their relatively minor side effects; they are also less toxic and require less dosage adjustment. They tend to work better than other antidepressants without the serious side effects, and physicians have fewer precautions in prescribing them to depressed patients. Similar to other antidepressants, SSRIs do not produce euphoria but act to decrease and eliminate symptoms of depression by raising levels of serotonin. Associated side effects include headache, nausea, drowsiness, agitation, and sexual problems. However, these side effects tend to lessen—often within a few days or weeks. In 2005, the FDA attached a "black box" warning label to all SSRIs when prescribed for children and adolescents. At times, seriously depressed youth—often those who have been considering suicide as part of their depressive illness—have engaged in sudden suicidal behavior shortly after commencing treatment with SSRIs. Children, adolescents, and even young adults should be monitored carefully in the first weeks of SSRI treatment to ensure that the sudden burst of agitation and energy associated with the drugs does not suddenly enable suicidal behavior in a person previously too depressed to execute a suicide plan.

Tricyclic Antidepressants

Among the original medications for depression, tricyclic antidepressants continue to be used today in cases of severe depression—typically when a person has been unresponsive to SSRI medication. Tricyclic drugs work by increasing the levels of the neurotransmitters serotonin and norepinephrine in the brain. They typically require between two and four weeks to reach maximal effect. Possible side effects from these medications are significant and include dry mouth, constipation, rapid heartbeat, blurred vision, weight gain, serious fatigue, bladder problems, and problems with sexual functioning. However, the potential for cardiac problems is of greater concern. Tricyclics are prescribed with great caution in patients with any history of or potential for heart problems. Finally, tricyclics can be used to overdose, as they are lethal in high doses. Suicidal parishioners should typically be given only a small supply at one time. It is also important for anyone taking these medications to avoid alcohol.

Monoamine Oxidase Inhibitors

Monoamine oxidase inhibitors (MAOIs) work by blocking enzymes that normally break down the neurotransmitters serotonin and norepinephrine in the brain. This increases the level of these neurotransmitters, which elevates the person's mood. Although MAOIs were once the primary alternative to tricyclics, they are rarely used today because of the dietary and medication restrictions required in order for them to be used safely. Patients who take MAOIs must strictly avoid certain foods and alcoholic beverages (e.g., cheese, beer, wine, foods containing MSG) and many common medications (e.g., cold and allergy medicines). If they do not, they risk a *hypertensive crisis,* which could involve a sudden increase in blood pressure, vomiting, severe headache, and possibly seizures or a stroke. In addition, MAOIs have other routine side effects—including many of those previously noted for tricyclic medications. Understandably, with these significant side effects and the dangerous risk of interaction with foods and medicines, MAOIs are used only in unusual cases of depression (e.g., depression with panic attacks) or when patients do not respond well to all other antidepressants.

Other Antidepressant Medications

Finally, four other antidepressants are chemically distinct from the categories discussed previously. *Wellbutrin* (bupropion) is unique in affecting the dopamine neurotransmitter system. *Effexor* (venlafaxine) affects both serotonin and norepinephrine. *Desyrel* (trazadone) antagonizes serotonin receptors and inhibits serotonin reuptake. *Remeron* (mirtazapine) antagonizes certain adrenergic receptors and certain serotonin receptors. Each of these medications has a unique profile of side effects and should only be prescribed by a psychiatrist with considerable experience using psychotropic drugs to treat serious depression. Following is a list of the most common psychiatric (psychotropic) medications prescribed for depression.

Common Antidepressant Medications

Trade Name (generic name)

Selective Serotonin Reuptake Inhibitors (SSRIs)

    Celexa (citalopram)
    Lexapro (escitalopram)
    Luvox (fluvoxamine)
    Paxil (paroxetine)
    Prozac (fluoxetine)
    Zoloft (sertraline)

Tricyclic Antidepressants

    Anafranil (clomipramine)
    Asendin (amoxapine)
    Elavil (amitriptyline)
    Norpramin (desipramine)
    Pamelor (nortriptyline)
    Sinequan (doxepin)
    Surmontil (trimipramine)
    Tofranil (imipramine)
    Vivactil (protriptyline)

Monoamine Oxidase Inhibitors (MAOIs)

    Nardil (phenelzine)
    Parnate (tranylcypromine)

Other Antidepressants

    Desyrel (trazadone)
    Effexor (venlafaxine)
    Remeron (mirtazapine)
    Wellbutrin (bupropion)

Antianxiety Medications

Anxiety is one of the most common human experiences. Anxiety disorders are frequently a concern of parishioners who present for professional mental health care. Some of these parishioners will have symptoms that are severe enough to merit consideration of antianxiety medications. High levels of anxiety or prolonged anxiety can become incapacitating and make the activities of daily life quite difficult. Generalized anxiety disorder, obsessive-compulsive disorder, panic disorder, and various phobias discussed in Chapter 3 all may be significant enough to warrant a trial of antianxiety medication.

Antianxiety medications help to calm and relax the anxious person and were originally called *tranquilizers* for this reason. The prevalence of anxiety disorders has made antianxiety medications widely prescribed psychotropic drugs. Today, the SSRI antidepressants (discussed earlier) are the most frequently prescribed antianxiety agents. SSRIs such as Prozac, Paxil, Celexa, and Zoloft have strong antianxiety properties. They are often prescribed for disorders such as posttraumatic stress disorder, panic disorder, obsessive-compulsive disorder, and social anxiety. Beyond the SSRIs, another class of antianxiety medications is the *benzodiazepines,* such as *Xanax* (alprazolam) and *Valium* (diazepam). Benzodiazepines—also called *anxiolytics*—work by stimulating special receptors in the brain that enhance the effects of the neurotransmitter gamma-aminobutyric acid (GABA), which inhibits brain arousal. Benzodiazepines are relatively fast acting and most take effect within hours. They are also relatively safe medically and even large overdoses are rarely fatal. Dosage is generally started at a low level and increased until the anxiety symptoms subside. These medications have relatively few side effects; however, side effects may include drowsiness, fatigue, mental slowing, and coordination problems. They should never be mixed with alcohol and may also be harmful when mixed with other medications. Benzodiazepines have the potential to produce strong psychological and physical dependence and therefore should be carefully monitored by the physician. However, they are less addictive than barbiturates (which are no longer prescribed for anxiety). In addition, patients should never discontinue benzodiazepines suddenly because withdrawal symptoms often occur. Instead, patients must take gradually decreasing doses of the medication under their physician's supervision.

BuSpar (buspirone) has become a major alternative to benzodiazepines for the treatment of anxiety, as it is considered free of the habit-forming properties of the other anxiolytic medications. On the downside, BuSpar cannot be taken on short notice; it must be taken continuously for a period of time before its effects are noticed. Finally, sleeping pills or "hypnotic" medications are sometimes prescribed for anxiety-related problems. These are also anxiolytic drugs with strong sedative effects. Like the benzodiazepines, these medications can produce increased tolerance and the potential for addiction and withdrawal. Following is a list of the most common psychiatric (psychotropic) medications prescribed for anxiety.[31]

Common Antianxiety Medications

Trade Name (generic name)

Antianxiety Agents

Ativan (lorazepam)
BuSpar (buspirone)
Centrax (prazepam)
Inderal (propranolol)
Klonopin (clonazepam)
Lexapro (escitalopram)
Librium (chlordiazepoxide)
Serax (oxazepam)
Tenormin (atenolol)
Tranxene (clorazepate)
Valium (diazepam)
Xanax (alprazolam)

Antipanic Agents

Klonopin (clonazepam)
Paxil (paroxetine)
Xanax (alprazolam)
Zoloft (sertraline)

Antiobsessive Agents

Anafranil (clomipramine)
Luvox (fluvoxamine)
Paxil (paroxetine)
Prozac (fluoxetine)
Zoloft (sertraline)

Mood-Stabilizing Medications

Mood-stabilizing medications work to help prevent wide swings in mood in either direction (toward depression or toward mania). In Chapter 3, we describe the essential features of bipolar disorder. Most persons with this disorder have cycling mood changes including severe highs (mania) and lows (depression). The cycles may be predominantly manic or depressive with normal mood between cycles. At times, the mood swings may follow each other closely or may be separated by months or even years. During a manic episode, the person will have increased energy and activity, euphoric feelings, decreased need for sleep, poor judgment, extreme irritability and distractibility, and unrealistic or grandiose beliefs in his or her abilities. Manic persons also engage in reckless and potentially harmful behavior. The depressions, which sometimes follow manic episodes for bipolar persons, are typical of other depressions (see the antidepressant section in this chapter for a description, or Chapter 3).

In the 1940s, an Australian physician observed that the chemical *lithium* calmed patients suffering from mania. Today, psychiatrists routinely prescribe lithium as the primary medication intervention for bipolar patients. As a naturally occurring mineral, lithium is distinct from other psychiatric medications, which are typically manufactured compounds. Although bipolar patients do not have a lithium deficiency, this mineral helps to even out both their manic and depressive mood swings. Typically, lithium will diminish severe manic symptoms within 5 to 14 days, yet it may take several months before the condition is well controlled. Although some parishioners with bipolar disorder may have only a single episode and be symptom free for years afterward, most will require continued maintenance on lithium or other mood-stabilizing agents for several years to control symptoms and prevent recurrences of full-blown mania.

Lithium remains the most effective medication for effectively preventing future manic episodes and suicidality for those with bipolar disorder by decreasing norepinephrine and increasing serotonin. Lithium is generally prescribed as lithium carbonate. It is essential that those taking it receive regular blood tests to ensure that the amount of the mineral in the body is within a therapeutic range. Blood level checks are also important because lithium can be potentially toxic at high levels. Signs of toxicity may include extreme thirst, fatigue, slurred speech, dizziness, dulling of consciousness, and severe tremors. If toxicity is not reduced, seizures, liver damage, brain damage, and cardiac problems may result. More routine side effects include increased thirst and urination, some fatigue, minor nausea, diarrhea, and a metallic taste in the mouth. Perhaps the biggest challenge in the medical treatment of bipolar patients is getting them to continue taking lithium. Because mania can be a frankly enjoyable (euphoric) state, many patients discontinue lithium shortly after they begin taking it for the first time. Of these, 50 percent relapse within four months.[32]

Anticonvulsant medications are also used as effective mood stabilizers. Typically used to treat seizures—such as those occurring in epilepsy—anticonvulsants are especially useful when lithium may not be a reasonable treatment alternative. This may be due to a medical condition (e.g., thyroid, kidney, heart disorders) or nonresponsiveness to lithium. In these cases, some bipolar patients have been found to respond favorably to anticonvulsant medications such as *Tegretol* (carbamazepine) and *Depakote* (divalproex sodium). Tegretol is widely used as an alternative to lithium, and it may be especially useful for bipolar patients who cycle very rapidly between mania and depression (over a period of days or even hours). Another promising anticonvulsant is Depakote. Research shows it works about as well as lithium at controlling cycling moods. Of course, both medications also produce some side effects including gastrointestinal upset, drowsiness, dizziness, confusion, and nausea. Long-term use also raises concern about liver damage, which should be assessed by a physician.

Here is the good news: between 40 and 70 percent of bipolar patients who remain on their mood-stabilizing medications are able to prevent future episodes of mania. Some research suggests that a combination of lithium and Tegretol may be more effective than either drug alone. It is clear that the parishioners who will respond best to these drugs have less severe bipolar disorder and continue to take their medications.[33] Following is a list of the most common psychiatric (psychotropic) mood-stabilizing medications prescribed.

Common Mood-Stabilizing Medications

Trade Name (generic name)

Depakene (valproic acid)
Depakote (divalproex sodium)
Eskalith (lithium carbonate)
Lamictal (lamotrigine)
Neurontin (gabapentin)
Tegretol (carbamazepine)
Zyprexa (olanzapine)

Antipsychotic Medications

In Chapter 3, we discuss the primary psychotic disorders, particularly schizophrenia, which may be the most debilitating of all the psychiatric disorders. Until the 1950s, little was available in the way of medical intervention for patients diagnosed with a psychotic disorder. These patients lost touch with reality, heard voices, and suffered from disorganized thoughts and bizarre delusions. In the 1950s, a French physician discovered *Thorazine* (chlorpromazine), which became the first of a class of antipsychotic drugs known as *phenothiazines,* and revolutionized the way psychotic patients were treated. Phenothiazines (also called *neuroleptic* medications or *typical antipsychotics*) work by blocking dopamine receptor sites in the brain. They generally help clear up and control the positive symptoms of schizophrenia (hallucinations, delusions, disordered thinking, and bizarre behavior) but do little to help alleviate the negative symptoms of schizophrenia (e.g., emotional apathy, social withdrawal).

A large number of neuroleptic drugs are available for the treatment of psychotic disorders. The primary difference among them is potency (the dosage prescribed to produce therapeutic effects). For example, Thorazine is comparatively low in potency, and psychiatrists may prescribe high doses (50 to 800 milligrams) for patients, while Haldol is higher in potency and would be prescribed at a much lower dosage (0.5–2.0 milligrams). The difficulty with long-term use of these phenothiazine antipsychotic medications is their potential for producing serious side effects. Common short-term side effects of these drugs include dry mouth, constipation, blurred vision, elevation in heart rate, muscle spasms, and restlessness. Unfortunately, long-term use of neuroleptic medications can cause the bizarre motor side effects that indicate *tardive dyskinesia,* an irreversible movement disorder which results directly from long-term use of these dopamine-blocking medications. Schizophrenic persons with tardive dyskinesia engage in facial grimacing, lip smacking, tongue thrusting, and flailing of the limbs, all of which are uncontrollable. Although it is generally true that schizophrenic patients are treated with typical antipsychotic medication for the shortest amount of time possible, schizophrenia is often a chronic disorder and long-term medication use may simply be unavoidable if there is any hope of reducing their psychosis and allowing them a somewhat normal lifestyle (outside an institution).

In 1990, *Clozaril* (clozapine), a new *"atypical"antipsychotic* medication for the treatment of psychotic disorders, was introduced. Clozaril and subsequent atypical antipsychotics often deliver treatment outcomes equivalent to phenothiazines and with fewer harmful side effects. Some chronic schizophrenic patients who had not responded well to phenothiazines demonstrated a very positive response to Clozaril, Zyprexa, Risperdal, and other common atypical antipsychotic drugs. These medications are quite sedating and are therefore started gradually. They may also produce some weight gain and metabolism changes. Additionally, Clozaril—still the most popular atypical antipsychotic—can cause a serious decline in white blood cell count, thereby weakening the person's ability to fight infection. Routine blood tests should be a standard part of the treatment protocol with these drugs. Following is a list of the most common psychiatric (psychotropic) antipsychotic medications prescribed.

Common Antipsychotic Medications

Trade Name (generic name)

Typical Antipsychotics

Haldol (haloperidol)
Loxitane (loxapine)
Mellaril (thioridazine)
Moban (molindone)
Navane (thiothixene)
Orap (pimozide)
Prolixin (fluphenazine)
Stelazine (trifluoperazine)

Atypical Antipsychotics

Clozaril (clozapine)
Geodon (ziprasidone)
Risperdal (risperidone)
Seroquel (quetiapine)
Zyprexa (olanzapine)

Stimulant Medications

It is unlikely that anyone reading this chapter has not encountered a person—typically a child or adolescent—who takes a stimulant medication for *attention-deficit/hyperactivity disorder* (ADHD; see Chapter 6). Persons with ADHD have difficulty with self-regulation and the ability to focus attention because of low levels of neurotransmitters in a key area of the brain, the prefrontal cortex. Stimulant medications—a class of amphetamine—increase activity related to the neurotransmitters dopamine and norepinephrine in the brain.[34] Because the frontal lobes are not as effective in these children (and adults), the ability to ignore distracting stimuli and inhibit impulsive thoughts and behaviors is diminished. Stimulants literally stimulate the frontal lobes so that the person is able to focus in a way that the rest of us take for granted. The most frequently prescribed ADHD medications include Adderall, Ritalin, and Concerta.

Here is the problem: it is clear that far too many children and adolescents are treated needlessly with stimulants. Too often, youth have been "diagnosed" by the local pediatrician or family practitioner who has little formal training and expertise in ADHD. And too often, the decision to medicate these children is based on complaints from a single source (e.g., academically demanding parents, a frustrated teacher). However, don't let the problem with overmedication in the population fool you: ADHD is real. It can be utterly debilitating. For children with carefully diagnosed and truly impairing levels of attention and impulse control problems, stimulant medication produces marked relief in 70 to 80 percent of cases. Over the course of your career in ministry, you will undoubtedly become familiar with children for whom you will know instantly whether they have missed their stimulant medication that morning (a Sunday school teacher frantically calling for backup might be a clue).

Although stimulants for ADHD are prescribed at doses far lower than might be abused or lead to tolerance, this class of medications does come with predictable side effects. These include decreased appetite, stomachaches, headaches, and difficulty with sleep. In most cases, the worst of these side effects diminish with time or can be addressed by lowering the dose or employing a slow-release version of the medication. In rare cases, children may develop difficulty with tics—typically around the face. In this case, a physician might consider a newer nonstimulant ADHD medication called *Strattera* (atomoxetine). Because Strattera is an antidepressant, doctors and parents must carefully monitor children for suicidal thoughts in the days and weeks following initiation of treatment.

Keep in mind that many children and adolescents do not "outgrow" ADHD symptoms. Although the hyperactivity component of the disorder is apt to decline, serious attentional problems may persist. Many adult parishioners may continue to use stimulant medications as a way of coping occupationally and socially with attention problems. Also, be aware that 20 percent of college students report illicit use of prescription stimulants, typically to enhance concentration for studying, pull all-nighters, or even to inhibit appetite to lose weight.[35] Following is a list of the most common psychiatric (psychotropic) stimulant medications prescribed.

Common Stimulant Medications

Trade Name (generic name)

Adderall (amphetamine and dextroamphetamine)
Concerta (methylphenidate)
Dexedrine (dextroamphetamine)
Ritalin (methylphenidate)
Strattera (atomoxetine)

Inpatient Hospitalization

At times, a parishioner may require the most restrictive treatment setting available: the psychiatric hospital. Inpatient psychiatric facilities range from small upscale private hospitals (most expensive) to large state mental hospitals (least expensive). For the most part, a mental health professional will not be inclined to hospitalize a parishioner whom you have referred for treatment unless the person's level of impairment is so severe that he or she cannot function well enough to adequately care for himself or herself. Also, MHPs may be legally obligated to pursue hospitalization for clients who present a clear danger to themselves (suicidal) or others (homicidal). In addition, some disorders are so acute in nature that treating them effectively may hinge on having the person in a closed environment where treatment can be comprehensive and quite intense. For example, severely alcoholic clients or adolescents with anorexia nervosa will often improve most rapidly with intensive inpatient care.

In most jurisdictions, MDs or ODs (psychiatrists) must officially admit patients to inpatient units. In some cases, psychologists may have admitting privileges, but most psychologists do not routinely admit patients to hospitals. The primary reason is that physicians must be responsible for a patient's physical exams and any psychiatric medications administered during hospitalization. Most psychiatric facilities provide a range of treatments including individual and group therapy, psychiatric medication, family therapy, recreational and occupational therapy, and *milieu* therapy. Milieu therapy is simply the use of the total environment as an important variable in helping the person improve. Ideally, patients become highly engaged with staff, other patients, therapy groups, and different MHPs while in the hospital.

Under ideal circumstances, hospitalization will be voluntary. The parishioner, with support from family, friends, and the church, will understand the importance of inpatient care for his or her own safety and long-term health. In other cases, parishioners may require involuntary commitment to a hospital. In this case, a physician, and later, a judge, will place a suicidal, homicidal, or obviously psychotic person on a legal hold, which keeps the patient hospitalized until he or she can be stabilized. Inpatient mental health treatment is a critically important form of mental health care for certain parishioners in certain circumstances. Ministers should become familiar with at least one psychiatrist with admitting privileges at a local psychiatric facility. Hospitalization is an expensive form of treatment, and large state hospitals are generally not known for high quality care; therefore, inpatient treatment should be reserved for very severe cases for which less restrictive alternatives are not adequate or risk the parishioner's safety.

Alcohol and Drug Treatment Programs

In Chapter 4, we discuss substance use disorders, including some of the primary forms of substance abuse treatment. However, because alcohol and drug problems are so prevalent in our culture and because they constitute such a potentially serious form of impairment, it is important for the minister to be familiar with the range of treatment options for substance-dependent parishioners. Although we focus primarily on treatment programs for alcoholism, there is tremendous overlap in treatment approaches for alcohol and other drug addictions. In fact, most treatment programs provide care for persons with any form of substance addiction.

Unfortunately, many substance-dependent parishioners will not admit that they have a problem until they "hit bottom." At this point, their lives have become entirely unmanageable and there may be a crisis that precipitates their willingness to finally consider treatment (e.g., a serious car accident, an arrest, severe financial problems, a threatened marital separation). Because alcoholics often react with denial and anger when confronted with their disorder, it is best to coordinate this confrontation so that all those invested in the alcoholic or addict can be involved (e.g., spouse, children, pastor, employer, parents).

Treatment options fall into several categories and include the following:

1. *Inpatient treatment programs,* which require a physician's admission order and generally keep patients for one to two months. The majority of these programs emphasize medical stabilization (especially important in the case of severe physical addiction), abstinence, and lifestyle changes. Staff members are typically medical professionals and addiction counselors. During the initial phase of hospitalization, emphasis is often placed on reducing the danger of withdrawal symptoms via tranquilizing medications (e.g., Valium, Librium). The intensity of inpatient programs has been lauded by its proponents as essential to giving the seriously addicted person a new start.
2. *Residential care programs* are transitional programs that may be helpful to the most seriously impaired alcoholics and addicts. They provide a transitional "group home" environment (often following inpatient care) in which the person is expected to remain abstinent and be actively engaged in various forms of counseling, occupational training, and peer support.
3. *Outpatient treatment programs* range widely in organization and intensity, but typically involve outpatient counseling (individual and group), Alcoholics Anonymous (or Narcotics Anonymous)

meetings, abstinence verification (e.g., via urinalysis), and so forth. The duration of these programs and the quality of the treatment and staff may vary widely.

4. *Self-help programs* include Alcoholics Anonymous (AA) and Narcotics Anonymous (NA). These programs are very popular and rely solely on the leadership and peer support by other recovering alcoholics and drug addicts. They emphasize recovery through the classic 12-step model, which includes admission of one's illness and powerlessness to overcome it, a reliance on God or a Higher Power for direction, unrelenting honesty, and a commitment to remain involved in the program for life. Members of AA are encouraged to view their "disease" as permanent, and complete abstinence is strongly emphasized.

Although inpatient hospital treatment has long been the standard as the initial form of treatment for someone identified with a substance addiction, research has not supported the value of inpatient care in comparison with less expensive and less invasive alternatives. Mental health professionals are increasingly aware of the benefits of outpatient treatment programs and quality self-help programs such as AA. Also, outpatient therapy (specifically, group therapy or cognitive-behavioral individual therapy) conducted by MHPs with expertise in substance disorders has been shown to produce promising outcomes. Finally, *Antabuse* (disulfiram) can be administered to alcoholics to deter them from drinking during the time they are trying to establish abstinence. If a person ingests alcohol while taking Antabuse, he or she will become violently ill. Unfortunately, the person can simply stop taking the medication, which often occurs.

We recommend allowing the MHP with expertise in alcohol and drug-related disorders to work with the parishioner and the family in determining the most appropriate treatment match. In more severe cases (especially those involving significant danger of withdrawal), inpatient care may be an important first step. In other cases, intensive involvement in AA and outpatient psychotherapy may be appropriate. Keep in mind that relapse rates following substance disorder treatment are high (around 50 percent or higher) and that alcoholic and drug-addicted parishioners may require long-term support and more than one episode of professional treatment.

Eating Disorder Treatment Programs

In Chapter 6, we detail the range of thorny treatment issues present when parishioners suffer from eating disorders. Not only are eating disorders potentially life-threatening, but they are also long-term in nature and often difficult to treat successfully. Although a range of psychotherapies have been developed for eating disorders, the pastor should be particularly attuned to inpatient programs for parishioners with anorexia. Hospitalization may be required to provide initial stabilization and intensive treatment.

When parishioners (typically adolescent or young adult females) suffer from anorexia or bulimia to the extent that they pose a danger to themselves because of chronic food restriction (starvation) or purging (vomiting or laxative abuse), immediate hospitalization should be carefully considered by a physician. Severely underweight anorexic clients will be a serious concern because of the danger of medical complications (e.g., cardiac problems, organ failure) related to starvation. Inpatient treatment for anorexic persons will involve mandatory fluid and nutrient intake (often using IVs initially), gradual increase in caloric intake, and monitoring of physical condition. Simultaneously, the patient will often be placed in a behavior-therapy setting in which all rewards (e.g., recreation, privileges) hinge on appropriate eating, involvement in individual, family, and group therapy sessions, and refraining from purging behaviors. The value of inpatient eating disorder programs is their intensity and their capacity to carefully control the patient's eating behavior to ensure safety while various psychotherapy approaches have time to take effect. Antidepressant medications may also be used during treatment to speed the recovery process—particularly when mood problems are clearly related to the eating disorder.

When hospitalization is not required, we recommend referral to a mental health professional with focused expertise in treating eating disorders. Of course, a physical examination should always be performed by a physician before a decision is made to proceed with outpatient care alone. Promising treatments for anorexia and bulimia include cognitive-behavioral, behavioral, and various group psychotherapies. The parishioner will be asked to focus on self-image, self-evaluation, distorted body image, and the recognition and maintenance of appropriate weight and body fat proportions. Family therapy is often a critical component of recovery. Treatment may focus on educating the family regarding the person's condition, identifying ways the parents inadvertently nurture a negative self-image in the child, and discerning ways the family system reinforces the eating-disordered member's behavior. Finally, group therapy is a cost-effective and extremely helpful form of treatment for eating-disordered clients. Group support, coupled with the perceptive confrontation of peers with similar behavior and thought processes, can be quite effective. An excellent MHP will typically combine multiple treatment components with eating-disordered clients.

Hypnosis

Hypnosis is an induced and altered state of consciousness in which one person responds to suggestions by another person to alter perception, thinking, feelings, and behavior. Hypnosis originated in the 1700s and was initially referred to as *mesmerism* after Franz Anton Mesmer, who first wrote about this altered state. A hypnotic state involves deep relaxation and high suggestability, which can be useful for some treatment purposes. Hypnosis is typically only effective with persons who are highly suggestible. Therapists who use this approach will assess whether a client is suggestible enough that this technique may have good effect. The MHP will use *induction techniques* to get a client into a hypnotic state characterized by heightened selective attention. Here, the client has tuned out stimuli that are not relevant and focuses solely on the therapist's suggestions. Induction techniques include progressive muscle relaxation, narrowing the client's gaze to a focused object or point, and directing the client's activities via suggestion (e.g., "You may now begin to feel very relaxed and your eyelids may become heavy").

Hypnosis may be used by MHPs for a variety of reasons. It has most frequently been used for creating *posthypnotic suggestions.* In this case, the therapist will suggest to the client that he or she will carry out or avoid some behavior later, while in a normal waking state. For example, a client who wishes to quit smoking may be told that he will become nauseated whenever he smells cigarette smoke and that whenever he has the urge to smoke, he will feel like chewing gum instead. Similarly, a medical patient may receive the hypnotic suggestion that she will experience very little postsurgical pain. Posthypnotic suggestions are frequently used quite successfully with a range of disorders, particularly behavioral and medical problems.

Hypnosis has also been used for recall of *repressed memories* and for *age regression.* This technique involves suggesting the client is at an earlier age while encouraging him or her to speak from that perspective to gain understanding regarding what events occurred and how he or she experienced life at that point in development. Unfortunately, age regression and memory recall are plagued by unreliability and significant research has shown that memories can be unintentionally fabricated. Competent MHPs who practice hypnosis would attempt these techniques with great caution.[36]

Hypnosis depends on both the suggestibility of the subject or client and on the skill of the hypnotherapist. MHPs who use hypnosis for clinical purposes should have focused specialty training in this technique. There is a board that certifies professionals who use hypnosis as one approach in their clinical practices, and board certification is a strong indication of the MHP's expertise with this treatment approach. It would not be at all unusual for parishioners to receive hypnosis for the purposes of pain management, smoking cessation, weight control, performance enhancement (it is quite common among athletes), relaxation training, and anxiety management. Research has shown, however, that hypnosis is primarily effective for involuntary problems (e.g., pain, headaches, asthma, stress-related skin conditions) and not as effective for voluntary problems (e.g., smoking, weight loss, athletic performance). Hypnosis would be less commonly used for routine counseling or psychotherapy issues.

Electroconvulsive Therapy

At times, a severely depressed parishioner—more often an older woman—who has not responded to psychotherapy, medication, or any other depression treatment may be encouraged by her psychiatrist to consider *electroconvulsive therapy* (ECT) as an option in the treatment of severe, unremitting, and often suicidal depression. Although ECT has been criticized in the professional literature and portrayed as barbaric in movies, research indicates that, for some very depressed patients, it may be a surprisingly effective, if not well understood, treatment approach. Because women are more prone to depression, about 70 percent of ECT patients are women.

ECT produces its curative effect on the depressed person by essentially creating a grand mal or generalized seizure in the brain that creates a state of amnesia; the client seems to "forget" about feeling depressed. To accomplish this, the person is put to sleep with an anesthetic and his or her muscles are paralyzed with another drug that prevents broken bones and other ill effects when the seizure occurs. Electrodes are placed at two locations on the scalp and an electric current is passed through the person's brain. The electric current lasts for only 2 seconds and the seizure lasts for about 30 to 60 seconds. Treatments are administered two or three times per week until the person's depression lifts or until it becomes clear the treatment is not working.[37]

Because severe biological depression in older adult clients may predict eventual suicide, ECT has a legitimate place in the psychiatrist's treatment arsenal (only psychiatrists are trained to practice this procedure). For some patients, ECT has produced dramatic results and complete remission of depressive symptoms. Research suggests that over half of those treated make substantial improvement in their depressive symptoms. Although ECT may produce good results, patients are prone to relapse and often require ECT sessions episodically. When ECT is combined with antidepressant medications, the relapse rate is lessened considerably. Be apprised that ECT is associated with memory difficulties in many patients, both retrograde (for events occurring before ECT) and anterograde (for events occurring after

ECT). When patients require multiple sessions of ECT to remain depression free, memory is more likely to be seriously impacted.

It is important not to dissuade parishioners or their families from considering ECT when they suffer severe major depression that has not been responsive to other forms of treatment. Although it is reasonable to pursue a second or third opinion before embarking on a trial of ECT, most psychiatrists would never consider ECT a first-order approach to handling complaints of depression.

Fads in Mental Health Treatment

During the past decade, MHPs have followed diagnostic fads including the overdiagnosis of ADHD and bipolar disorder in children and multiple personality disorder (now *dissociative identity disorder*) in adults. For a time, many MHPs believed that satanic ritual abuse was occurring in epidemic proportions and they wrongly diagnosed clients as victims of such abuse, often attempting to elicit abuse memories via age regression under hypnosis. The effect of these diagnoses and treatments on the lives of clients was harmful, to say the least. With the American Psychiatric Association's release of the most recent *Diagnostic and Statistical Manual of Mental Disorders* (*DSM-5*),[38] several prominent psychiatrists, including the chair of the *DSM-IV*, Allen Frances, have issued stern warnings regarding the worsening culture of overdiagnosis in the mental health field.[39] Like all fallible human beings, mental health professionals may also fall prey to fleeting fads and bizarre trends in mental health treatment. In fact, over the years, numerous bright and well-trained MHPs have endorsed "therapeutic" approaches such as naked encounter groups, hallucinogenic drug experimentation, and "primal scream" therapy. Of course, none of these approaches were particularly useful and some were simply unethical and possibly harmful.

Unfortunately, as long as there are fads and "breakthrough" treatment approaches, MHPs will be duped, and may attempt to apply these magical cures to all their clients and client problems. We recommend being wary of MHPs who use only one approach with clients or who claim to have "one of a kind" or exclusive therapeutic powers and techniques. We consider any approach to treatment that lacks careful, valid scientific research to be questionable at best and faddish at worst. Of course, most of these "rages" disappear and MHPs will recognize that author M. Scott Peck was right— "Life is hard" and there really are no therapeutic shortcuts.[40] Your troubled parishioners will get better when they work hard in therapy to understand themselves, learn new skills, and modify self-defeating beliefs, behaviors, and emotions.

Notes

1. Ellis, A. (1970). *Reason and emotion in psychotherapy*. New York, NY: Lyle Stuart.
2. Bohart, A. C., & Wade, A. G. (2013). The client in psychotherapy. In M. J. Lambert (Ed.), *Bergin and Garfield's handbook of psychotherapy and behavior change* (6th ed.) (pp. 219–257). New York, NY: Wiley.
3. Eysenck, H. J. (1952). The effects of psychotherapy: An evaluation. *Journal of Consulting Psychology, 16*, 319–324.
4. Lambert, M. J. (2013). The efficacy and effectiveness of psychotherapy. In M. J. Lambert (Ed.), *Bergin and Garfield's handbook of psychotherapy and behavior change* (6th ed.) (pp. 169–218). New York, NY: Wiley.
5. Smith, M. L., Glass, G. V., & Miller, T. I. (1980). *The benefits of psychotherapy*. Baltimore, MD: Johns Hopkins University Press.
6. Wampold, B. E. (2001). *The great psychotherapy debate: Models, methods, and findings*. New York, NY: Routledge.
7. Craske, M. G., & Barlow, D. H. (2007). *Mastery of your anxiety and panic: Therapist guide* (4th ed.). New York, NY: Oxford.
8. Gabbard, G. O. (2005). *Psychodynamic psychiatry in clinical practice*. Arlington, VA: American Psychiatric Publishing.
9. Consumer Reports. (1995, November). *Mental health: Does therapy help?* 734–739.
10. Jones, S. L., & Butman, R. E. (2011). *Modern psychotherapies: A comprehensive Christian appraisal* (2nd ed.). Downers Grove, IL: InterVarsity Press.
11. American Psychiatric Association. (2013). *Diagnostic and statistical manual of mental disorders* (5th ed.). Washington, DC: Author.
12. Smith, E. W. L. (2003). *The person of the therapist*. Jefferson, NC: McFarland.
13. Trull, T. J. (2005). *Clinical psychology* (7th ed.). Belmont, CA: Wadsworth/Thomson.
14. Anastasi, A., & Urbina, S. (1997). *Psychological testing* (7th ed.). New York, NY: Macmillan.
15. Murphy, L., Geisinger, K. F., Carlson, J. F., & Spies, R. A. (2011). *Tests in print VIII*. Lincoln, NE: Buros.
16. Spies, R. A., Carlson, J. F., & Geisinger, K. F. (2010). *The eighteenth mental measurements yearbook*. Lincoln, NE: Buros.
17. Shea, S. C. (2011). *The practical art of suicide assessment: A guide for mental health professionals and substance abuse counselors*. New York, NY: Wiley.
18. Wedding, D., & Corsini, R. J. (2013). *Current psychotherapies* (10th ed.). Belmont, CA: Cengage Learning.
19. Jones, S. L., & Butman, R. E. (2011). *Modern psychotherapies: A comprehensive Christian appraisal* (2nd ed.). Grand Rapids, MI: Intervarsity Press.
20. Gabbard, G. O. (2010). *Long-term psychodynamic psychotherapy: A basic text* (2nd ed.). Washington, DC: American Psychiatric Publishing.
21. Antony, M. M., & Roemer, L. (2011). *Behavior therapy*. Washington, DC: American Psychological Association.
22. Ellis, A., & Dryden, W. (2007). *The practice of rational emotive behavior therapy* (2nd ed.). New York, NY: Springer.
23. Koerner, K. (2011). *Doing dialectical behavior therapy: A practical guide*. New York, NY: Guilford.
24. Rogers, C. R. (2003). *Client-centered therapy: Its current practice, implications, and theory*. London, England: Robinson Publishing.
25. Gottman, J. (1995). *Why marriages succeed or fail: And how you can make yours last*. New York, NY: Simon & Schuster.
26. Haley, J. (1962). Whither family therapy. *Family Process, 1*, 69–100.
27. Minuchin, S. (1974). *Families and family therapy*. Cambridge, MA: Harvard University Press.
28. Healy, D. (2004). *The creation of psychopharmacology*. Cambridge, MA: Harvard University Press.
29. PDR Network. (2013). *The physician's desk reference* (68th ed.). Montvale, NJ: Author.

30. Kirsch, I., Moore, T. J., Scoboria, A., & Nicholls, S. S. (2002). The emperor's new drugs: An analysis of antidepressant medication data submitted to the U.S. Food and Drug Administration. *Prevention & Treatment, 5.*
31. National Alliance on Mental Illness. (2013). *Commonly prescribed psychotropic medications.* Retrieved from www.nami.org/Template.cfm?Section=Policymakers_Toolkit&Template=/ContentManagement/HTMLDisplay.cfm&ContentID=18971
32. Baker, J. P. (1994). Outcome of lithium discontinuation: A meta-analysis. *Lithium, 5,* 187–192.
33. Baldessarini, R. J., Perry, R., & Pike, J. (2008). Factors associated with treatment nonadherence among US bipolar disorder patients. *Human Psychopharmacology, 23*(2), 95–105.
34. Fone, K. C., & Nutt, D. J. (2005). Stimulants: Use and abuse in the treatment of attention deficit hyperactivity disorder. *Current Opinion in Pharmacology, 5*(1), 87–93.
35. Judson, R., & Langdon, S. W. (2009). Illicit use of prescription stimulants among college students: Prescription status, motives, theory of planned behaviour, knowledge, and self-diagnostic tendencies. *Psychology, Health, and Medicine, 14*(1), 97–104.
36. Lynn, S. J., & Kirsch, I. (2005). *Essentials of clinical hypnosis: An evidence-based approach.* Washington, DC: American Psychological Association.
37. Mankad, M. V., Beyer, J. L., Weiner, R. D., & Krystal, A. (2010). *Clinical manual of electroconvulsive therapy.* Arlington, VA: American Psychiatric Publishing.
38. American Psychiatric Association. (2013). *Diagnostic and statistical manual of mental disorders* (5th ed.). Washington, DC: Author.
39. Frances, A. J. (2010, June). *DSM-5 in distress: Psychiatric fads and overdiagnosis. Psychology Today.* Retrieved from www.psychologytoday.com/blog/dsm5-in-distress/201006/psychiatric-fads-and-overdiagnosis
40. Peck, M. S. (1977). *The road less traveled.* New York, NY: Simon & Schuster.

3 The Parishioner in Distress

Major Psychological Disorders, Part I

In this chapter, we briefly describe the most prevalent psychiatric disorders that the pastor may encounter in the congregation. We include the following disorder categories: anxiety disorders, mood disorders, psychotic disorders, neurocognitive disorders, and somatic symptom disorders. In Chapter 4, we describe several additional disorders that are somewhat less prevalent, yet still reasonably common. Although other psychiatric disorders may be found in the American Psychiatric Association's *Diagnostic and Statistical Manual of Mental Disorders, Fifth Edition,* (*DSM-5*),[1] we believe our list is fairly comprehensive and that most of the serious mental health problems among adult parishioners can be located in these two chapters.

For each of the major disorder categories, we offer a *presenting complaints* section, which provides several examples of how this class of disorders might look in everyday life. In other words, we describe how the minister might first become aware that a parishioner is suffering from a disorder of this type. Next, we summarize the *common features and symptoms* of this class of disorder. We then offer short descriptions of the different *subtypes* of the disorder, including the main symptoms and indicated treatments. For each disorder subtype, we have included a *key indicators* box, which highlights the most important diagnostic criteria. Although many of these key indicators are similar to those in the *DSM-5*, we have modified them to enhance readability and reduce technical jargon. For the official diagnostic criteria for each psychiatric disorder, pastors should directly consult the *DSM-5*. We conclude our discussion of each disorder with a *summary and guidelines* section, which briefly highlights the major characteristics of the disorder category and recommends specific things for the minister to consider in caring for the parishioner who may suffer from a particular disorder.

Anxiety Disorders

Presenting Complaints

Mary is a single 48-year-old who has not attended church services for several years. In a conversation with Mary's daughter, you learn Mary has not been outside her house for nearly three years and that her daughter is growing weary of having to take her mother groceries and other goods. She notes that her mother would love to return to church but that "leaving the house makes her fall apart."

Todd is a 21-year-old college senior with excellent grades and tremendous people skills. He has expressed strong interest in becoming a pastor but now seems to avoid the topic altogether. When you bring this change to Todd's attention, he tearfully describes an inability to speak in front of others without trembling, forgetting his speech, and feeling nauseated. He claims to have tried everything to reduce his anxiety but nothing has seemed to help.

Arthur is 35 years old and is known in the church as "Mr. Clean." He has never had a serious relationship and has been deemed by his fellow church board members as "impossible to work with." It seems that Arthur becomes obsessed with the minute details of any decision the board must address. He checks and rechecks all figures, will sometimes seek up to 20 bids for minor repair jobs, and cannot delegate work to others. At home, Arthur adheres to rigid rituals for eating and cleaning. He becomes very distressed when things are out of place.

Common Features and Symptoms

Anxiety is a universal human emotion. It is a general feeling of apprehension about possible danger. Nearly all human beings experience anxiety from time to time, and research indicates that some anxiety may be optimal for many kinds of tasks and performances. It is only when anxiety becomes overwhelming or chronic that it may be classified as an *anxiety disorder.* Each of the major disorders in this category share a common characteristic: an unrealistic, irrational fear or anxiety of distressing or disabling intensity. Some of the anxiety disorders are characterized by extreme fear or *panic.* Panic is a basic and primitive emotional state that involves activation of the "fight or flight" response of the sympathetic nervous system.

Like all human emotions, anxiety has three primary components: physiological (biological), subjective (cognitive), and behavioral. The physiological symptoms are those nervous system responses that are normally triggered in all of us when exposed to sudden threat (e.g., sudden air turbulence while flying, the sound of someone approaching rapidly from behind when walking down a darkened street). These symptoms include sweating, rapid heart rate, shortness of breath, nausea, dizziness, hot or cold flashes, trembling, dry mouth, and difficulty swallowing.

Subjective or cognitive components of anxiety are less directly observable from the outside, and we must often rely on the person's direct report of these experiences. Such internal experiences of anxiety include worrying, dread, fear of dying or being humiliated, feeling tense, feeling that things are not real, and the ongoing fear that something awful is about to happen.

The behavioral components of anxiety are more easily observed from the outside. These behaviors may include pacing; increased speed, volume, and intensity in speech; being easily startled; and a variety of avoidance behaviors. Avoidance behaviors are attempts by the person to avoid those situations viewed as threatening as a means of reducing anxiety. Unfortunately, avoidance usually has some negative consequences. For example, the agoraphobic is fearful of wide open spaces and crowds and therefore avoids the possibility of being in an open or crowded place by staying at home. Obviously, refusing to leave one's home is likely to have adverse occupational and social consequences.

Large-scale population studies of psychiatric disorders in the United States have shown that roughly 18 percent of the population suffers from anxiety disorders in any given year and that over the course of our lives, 28 percent of us will have an anxiety disorder at some point.[2] Anxiety problems and chronic worries or fears are among the most frequent counseling problem reported by pastors.[3]

As a minister, it is likely that many of the parishioners you see will suffer from anxiety at one time or another. In addition, anxiety is a common symptom of other types of psychiatric disorder and anxiety symptoms should be a signal that the person is suffering and may need further assistance. A calm and reassuring demeanor is always indicated when exploring the experience of anxiety with a parishioner.

Subtypes

Specific Phobia

A phobia is a persistent and disproportionate fear of some specific object or situation that presents little or no actual danger. In any year, 7 to 9 percent of the U.S. population suffers from various phobias.[1] There are three major types of phobias: *specific phobia, social phobia,* and *agoraphobia.* We describe specific and social phobia here and cover agoraphobia in the section on panic disorder.

Specific Phobia: Key Indicators

- Marked, excessive, unreasonable, and persistent fear of a specific object or situation (e.g., animals, storms, sight of blood, heights).
- Exposure to the object or situation provokes an immediate anxiety response, which can be as severe as a panic attack.
- The person's anxiety is clearly out of proportion to the actual threat presented by the object or situation.
- The person avoids the feared object or situation if at all possible or else endures it with intense distress.
- Avoiding the anxiety significantly disrupts the person's normal activities (e.g., work, school, social activities, relationships), or the person is quite distressed about having the fear.

Parishioners with any of the specific phobias will usually demonstrate intense, and sometimes incapacitating, anxiety in the presence of the feared object or situation. Interestingly, the person understands the irrational nature of the fear, yet can do little on his or her own to overcome it. Although people can develop phobias to nearly anything, some phobic syndromes are much more common in the population. For example, nearly half of all Americans are fearful of snakes. Other common forms of specific phobia include *acrophobia* (fear of heights), *claustrophobia* (fear of enclosed places), *mysophobia* (fear of contamination or germs), and *nyctophobia* (fear of darkness).

Treatment for specific phobias generally involves referral to a practitioner with expertise in the use of behavioral and cognitive techniques for anxiety disorders. Systematic desensitization (gradual) and prolonged exposure or flooding (brief and intense) are the most common behavioral techniques for treating phobias. These approaches are relatively short term and very often successful. Psychiatrists and other physicians may also prescribe low doses of antianxiety medication for use when the parishioner must face the feared object or situation. However, because phobias are highly treatable with psychotherapy, medication should not generally be the first approach to treatment.

Social Phobia (Social Anxiety Disorder)

Socially phobic individuals are extremely anxious about being exposed to the scrutiny of others. They fear they will act in an embarrassing or humiliating manner in front of others. For example, persons with social phobia may be intensely frightened about speaking in front of others, urinating in a public bathroom, or eating or writing in public. Obviously, social phobia could pose a major problem for individuals who desire to serve actively in church leadership. These individuals are likely to avoid social events, opportunities to speak, and even any situation involving public eating or drinking. Although they may appear disinterested in social interaction, they are actually quite fearful.

Social Phobia (Social Anxiety Disorder): Key Indicators

- A marked and ongoing fear of one or more social or performance-focused situations in which the person believes he or she will be evaluated or scrutinized by others.
- The person fears that he or she will act in a way that will be humiliating or embarrassing.
- When exposed to the feared social situation, the person experiences intense anxiety, which may be as severe as a panic attack.
- The person attempts to avoid the feared social situation at all costs or endures it only with great discomfort.
- Avoiding the anxiety significantly disrupts the person's normal activities (e.g., work, school, social activities, relationships), or the person is quite distressed about having the fear.

Treatment of social phobia can be very successful with cognitive-behavioral therapies. Most often, these treatments involve a mixture of exposure to social situations (in vivo training) and cognitive challenges to the person's extreme thinking (e.g., "If people saw me trembling, it would be absolutely awful!"). In severe cases, antianxiety medications can be used to reduce anxiety symptoms during performances. For example, many entertainers use *Inderal* (propranolol) before major performances or speeches to control the symptoms of speaking anxiety.

Panic Disorder and Agoraphobia

Although panic disorder and agoraphobia are distinct psychiatric disorders, they often coexist and are therefore highly linked in most diagnostic systems. We discuss them both here and explain why they are so closely connected.

Panic Disorder: Key Indicators

- Unexpected and recurring panic attacks. Panic attacks typically last 10 minutes or less and involve intense fear or discomfort in which at least four of the following symptoms of panic are present: (1) palpitations, pounding heart, or accelerated heart rate; (2) sweating; (3) trembling or shaking; (4) sensations of shortness of breath or smothering; (5) feeling of choking; (6) chest pain or discomfort; (7) nausea or abdominal pain; (8) feeling dizzy, lightheaded, or faint; (9) feelings of unreality or feeling detached from oneself; (10) fear of losing control or going crazy; (11) fear of dying; (12) numbness or tingling sensations; (13) chills or hot flashes.
- Following the initial panic attack, the person may have persistent concerns about additional attacks, concern about the health implications of the attack, or a seriously restricted lifestyle in anticipation of further attacks.
- The attacks cannot be explained by substance abuse or other medical problems.

Persons with panic disorder live in perpetual fear of experiencing a panic attack. For some, the attacks seem to come "out of the blue" with no apparent warning or trigger (uncued), while for others, the intense episodes are linked to a specific location or situation (e.g., driving over a bridge, flying in an airplane). As you can discern from the list of physical symptoms in the key indicators, the panic attack experience can be quite distressing, and individuals often report that they believed they were going to die or that they were surely "going crazy." Following their first attack, sufferers will often consult many different doctors searching for explanations. When nothing physical is discovered, the person may live in constant fear of the next episode; this can make panic disorder particularly debilitating. Panic disorder normally begins in young adulthood (ages 20–24) and occurs in 2 to 3 percent of the U.S. population.[1]

Agoraphobia: Key Indicators

- The person is extremely anxious about being in situations in which escape might be difficult or embarrassing, or situations in which help may not be immediately available should a panic attack occur.
- The most commonly feared situations include being outside the home alone, being in open spaces, being in a crowd or standing in a line, or being in an enclosed space.
- The person can endure these situations only with great difficulty and usually requires a great deal of reassurance.

Agoraphobia and panic disorder often occur together. In fact, agoraphobic avoidance of situations and places is often triggered by experiences of panic as well as the ongoing and increasing anxiety that the person will panic again in a crowded or inescapable situation. Evidence confirms that agoraphobia is much more common in persons with panic disorder.[4] As the person avoids more and more anxiety-provoking situations, his or her life can become extremely restricted. In the worst cases, a person may be literally "self-imprisoned" at home. Agoraphobia can also occur without panic attacks. In these cases, the pattern is one of gradually increasing fearfulness of environments outside the home.

As with most psychiatric disorders, the exact causes of panic disorder and agoraphobia are not clear. However, there is strong evidence that both genetic and situational factors play a role. It has been estimated that as many as 80 percent of persons who experience a panic attack have had a stressful life event in the period immediately preceding the attack. Parishioners who suffer from these disorders are bound to be experiencing a great deal of distress. Treatment is more extensive than for phobias and may require a combination of cognitive-behavioral therapy and medication to alleviate the panic symptoms initially. Referrals to both a physician and a practitioner with expertise in treating anxiety disorders are indicated.

Generalized Anxiety Disorder

People with generalized anxiety disorder (GAD) have persistent, uncomfortable, uncontrollable anxiety, the source of which cannot be identified. Freud originally called GAD "free-floating" anxiety because the anxiety did not seem to be connected to a specific object or situation as with specific or social phobias. GAD is characterized by chronic, excessive worry about many potential problems and catastrophes. These parishioners will be continually tense, worried, and physically upset or anxious. They often worry about bad things that might happen (e.g., loss of a job, financial failure, injury or death of children). In general, these parishioners live with constant suffering from tension, worry, and vague uneasiness.

Generalized Anxiety Disorder: Key Indicators

- Excessive anxiety and apprehension about a range of events or activities.
- The person finds it difficult to control the worry.
- The anxiety or worry is usually associated with symptoms such as restlessness, fatigue, poor concentration, irritability, muscle tension, and sleep disturbance.
- The anxiety is usually severe enough to interfere with the person's work or relationships.

Parishioners with GAD will truly be suffering. The various symptoms of tension and apprehension associated with this disorder are nearly always unpleasant and, cumulatively, they can fatigue and overwhelm a sufferer. Beyond their verbalized worries and ruminations, look for evidence of an inability to relax, tension, poor concentration, agitation, feeling frightened, fear of losing control, fear of being rejected, and an inability to control repetitive anxious thoughts in these parishioners. It is likely that effective treatment will require a cognitive-behavioral or interpersonal approach. Referral to a physician is also indicated to rule out a physical explanation for these symptoms.

Obsessive-Compulsive Disorder

Persons with obsessive-compulsive disorder (OCD) are caught in a vicious cycle of obsessions and compulsions. *Obsessions* are persistent, intrusive, unwanted, and inappropriate *thoughts* that cause the person significant anxiety and distress. The person views these thoughts as beyond his or her control and the thoughts appear quite at odds with things the person might normally think about. Common obsessions include repeated thoughts about becoming contaminated by dirt, germs, or toxins; fearful thoughts that something terrible is about to happen; aggressive or horrible impulses (killing a spouse, parent, or child; shouting blasphemies in church); and sexual thoughts (pornographic images). The obsessive thoughts are usually extremely distressing to the person and may be in obvious conflict with religious values.

Compulsions are either repetitive *behaviors* or mental activities, the goal of which is to reduce or avoid anxiety and distress—often produced by obsessions. Compulsive acts are not pleasurable for the person, but feel absolutely necessary in order to ward off intense anxiety. Examples of repetitive behaviors include hand washing, placing things in order, counting, and checking. Mental acts may include compulsive praying, counting, or repeating words or phrases.

> **Obsessive-Compulsive Disorder: Key Indicators**
> - The person has recurrent obsessions or compulsions.
> - In most cases, the obsessions or compulsions cause substantial distress, take a great deal of the person's time, and seriously interfere with the person's normal routine and relationships.
> - During the episodes, the person may or may not have insight about the excessive or unreasonable nature of the obsessions or compulsions.

Freud referred to OCD as the "doubting disease," perhaps because many OCD clients seemed to doubt whether they had already checked things around the house (e.g., "is the stove off? . . . is the door locked?"). A symbolic connection often exists between a particular obsession and its accompanying compulsion. For example, a person obsessed with dirt and germs may wash his or her hands until the skin is raw. Another person may avoid persistent obsessive thoughts about pornography only by chanting several scriptures in a specific order many times. These compulsions may cause extreme disruption in the person's life and relationships. It is likely that OCD has several contributing causes, some of which are biological and genetic. Very often, psychiatric medication is required for the person to experience full relief from OCD symptoms. Behavioral approaches, involving exposure to the feared thoughts while preventing the usual compulsions, can also be effective with many sufferers.

Summary and Guidelines

Although the anxiety disorders include a range of specific and distinct syndromes, they are united by the underlying presence of fear or panic as the core emotional state. Panic involves activation of the autonomic nervous system and a number of very primitive self-protective bodily responses, whereas anxiety is a more diffuse emotional state characterized by worry, unrest, and a less specific sense of danger. Parishioners with anxiety disorders may be fearful of specific situations and objects, and each of the disorders is characterized by irrational and excessive evaluation of the danger these situations present.

In nearly every case, we recommend referral of parishioners with extreme and unrelenting anxiety to a physician. Certain cardiologic, neurologic, and endocrine-based illnesses may produce anxiety symptoms that mimic these psychiatric problems. Once these potential problems are ruled out, referral to a mental health service provider with expertise in treating anxiety disorders is recommended. Certain anxiety disorders (e.g., generalized anxiety disorder, panic disorder, obsessive-compulsive disorder) have been shown to respond best to a combination of drug and psychological therapies. For example, minor tranquilizers (anxiolytics) such as Valium or Xanax have been helpful in creating initial reductions in the severe symptoms of panic so that persons can respond to other interventions. Also, antidepressant medications have been used successfully with panic disorder, and *Anafranil* has shown marked promise in reducing the intensity of OCD symptoms. Of course, certain antianxiety medications can be quite addictive (e.g., benzodiazepines) and their use should be closely supervised by a physician.

Cognitive-behavioral therapies are perhaps the best researched and most often practiced approaches to treating anxiety disorders.[5] Psychologists, psychiatrists, social workers, and others with expertise in this area will help parishioners to reduce maladaptive behaviors, reduce the thoughts that tend to produce anxiety, learn and sharpen adaptive skills (e.g., relaxation, assertiveness), and approach objects and situations that they have previously avoided. As a minister, it is critical to communicate to the parishioner that these disorders are highly treatable and that effective treatment is often quite brief. Helping the person to realize that the experience of anxiety is neither abnormal nor catastrophic is an important starting place.

Mood Disorders

Presenting Complaints

Frank, a 28-year-old parishioner who is relatively new to the congregation, calls you in the middle of the night and excitedly begins to tell you about a wonderful plan he has developed to make the church and the entire denomination completely financially secure by the end of the year. His speech is rapid and pressured, and you find it nearly impossible to interrupt his wildly rambling discussion. Frank acknowledges that he has not slept for two days and states that God has given him the "energy of a million men." Frank mentions some annoyance at having received three speeding tickets earlier in the day. He insists that nothing must be allowed to thwart his master plan for the church.

Emma is a single 34-year-old who is feeling "down" and "blah." In your meeting with Emma, you learn she has nearly always felt this way. She denies despair or suicidal thinking and insists her low mood has never caused her to miss work or any other significant event. She appears matter-of-fact in describing her mood as "always on the down side."

Robert is a 58-year-old insurance broker who has been extremely healthy all his life. Following a significant demotion at work, he begins to feel increasingly depressed. Eventually, Robert's appetite and ability to sleep are so diminished that his wife becomes alarmed. Robert describes a constant depressed mood, a sense of hopelessness about the future, significant guilt about his inability to correct his mood, and loss of interest in all the activities he once enjoyed. He has begun to perform poorly at work and spends most of his waking hours in bed. For the first time, Robert admits thinking about suicide.

Common Features and Symptoms

Mood disorders are among the most common of all mental health problems in the United States.[1,2] The most prominent symptom is a disturbance of mood that is intense and persistent enough to be clearly maladaptive. In each of the major mood disorder types, the parishioner will suffer extremes of emotion (also called *affect*) that dominate his or her appearance and behavior. These emotional extremes may range from soaring elation, or *mania,* to deep *depression.* Depression refers to feelings of extreme sadness and dejection, and mania refers to the experience of intense and unrealistic excitement and euphoria. Most people suffering from a mood disorder have a *unipolar* disorder, which means they experience only depressive feelings. Others will experience both manic and depressive episodes and are considered to suffer from a *bipolar* disorder.

Most parishioners (and ministers!) will experience periods of depressed mood during their lifetime. So-called "normal depression" is quite common and is most often associated with some sort of life stress. Following episodes of loss (e.g., death of a loved one, divorce, retirement, job loss, separation from a friend), depressed mood related to grief and normal adjustment is reasonably ordinary and would not be considered indicative of a psychiatric problem. In this section, we discuss the major mood disorders with an emphasis on their defining symptoms.

In any 12-month period, roughly 9 percent of the U.S. population suffers from a mood disorder of some sort; the lifetime prevalence is approximately 20 percent.[2] It is not surprising that depression was the second most common counseling problem reported by ministers.[3] Mood disorders may also be evident in parishioners who present to the minister with other problems such as substance abuse, chronic illness, marital conflict, and marital dissolution. Beginning in adolescence, women are roughly twice as likely as men to suffer from serious depression.[1] The rates are reversed for alcoholism, leading some to speculate that males are more inclined to self-medicate depressive symptoms while women are more willing to express these symptoms and seek help. Rates for bipolar mood disorders are considerably lower (between 1 and 2 percent). Parishioners of all ages can become depressed. Even infants may experience a form of depression if separated for a prolonged period from their parents.[6]

Mental health professionals with the necessary expertise in treating mood disorders recognize that they are caused by a complex interaction of several factors. These causative agents include genetics, biochemistry, past experience, faulty thinking patterns, and situational stressors (especially losses). If a therapist suggests that depression is "always" caused by any single factor, be very cautious. Research has convincingly demonstrated that mood disorders run in families and that having parents with either unipolar or bipolar mood problems significantly increases the probability that a person will suffer from a similar disturbance. It is also clear that a significant imbalance in brain neurotransmitters (e.g., serotonin, norepinephrine) will produce depressed or manic symptoms. Each of the antidepressant medications, which can be so effective in treating severe depression, work to correct neurotransmitter imbalances in the depressed person's brain. Finally, research from cognitive psychology has demonstrated that depressed persons make excessively negative evaluations of themselves, their environments, and their futures. The point here is that mood disorders are complex in origin. A minister, like any professional, should avoid assumptions regarding "why" a parishioner is depressed.

Subtypes

Major Depressive Disorder

The criteria for diagnosing major depression require that individuals have numerous severe depressive symptoms, and that they cause significant distress and life impairment. These parishioners will have very depressed moods and/or loss of interest in pleasurable activities nearly all of the time. A major depressive episode is typically associated with changes in appetite, weight, and sleep. If a parishioner reports suicidal thinking, assume major depression until proven otherwise. Major depression is a potentially fatal problem and should be taken quite seriously by those who know the depressed person. Roughly 3.5 percent of persons with this disorder die as a result of suicide.[7]

Major depression may strike parishioners in any age, gender, or racial group, but it is particularly notable in those over the age of 50; older men constitute an especially vulnerable group. Major depression may be mild, moderate, or severe. A few people with major depression can become so severely depressed that they begin to have psychotic symptoms such as delusions (fixed beliefs that are incongruent with reality). The themes of these delusions would usually be *mood-congruent* and include personal inadequacy, guilt, deserved punishment, death, and disease. A parishioner may be suffering his or her first episode of major depression—in which case it is described as a *single episode.* Major depression may also be *recurrent* and occur episodically. In either case, most major depressive episodes are time-limited. With appropriate assistance, the parishioner may be expected to return to a more normal mood state.

Major Depressive Disorder: Key Indicators

- The person reports either seriously depressed mood or loss of interest or pleasure in usual activities for at least a two-week period.
- At least five of the following specific symptoms are present: (1) depressed mood most of the day, nearly every day; (2) markedly diminished interest in all or almost all activities most of the day; (3) significant weight loss, weight gain, or either decrease or increase in appetite every day; (4) insomnia or hypersomnia nearly every day; (5) obvious agitation or slowing in physical movements; (6) fatigue or loss of energy nearly every day; (7) feelings of worthlessness or excessive or inappropriate guilt nearly every day; (8) poor concentration or increased indecisiveness; (9) recurrent thoughts of death or committing suicide.
- These symptoms significantly interfere with the person's social well-being and his or her performance at work or school.

The severely depressed person may or may not be a self-referral to the minister. Very often, a family member may be the first one to contact you about the person's deteriorated mood and poor functioning. Of course, the specter of suicide should be of concern. Although hopelessness is common in those with major depression, it is also a risk factor for suicide, as are increased alcohol use, prior history of suicidal behavior, and subtle or overt attempts to "say good-bye" to loved ones. In the case of major depression, the pastor may need to make an emergency mental health referral (including hospitalization), particularly when the parishioner has articulated some suicidal thinking or their level of functioning is so impaired that they require intensive and monitored treatment.

Dysthymia (Persistent Depressive Disorder)

Dysthymia is basically "mild and chronic depression." The forlorn character Eeyore in *Winnie the Pooh* is a classic example of the dysthymic character. Eeyore is rarely happy, hangs his head frequently, and generally expects things to go poorly. Yet Eeyore is neither severely depressed nor suicidal. Dysthymia is a milder but more chronic problem than major depression. The dysthymic person often reports a lengthy history of low mood with accompanying thoughts of guilt, worthlessness, and pessimism about the future. More severe indicators of depression are usually not present, and the person often maintains a reasonable level of functioning, even though his or her poor mood interferes with relationships or work performance. Parishioners with dysthymia will have intermittent periods of normal mood (those with severe depression usually do not). They will report a long-standing history of mood problems, and they must have suffered with the problem for at least two years to be diagnosed with the disorder.

Dysthymia (Persistent Depressive Disorder): Key Indicators

- The person has depressed mood for most of the day, most of the time, as indicated by his or her own report or that of others.
- This low mood pattern has persisted for at least two years.
- While feeling depressed, the person reports at least two of the following: (1) poor appetite or overeating; (2) insomnia or hypersomnia; (3) low energy or fatigue; (4) low self-esteem; (5) poor concentration; (6) feelings of hopelessness.
- The person is not without the symptoms for more than two months.

Of course, the minister must be cautious not to assume that all who describe themselves as sometimes "down in the dumps" have a depressive disorder. As we noted previously, nearly all of us will feel depressed now and then. The difference is that this becomes a way of life for the dysthymic person. Various kinds of therapy (primarily cognitive, behavioral, or interpersonal) are likely to be helpful and antidepressant medication may also help. Such parishioners are unlikely to present in "crisis," but are more likely to come to the minister's attention because of the adverse social and occupational effects of dysthymia.

Adjustment Disorder With Depressed Mood

Adjustment disorders involve the development of a significant emotional and/or behavioral syndrome that is clearly in response to an *identifiable stressor*. The parishioner who has lost a loved one, begun divorce proceedings, or been seriously injured may suffer an understandable and even predictable adjustment reaction to that stressful event. Someone suffering from an adjustment disorder with depressed mood may appear to have dysthymia or major depression. The critical difference is that the person with an adjustment disorder is responding to an identifiable loss or stressor. Also, the adjustment problem must have begun within three months of the stressful event and, after termination of the stressful event, the problem should resolve within six months. If not, it may be something more serious.

Adjustment Disorder With Depressed Mood: Key Indicators

- The person has developed depressive symptoms (see Dysthymia Key Indicators) within three months from the start of the stressor(s).
- These depressive symptoms and behaviors are either in excess of what could be expected following the stressor, or their presence impairs social relationships or occupational functioning.
- Once the stressor ceases, the symptoms do not persist for more than six months.
- The symptoms do not represent normal bereavement (which should not be diagnosed or considered pathologic).

Helping the person suffering an adjustment disorder to view depressive symptoms more tolerantly may be the most important therapeutic task for ministers and therapists. Although determining which stressors qualify as likely to induce an adjustment disorder is somewhat subjective, many life events may be stressful enough to cause adjustment problems—particularly in parishioners with few resources and low resilience. If the person's symptoms are quite severe or seem not to resolve quickly, a referral for the same types of services noted for dysthymia and major depression is indicated.

Bipolar ("Manic-Depressive") Disorder

Bipolar disorder is distinguished from major depression by the presence of one striking and unique syndrome—the *manic episode*. *Mania* is an extreme mood condition, and it nearly always interferes with social and occupational functioning. A person who experiences a manic episode has a markedly elevated, euphoric, and expansive mood, often interrupted by occasional outbursts of irritability or even rage—especially when others refuse to go along with the sufferer's odd plans or behavior. Manic individuals may also have seemingly boundless energy and restless thoughts that seem to "race." Their speech is often extremely rapid, and they have great difficulty focusing on one topic. Persons with this disorder typically alternate between depressive episodes (see the Major Depression Disorder Key Indicators) and manic (or, slightly milder, *hypomanic*) episodes, which will be less frequent and shorter in duration. Although mental health professionals differentiate between bipolar disorder *Type 1* (characterized by more extreme manic episodes—see following key indicators) and *Type 2* (characterized by somewhat less extreme hypomanic episodes but very predictable swings between hypomanic and depressive episodes),[1] it is often very difficult—and probably unnecessary—for the minister to try to differentiate the two. For the most part, treatment options will be similar.

Bipolar ("Manic-Depressive") Disorder: Key Indicators

- For a period of at least one week, the person has persistently elevated, expansive, or irritable mood.
- During this time, at least three of the following symptoms are present: (1) inflated self-esteem or a grandiose assessment of oneself; (2) decreased need for sleep; (3) more speech, and speech that seems "pressured"; (4) racing thoughts; (5) distractibility; (6) increased goal-directed activity (socially, at work or school, or sexually) or increased physical-motor agitation; (7) excessive involvement in pleasurable activities that have high potential for painful consequences (e.g., unrestrained buying sprees, sexual indiscretions, foolish business investments).
- The person's relationships or work performance are impaired.
- There is typically some history of previous episodes of major depression (although it is possible to have manic episodes in the absence of depression).

The manic parishioner will likely be quite disruptive at work, in relationships, and in the church. He or she will engage in very uncharacteristic and potentially injurious behaviors. Often, these high-risk and inappropriate behaviors will be a source of great shame and embarrassment after the person has received treatment and the manic episode has resolved. It is important to keep in mind that this person needs professional treatment immediately. A referral to a psychiatrist is indicated so that the person can begin a trial of medication, usually lithium or another mood-stabilizer. Once the current manic episode has been treated, the real challenge may be encouraging the person to remain on medication (as long as the physician recommends) to prevent further occurrences.

Summary and Guidelines

Mood disorders are among the most common problems the pastor will see in day-to-day interaction with parishioners. Such disorders may range from "normal" depression to major depression with suicidal planning. Although bereavement, adjustment disorders, and, in some cases, major depression may have specific precipitating causes, most severe mood disorders are caused by a combination of biological, genetic, social, and even cultural factors. In the case of mild forms of depression, the pastor must consider how well prepared he or she feels to counsel a parishioner with mood problems. Good social support, good insight about the problem, and a willingness to seek and engage in assistance through the church are all positive indicators.

In the case of more serious mood problems such as major depression and bipolar disorder, the minister should nearly always encourage the parishioner (and the parishioner's family) to pursue professional mental health treatment. Again, a joint referral to a physician (preferably a psychiatrist) and a mental health provider with expertise in psychotherapy for mood disorders is highly recommended. It is quite likely that antidepressant medications will be prescribed for the person with a major depressive episode. Increasingly, physicians prescribe SSRIs (selective serotonin reuptake inhibitors), which change levels of the neurotransmitter serotonin in the brain and often create remarkably positive changes in mood (see Chapter 2 for a summary of medications most often prescribed for mood disorders). Antidepressant medications may play a critical role in an individual's recovery from severe depression. Unfortunately, antidepressant medications often come with a host of unpleasant side effects including nausea, headache, agitation, and increased risk of self-harm for children and adolescents.[8] SSRIs usually require several weeks to take effect. In the meantime, the severely depressed person may require hospitalization (especially if suicidal) or other intensive care to ensure their well-being and safety. In the most severe cases of major depression—when other avenues to treatment have been exhausted—a psychiatrist may employ electric shock treatment *(electroconvulsive therapy,* or *ECT)*. Electroconvulsive therapy is typically used only with older adults with unremitting depression.

Lithium therapy is the medical treatment most likely to be effective in treating bipolar illness, although it is also used in some cases of major depression. Lithium is often effective in preventing the cycling between manic and depressive episodes common among persons with this disorder. Other medications—including anticonvulsant drugs—may have value as mood-stabilizing agents.[9]

A range of psychotherapies, most preferably cognitive-behavioral, are also helpful in treating major depression. These therapies often focus on helping depressed persons to change their depressing self-statements and irrational beliefs. They may also address the sufferer's lack of rewarding experiences during the day and his or her need for more social reinforcement. Most often, a combination of therapy and medication will produce the most rapid recovery.

Finally, the minister must recognize that he or she can often play a critical role in the parishioner's recovery from depression.[10] This may involve making an immediate referral in the case of the severely depressed parishioner, serving as a supportive person in the parishioner's environment, and helping the parishioner and his or her family negotiate conflicts and understand the common symptoms of the disorder. The pastor will often be very influential in encouraging the afflicted person to seek treatment and in helping him or her deal with the guilt and shame that can often accompany depressive syndromes. Finally, the use of spiritual resources, prayer, and religious imagery has been shown to be very helpful for parishioners suffering from depression.

Psychotic Disorders

Presenting Complaints

Arthur, a 23-year-old parishioner, has been a member of the church since childhood. During the past two years, he has evidenced some odd changes in behavior. Arthur began withdrawing from social activities, stopped attending church, and began spending most of his time in his college dorm room. He appeared emotionally "blank" and stopped basic personal hygiene. Eventually, Arthur dropped out of college and has been living with his parents. His parents report that Arthur now hears voices calling him bad names. He believes that authorities from his college are attempting to kill him using microwaves.

Linda, age 32, comes for counseling with her husband. Her husband is exasperated by Linda's constant preoccupation with Tom Cruise.

It seems Linda believes this actor is deeply in love with her and that he communicates to her via subtle comments and gestures (which only she can translate) in his various movie roles. When she reads interviews with the actor, Linda detects "special notes" to her. Linda appears normal with the exception of her firm belief that Mr. Cruise is communicating intense love for her.

You are asked to visit 50-year-old Reggie in the hospital. He has apparently "gone crazy" after accidentally hitting and killing a child who ran out in front of his car. In the hospital, Reggie is staring and mumbling to himself. He does not respond to you or anyone else. One week later, Reggie is back in church. He has fragmented recall of the accident and your visit and he appears to have completely returned to normal.

Common Features and Symptoms

The psychotic disorders represent the ultimate in psychological breakdown. Parishioners who are psychotic will present with some of the most extreme and disturbed behaviors the minister will ever see. The term *psychosis* implies a profound loss of contact with reality. In essence, the psychotic person has become detached from basic connection points with the real world.

To people who interact with them, psychotic persons appear bizarre, incomprehensible, and even frightening. Psychotic individuals are so detached from reality that they are sometimes not held responsible for acts committed while psychotic. Hospitalization and medication are nearly always indicated. In this section, we describe *schizophrenia* (undoubtedly the most common and well-known of the psychotic disorders), *delusional disorder,* and *brief psychotic disorder.*

Subtypes

Schizophrenia

Schizophrenia is a debilitating psychotic disorder that occurs in all cultures. This disorder is among the most costly of world health problems with respect to financial loss, personal suffering, and treatment intensity.[2] The cost of caring for schizophrenic persons in the United States each year exceeds 60 billion dollars.[11] About 1 percent of the U.S. population suffers from schizophrenia.[1] The word *schizophrenia* means "split mind," and the disorder is characterized by disorganized thought processes, lack of coherence between thought and emotion, and an inward movement away from reality. The disorder is particularly tragic because its onset is typically in late adolescence or early adulthood, and the prognosis for full remission is poor.

Schizophrenia typically develops gradually. The afflicted person becomes progressively more reclusive, loses interest in the outside world, and the capacity for emotional responsiveness declines. Although most cases show this gradual onset in late adolescence or early adulthood, a smaller percentage are more sudden in onset and may be triggered by a stressful life event. Although the causes of schizophrenia are not well understood, research has confirmed a strong genetic component. For example, when one identical twin has the disorder, a 55 percent chance exists that the other will also have it—even when the two are reared apart. Undeniable evidence indicates that brain chemistry plays a central role in causing this disorder. An excess of the neurotransmitter dopamine has been a consistent finding among schizophrenic patients. The medications that effectively treat this disorder do so by lowering dopamine levels.

Schizophrenic symptoms are usually divided into *positive symptoms* and *negative symptoms*. Positive symptoms are behavioral excesses such as motor agitation, inappropriate emotional expression, disorganized speech and behavior, and the two hallmark symptoms of schizophrenia, *hallucinations* and *delusions*. Hallucinations are false perceptions such as voices, sights, or smells that no one else perceives. Delusions are clearly false beliefs such as "my thoughts are being broadcast to the CIA" or "someone is using microwaves to control me." Inappropriate emotional expression refers to such things as giggling when describing something morbid (e.g., the death of a family member). Disorganized speech refers to the fact that the schizophrenic's speech does not make sense (sometimes called "word salad"). Negative symptoms are behavioral deficits in such areas as emotional expression (flatness of expression), communicative speech (low verbal output), reactivity to the environment (withdrawal, fantasy, daydreaming), and goal-directed activities (apathy, poor hygiene).

Schizophrenia: Key Indicators

- At least two of the following must have been present most of the time for at least one month: (1) delusions; (2) hallucinations; (3) disorganized speech; (4) disorganized behavior; (5) negative symptoms (see aforementioned text) such as loss of emotional expression.
- The symptoms cause interference in the person's social and/or occupational functioning.
- There must be continuous signs of the disturbance for at least six months (including at least one month of the aforementioned symptoms), perhaps followed by periods of less intense disturbance.

It is worth noting that parishioners who suffer from schizophrenia do not always exhibit the same symptoms. In addition to the varied causes of this disorder (genetics, biology, social stressors, trauma, etc.), it has several subtypes. *Paranoid schizophrenia* is characterized by bizarre and illogical delusions, which often have a grandiose or suspicious quality (e.g., "I am God's chosen one, and many are jealous of that and trying to kill me."). A great deal of impaired judgment, erratic behavior, and even dangerous acting out occurs. Although the paranoid schizophrenic is less withdrawn socially, he or she may be more hostile and dangerous by interpreting the behavior of others as a direct personal threat. The *disorganized schizophrenic* is likely to develop the disorder at an earlier age and is considered more seriously fragmented than other types. Symptoms of emotional distortion and inappropriateness, bizarre behavior, and odd mannerisms are most common with this subtype. Finally, a person with *catatonic schizophrenia* may remain motionless for hours or even days—seemingly entirely cut off from external reality. These periods of *stupor* may alternate with periods of excitement as well as emotional and physical acting out.

Treatment for schizophrenia nearly always begins with hospitalization. This is especially true during initial episodes when the person begins acting quite erratically. For example, the person may be hearing voices or staring vacantly while ignoring basic self-care. Stabilizing schizophrenics often involves having them carefully monitored lest they harm themselves or others. In most states, there are provisions for hospitalizing psychotic persons, involuntarily if necessary, in order to protect and treat them. Antipsychotic medications are nearly always indicated and long-term management by a psychiatrist should be expected. Although medications will often help alleviate the most severe symptoms of schizophrenia, family members and friends should anticipate a long road to recovery. About two-thirds of those with this disorder will evidence at least mild symptoms for the rest of their lives.

Delusional Disorder

Delusional disorder is much less serious than schizophrenia. The psychotic person with this disorder may be able to function reasonably well both socially and at work. The hallmark symptom of delusional disorder is the presence of *delusions,* fixed beliefs that are not amenable to change in light of conflicting evidence, that persist for at least a month. A person who has other psychotic symptoms or has ever been diagnosed with schizophrenia cannot be diagnosed with this disorder.

The delusional person often feels singled out and taken advantage of, plotted against, stolen from, spied on, ignored, or otherwise mistreated. The delusions to which this person firmly clings involve situations that can conceivably occur in real life (e.g., being followed, poisoned, infected, loved at a distance, deceived by one's spouse or lover).[1] The delusional system usually centers on only one of these themes. For example, a parishioner may believe that his coworkers are attempting to steal his plans and that they have begun following him, tapping his phone, and collaborating with government agencies to collect information about him. Another parishioner may believe her husband is being unfaithful, although no real evidence for this exists. Because he returns 10 minutes late from the store one evening, she concludes he has rendezvoused with a lover. She becomes convinced that each of his behaviors (taking slightly more time in the shower, smiling when a certain song plays on the radio, or wearing a specific tie to work) hints at his unfaithfulness. She will be unresponsive to reason from others and will hold firmly to the belief that he is unfaithful.

Several subtypes of delusional disorder are as follows:

- *Persecutory type:* The person believes that he or she, or a loved one, is being subjected to maltreatment such as spying, stalking, or spreading of false rumors. The person may take legal (or more hostile) actions against those believed to be responsible.
- *Jealous type:* The person believes firmly that his or her sexual partner is being unfaithful.
- *Erotomanic type:* Someone of higher status (e.g., a movie star) is believed to be deeply in love with the person and interested in a sexual relationship (some people who "stalk" celebrities may fit this category).
- *Somatic type:* This person has an unshakable belief that he or she suffers from some physical illness—often of a very exotic nature (e.g., one's arm has been replaced by an alien appendage).
- *Grandiose type:* The person has a fixed belief that he or she has extraordinary status, power, ability, talent, beauty, and so forth.

Delusional Disorder: Key Indicators

- Delusions (extremely rigid bizarre thoughts) for at least six months.
- The person has never been schizophrenic.
- Aside from the impact of the delusions (e.g., rejection by others), there is no obvious impairment in functioning and behavior is not otherwise odd or bizarre.

The exact causes of delusional disorder are unclear. We do know that these persons have often gone through life feeling unappreciated, frustrated, and unjustly treated. As children, they were probably aloof, suspicious, stubborn, secretive, and resentful of punishment. They rarely have warm relationships with others.[1] Once a delusional disorder is firmly in place, it is very difficult to help these people. They may be quite frustrating for the pastor and their own family members because they seldom seek treatment; they are much more interested in seeking justice for all the wrong that has been done them. Because their lives may remain marginally intact, in spite of their fixed false beliefs, they may effectively thwart all attempts at intervention; they are seldom at such great risk that they merit involuntary hospitalization. They cannot be "talked out of" their delusions and attempts to do so may merely convince them that the minister is an accomplice to those who persecute them. Although some medications may be helpful, it is seldom that a person with this disorder will consent to take them. Unconditionally accepting the delusional parishioner and providing support for the family may be key pastoral roles.

Brief Psychotic Disorder

On very rare occasions, a person may become psychotic only for a brief time. In these unusual cases, the individual appears to be fine one day and delusional, disorganized, or hearing voices the next. The symptoms last only a short while, and the person can be expected to return to normal functioning again. The person does not have schizophrenia or a delusional disorder, but does evidence one or more of the common psychotic symptoms for a brief period of time. Most often, an identifiable stressor precipitates the psychosis (e.g., loss of a loved one, combat experience), but an identifiable stressor is not required for this brief disturbance to occur. Finally, there are some cases of these brief reactive states in women shortly after giving birth (postpartum onset).

Brief Psychotic Disorder: Key Indicators

- The person experiences at least one of the following symptoms: (1) delusions; (2) hallucinations; (3) disorganized speech; (4) grossly disorganized behavior.
- Symptoms last for at least one day but less than one month.
- The person returns to a completely normal level of functioning.

It is important to be sure that the parishioner who demonstrates sudden psychotic behavior has not been using illicit drugs or prescription medications that might explain his or her symptoms. Sudden symptom onset also raises concerns about medical problems such as brain accidents (e.g., strokes). Also, there are cultural explanations for certain behaviors that might otherwise seem bizarre. These *culture-bound syndromes* include the belief that sleeping in a room with an electric fan will be fatal, or that one's penis will suddenly shrink into the abdomen causing death.[12] Certain religious ceremonies and religious groups may endorse speaking in tongues, "receiving a word" from outside of oneself, or having spiritually based experiences such as visions. The minister should be sensitive to the specific symptom and its meaning to the parishioner in the context of his or her religious community.

Summary and Guidelines

Psychotic disorders are extremely serious. They are chronic mental health afflictions. As a minister, you may be the first to recognize signs of psychosis in a parishioner. You may be the one to organize and leverage hospitalization for a seriously disorganized and potentially dangerous person. More often, you will be called upon to support this person's family as they struggle to understand the gravity of their loved one's illness. Alleviating guilt or shame for the family is important as parents may often assume that they have "caused" schizophrenia in their child. Helping the family to understand the potent genetic and biological contributions to psychosis, the need for psychiatric treatment, and the long-term nature of the disorder are critical tasks. Research has shown that helpful communities for schizophrenic persons are gentle, accepting, consistent, and knowledgeable about the signs and treatments of the disorder. Larger churches or groups of churches might consider establishing day treatment or support programs for schizophrenic members and their families. The pastor should keep in mind that psychiatric medications are typically a must in the effective treatment of these disorders and that hospitalization can be critical as well. Understanding the chronic nature of schizophrenia while also maintaining and expressing hope for recovery is essential.

Neurocognitive Disorders

Presenting Complaints

Sally is a 61-year-old mother of four. She has always been exceptionally active in the church and a leader in many areas. During the last year, Sally's family has grown concerned about her slow withdrawal from social activities. Sally has some trouble remembering new things. She seems more fatigued and less alert than before. Her husband is especially concerned that Sally has slowly grown less concerned with hygiene and the appearance of their home. Her daughter wonders why her mother has become more childlike in her emotional expression. The family asks if you will "counsel" Sally.

Earl is a 70-year-old church member. His wife, Mildred, phones you from the hospital where Earl has been recovering from hip replacement surgery. She is beside herself. She blurts out that during the past 24 hours, Earl has become disoriented, agitated, and appears to be hallucinating. He doesn't appear to recognize Mildred, has cursed at her for the first time in 50 years, and is trying to hit nurses and orderlies who get too close. Earl's words are nonsensical. Mildred requests your presence. She is terrified that Earl has gone "crazy."

Stephen is a 47-year-old accountant. He has been a steady and reliable parishioner for many years. He is a model family man and a responsible member of the elder board. Stephen's wife demands that he accompany her to see you for counseling. During the past week, Stephen has behaved in a very uncharacteristic fashion. His mood fluctuates rapidly and can swing from irritability to tearfulness with little warning. He has also made inappropriate sexual comments at home and at work. Stephen admits being involved in a "fender bender" the week before, but he minimizes the "tiny bump on the head" he received.

Common Features and Symptoms

In contrast to other varieties of psychiatric impairment, *neurocognitive disorders* are nearly always a consequence of structural defects or damage to brain tissue—often the result of injury or disease. This loss of integrity of brain tissue (destruction of nerve cells in the brain) results in emotional and behavioral disorders that, at times, mimic other psychiatric problems. Neurocognitive disturbances are referred to as *organic* disorders. Delirium and neurocognitive disorders caused by dementia, traumatic brain injury, or other diseases always indicate damage, deterioration, imbalance, or infection of the brain. Brain impairment may result from focal damage (e.g., a bullet wound) or from diffuse damage resulting from disease, exposure to toxic substances, oxygen deprivation, or a head injury that affects more than a single region.

Persons with "organic" brain disorders often share certain presenting symptoms, although these will vary in each case. Symptoms may include memory impairment (especially for more recent events), forgetting one's own identity or the identities of loved ones, inability to learn new material, poor judgment (behavior becomes improper or unethical), apathy, lack of initiation of behavior (e.g., working, conversing), poor visual-spatial perception, and prob-lems understanding and using language.[13] Differentiating normal decrements in memory, cognitive processing speed, and judgment from those associated with a neurocognitive disorder often requires a careful professional assessment.

Parishioners with organic brain disorders will often be elderly. One of the premier challenges to clergy is to provide good support and direction to family members who may be understandably horrified by or depressed about the progressive (and often irreversible) changes to the personality of their loved one. In many cases, organic brain disorders are progressive and terminal. In others, they result in only temporary disability followed by return to previous levels of functioning (e.g., delirium).

Subtypes

Delirium

Many ministers reading this book may recall an episode from earlier in life in which they suffered a high fever, dehydration, concussion, or sedation, after which loved ones reported that their behavior during the episode was "weird, bizarre, or crazy." Those readers will appreciate the experience of a *delirium,* a temporary state of cognitive impairment characterized by dimin-ished attention, memory, and awareness of surroundings. A delirious parish-ioner will have trouble interacting lucidly and seem unaware of events going on around him or her. The terms *disorientation* and *clouded consciousness* are often used to summarize this person's presentation. Here is the good news: a delirium has a rapid, sudden onset and the impairment it creates will be short-lived. Once the biological cause of a delirium fades (e.g., anesthesia, an illicit substance, dehydration, fever, exhaustion) or is treated medically (e.g., bacterial or viral infection), the parishioner should make a full recovery.

Delirium: Key Indicators

- The person has trouble directing, focusing, and sustaining attention.
- Awareness of the surrounding environment is diminished; the person appears disoriented.
- There may be additional problems with memory, language, and odd perceptions.
- The onset is rapid and caused by an organic or biological problem.

Onset of a delirium in a loved one will no doubt be upsetting. The person moves from normal to quite impaired with little warning. If the organic cause is not immediately apparent, parents and others may worry that the symptoms indicate schizophrenia or sudden onset of dementia. The minister should reassure parishioners that neither of those disorders have a sudden onset. Immediate medical attention—often in the emergency room—is indicated.

Neurocognitive Disorder Caused by Alzheimer's Disease

In the latest edition of the *Diagnostic and Statistical Manual for Mental Disorders*, serious organic brain disorders such as Alzheimer's dementia and traumatic brain injury have been categorized as *Major* or *Mild Neurocognitive Disorders*.[1] *Dementia,* certainly the most common and feared organic brain disorder among older adults, is now labeled a neurocognitive disorder, perhaps *mild* shortly after onset and eventually, *major,* as the person becomes progressively impaired. In contrast to delirium, which develops quickly, dementia involves the progressive deterioration of the brain sometime after early adulthood. The cognitive deficits associated with dementia are chronic, slowly developing, progressive, and irreversible.[14] The parishioner with dementia will typically be elderly, although the disorder can strike people as young as 40. The earlier the onset of a dementia process, the more rapid the progression.

Recent data suggests that roughly 14 percent of adults 71 and older will suffer some sort of progressive dementia, and that percentage climbs to 37 percent for those over the age of 90.[15] Although neurocognitive disorders leading to dementia can be caused by vascular disease (stroke), Parkinson's disease, Huntington's disease, Lewy body disease, and HIV infection—among many other causes—Alzheimer's disease is by far the most common source of progressive dementia in older parishioners.[1]

Alzheimer's dementia is a very subtle disorder, which develops slowly in most cases. In early stages, the person remains reasonably alert and aware, though he or she may have trouble remembering some recent events. This subtle beginning often makes the onset of dementia nearly impossible to date. As the disorder progresses, the person experiences difficulty with abstract thinking, learning new things, judgment, problem solving, and impulse control. His or her personality may begin to deteriorate, emotional control declines, and the person appears to lose motivation in most areas. Persons with Alzheimer's dementia may become upset by changes to their routine. They become progressively more childlike, unaware of hygiene, and ultimately entirely dependent on others for care.

Neurocognitive Disorder Caused by Alzheimer's Disease: Key Indicators

- The person develops several cognitive problems such as loss of memory, an inability to use language, failure to recognize or identify objects or people that he or she should be familiar with, loss of ability to effectively plan or organize, and disturbances in motor functioning.
- In later stages, the person disengages from activities and interests previously enjoyed, becomes less alert, less emotionally balanced, and inflexible with regard to daily routine.
- These changes cause disruption in the person's social or occupational functioning and represent a loss or decline.
- The development of the symptoms is gradual and progressive.

Unfortunately, this disorder is terminal and slowly decreases the parishioner's quality of life until death. Regardless of the cause, the disorder will gradually diminish the person's ability to enjoy relationships, remain independent, and even understand who he or she is. Not only may the pastor be called upon to assist the parishioner with accepting and coping with this frightening disorder, the family typically has a substantial need for support and encouragement from the pastor as they deal with grief issues, adjustment to caretaking, and preparation for gradual loss of a parent or spouse. The person's faith, and that of his or her family members, may be understandably shaken at times during this process. The now-classic book for caregivers, *The 36-Hour Day*, nicely captures the challenges associated with caring for a family member with Alzheimer's.[16] It may also be useful to ministers who care for caregivers. Although there is no cure for dementia, the pastor may refer the parishioner to a physician with expertise in gerontology who may prescribe Cholinesterase Inhibitors (e.g., Aricept, Exelon, Razadyne) to slow the progression of memory deficits in the early stages of the disease. In the later stages, referral of the parishioner and family for appropriate social services (such as adult day care) is highly recommended.

*Neurocognitive Disorder Caused
by Traumatic Brain Injury*

There are three types of head injuries. In *closed-head* injuries, the cranium remains intact, but damage occurs to brain tissue nonetheless. Closed-head injuries are by far the most common organic brain disorders. Auto accidents, accidental falls, sports-related injuries, and many other events frequently result in closed-head trauma, which may be quite mild or life threatening depending on severity of damage to brain tissue. Less common head injuries include *penetrating* injuries (such as those from bullets or shrapnel in combat situations) or *skull fractures* in which the impact is substantial enough to break the skull bone.

Regardless of the cause of the injury to a person's brain, brain damage caused by head injury can produce some predictable symptoms. The most common are *retrograde amnesia* (loss of memory for events immediately preceding the injury), *anterograde amnesia* (inability to effectively store new memories following the injury), poor concentration, problems with speech, impaired judgment, poorly controlled moods, increased or decreased sleep, fatigue, irritability, dizziness, and headaches. Any of these symptoms, if sudden in onset, may be an indicator of a head injury. It is a good idea for the minister to inquire about recent accidents. In some instances of closed-head injury, a parishioner may have received what he or she believes was merely a "bump on the head," when in fact there is sustained bleeding inside the brain which produces pressure on the brain tissue, impairment, and the necessity of surgery to relieve the pressure. It is also important to note that these symptoms could be indicative of a brain tumor—particularly when accompanied by headaches, nausea, and dizziness.

Neurocognitive Disorder Caused by Traumatic Brain Injury: Key Indicators

- The person has sustained some injury to the brain, even when the event was apparently not traumatic (e.g., may or may not result in loss of consciousness).
- Following the injury, the person experiences symptoms such as impaired memory, confusion, poor control of emotions, impaired judgment, changes in sleep pattern, fatigue, poor concentration, headaches, dizziness, and anxiety.

Traumatic brain injuries are a distinctly medical matter. When the pastor becomes concerned that a parishioner is experiencing symptoms related to a recent injury to the head, an immediate referral to a physician is indicated. If the symptoms appear severe, transportation to a hospital or consultation with a neurologist is recommended. Prognosis for recovery hinges on the extent of damage to the brain and the speed at which medical intervention occurs. Prognosis is nearly always more positive in children, as younger brains have greater potential for recovery and adaptation.

Summary and Guidelines

Neurocognitive disorders or "organic" mental health problems may be among the most tragic and difficult for the minister and family members to address. Because these disorders involve the structure and functioning of the brain itself, they are sometimes not treatable. Perhaps the most important task for the minister is helping brain-impaired parishioners and their families with acceptance. Helping young parents accept the cognitive limitations of a brain-injured child, helping adult children accept the steady and permanent decline of a parent with Alzheimer's, and helping a spouse accept the steady loss of functioning in a spouse with early dementia are examples of this task. Modeling patient acceptance and sturdy faith in the face of such adversity can be powerful interventions.

Serving as an effective referral source is another critical pastoral role. As a minister, you may be the first to recognize the signs of a stroke or subtle head injury and should initiate an immediate referral to a physician. You may be the first to spot signs of "caretaker stress" in the spouse of a parishioner with dementia. In this case, you might recommend a day care facility for such impaired church members or even work with other local churches to create a day care consortium for Alzheimer's patients.

Somatic Symptom Disorders

Presenting Complaints

Marla is the young mother of a 1-year-old. Her husband brings her to see you as a result of his exasperation with her concerns about her appearance and her startling weight loss. Following the birth of her child, Marla became convinced that her abdomen continued to protrude in an unsightly way. She initiated a fanatical exercise routine and a rather severe diet. Now, one year later, she appears extremely skinny. There is no evidence of the slightest excess weight around her abdomen. Nonetheless, she looks at you with an expression of shame and distress and says, "As you can see, I can't lose the baby weight; I can't stand looking at my own disgusting stomach anymore."

Dave comes to your attention when a lay group leader complains that Dave has been attending the church's cancer support group for nearly five years. It has come to the leader's attention that Dave may not have cancer at all. Although he is convinced that he suffers from brain cancer—based on his own obsessive reading of medical journals and online medical webpages—Dave complains that no doctor has been competent enough to accurately diagnose him yet. In spite of his apparent good health, Dave insists that he suffers undiagnosed cancer, frequently dominates group discussions, and requests prayer for healing.

Common Features and Symptoms

Depending on the size of one's religious community, it is nearly certain that some members will be suffering preoccupation, anxiety, and sometimes, constant rumination about physical illness. *Somatic symptom disorders*—previously called *somatoform* disorders—form a related cluster of syndromes with this common feature: the parishioner complains of physical problems or concerns about medical illness.[1] Here is the catch: people with these disorders do *not* have an actual biological condition that can explain their physical symptoms. Parishioners with somatic symptom disorders will tend to communicate psychological distress through physical complaints and to display a lengthy track record of seeking medical help for their unexplained symptoms. According to some estimates, persons with these syndromes may account for 23 percent of people with medically unexplained symptoms seeking medical care.[17] Fixated on physical problems, unsatisfied with medical care, and prone to worry about their condition ceaselessly, these parishioners may be a handful for the minister.

Subtypes

Somatic Symptom Disorder

Physicians sometimes refer to persons with somatic symptom disorder as hypochondriacs or "organ recital patients." The reason is simple: these parishioners frequently complain of multiple bodily symptoms that cause them great worry and constant distress. Most of us are aware of a twinge here and a pain there, but the person with this disorder becomes thoroughly preoccupied with a laundry list of bodily symptoms such as pain (e.g., back, neck, pelvis, muscles), fatigue, shortness of breath, dizziness, and heart palpitations. There is no physical basis for these complaints, and the parishioner is likely to seek frequent doctor visits, even hospitalization, for the symptoms.

Somatic Symptom Disorder: Key Indicators

- The person complains of several persistent bodily symptoms that are distressing or disrupt daily functioning.
- The person worries about the seriousness of the symptoms, shows a high level of anxiety about them (e.g., needs to discuss them frequently), and spends an inordinate amount of time devoted to health concerns (e.g., researching the symptoms on the Internet).
- Physical exams reveal no biological cause for the symptoms.

As with all somatic disorders, it is imperative that the minister remains calm and patient with the somatic symptom disorder sufferer. This person will feel compelled to talk about symptoms frequently, which may frustrate friends and family members. The pastor may help the parishioner to "rest" in faith, using prayer, imagery, and scripture to counteract the tendency to engage in catastrophic thinking about the implications of various symptoms.

Illness Anxiety Disorder

Closely related to somatic symptom disorder, *illness anxiety disorder* is differentiated by the fact that the parishioner will become preoccupied with a specific illness—typically a fatal condition. This person will be preoccupied or fearful of having some serious disease that may explain various perceived bodily symptoms. A key element of the disorder is continued preoccupation and worry even *after* a careful physical exam has proven otherwise. This parishioner is likely to suffer *autosuggestibility*, the tendency to become alarmed by news stories or conversations about someone else suffering from a fatal illness.[18] Despite reassurances from one or more physicians that they do not suffer a life-threatening illness, these parishioners will spend considerable time researching the disease, diagnosing themselves, and talking about their illness conviction with anyone who will listen.

Illness Anxiety Disorder: Key Indicators

- The person has an excessive and unreasonable preoccupation with having or developing a serious illness.
- There is significant anxiety about the illness and the person will be easily alarmed by small changes in health status.
- Despite reassurances from medical professionals, the person remains anxious, preoccupied, and prone to frequent symptom checking.

Illness anxiety disorder can cause serious impairment in a parishioner's relationships, job effectiveness, and quality of life. Sadly, this person suffers needlessly. The minister must stand ready both to confront this parishioner with the "evidence" from physicians that no serious illness exists and offer support for the person's chronic worry about such. A referral to an MHP that can help the parishioner get to the source of their underlying anxiety is often indicated.

Body Dysmorphic Disorder

Although many of us worry about our looks, specific body features, and the occasional "bad hair day," roughly 3 percent of the population becomes obsessed and preoccupied with some imaginary or slight "defect" in their appearance.[1] Parishioners with body dysmorphic disorder (BDD) will check themselves constantly and seek frequent reassurance from others about how they look. They often worry excessively about specific aspects of their appearance such as facial features, wrinkles, hair, skin spots, and the size of certain body parts (e.g., nose, ears, muscles).[19] BDD is far more prevalent in younger adults. Research suggests that nearly a quarter of college students express significant concern about body image, though only fraction of these will develop BDD. There is a strong link between obsessive-compulsive disorder and BDD; the parishioner will obsess about perceived defect(s) and attempt to manage the anxiety this obsession provokes by compulsive checking and grooming. Those with the financial means may seek plastic surgery to address the "problem," but they are rarely happy customers and often seek multiple surgeries. Be advised that when BDD persists untreated, the parishioner may become so hopeless that suicide emerges as a serious risk.

> **Body Dysmorphic Disorder: Key Indicators**
> - The person is preoccupied with perceived defects in physical appearance that are unobservable or appear slight to others.
> - There is evidence of obsessive worry about the perceived defect as well as repetitive behaviors (e.g., mirror checking, reassurance seeking, excessive grooming) in response to the perceived appearance flaw(s).
> - The pattern of behavior is distressing for the person and maladaptive (e.g., causes the person to be late to work or socially isolated).

Parishioners with BDD will suffer a private agony. Although friends and loved ones typically see no problem with the person's appearance, he or she remains convinced that some aspect of appearance is disturbing to look at. They suffer needless embarrassment and shame. Yet, much like the adolescent with anorexia nervosa, the BDD parishioner will be impervious to reassurance. When the BDD sufferer resists positive feedback regarding appearance, the minister should remember that this parishioner actually perceives his or her body differently, and that he or she is not obstinate! The person's perceptual apparatus is distorted, generating tremendous anxiety.

Factitious Disorder

All of the somatic symptom disorders discussed earlier are sincere or authentic in the sense that the parishioner is not conscious of translating stress into anxiety and bodily preoccupation. But on occasion, a minister may encounter a person who deliberately produces physical or psychological symptoms for the sole purpose of receiving attention, pastoral care, or even medical treatment. Persons with *factitious disorder* deliberately lie about or even cause physical or psychological problems.[1,20] For instance, this person may injure himself, drink a toxic substance, or merely fabricate reports of seizures, pain, or suicidal depression. Attention from others—including medical professionals and ministers—is the objective. Consider the 78-year-old widower who suffers chest pains while shoveling his driveway. During a subsequent hospitalization for evaluation, his distant children visit, church members hover at his bedside, and kind nurses dote around the clock. Although he receives a clean bill of health, he experiences several subsequent "spells" resulting in hospitalizations in the following year. It becomes apparent this lonely parishioner finds all the care and attention associated with his hospitalizations to be quite emotionally gratifying; members of the medical and church community begin to suspect that he is faking his symptoms.

Factitious Disorder: Key Indicators

- The person deliberately falsifies physical or psychological symptoms or induces injury or disease in order to receive care and attention.
- The person presents to others as injured, ill, or impaired.
- The motivation is attention, not money or another external reward.

There is no specific treatment for factitious disorder.[20] It is important for the minister to balance holding the parishioner accountable for deliberate deception—once this is firmly established—with a good measure of empathy for the person's intense need for care and attention.

Summary and Guidelines

Somatic symptom disorders were first discussed by Freud and the psychoanalysts. There term "hysteria" was used to capture certain somatic presentations. It is possible that parishioners with somatic disorders (with the exception of factitious disorder) are struggling with unconscious sources of anxiety that happen to find expression in bodily symptoms and complaints. Psychodynamic therapy may help these parishioners to explore the psychological conflicts generating somatic symptoms. Cognitive-behavioral therapies are often useful for relieving this underling *health anxiety* by helping sufferers to question their illness beliefs and interpret their body's reactions in more rational terms. Raising levels of serotonin in the brain through the use of SSRI antidepressants may also be useful in cases involving extreme rumination and obsessiveness. At times, remaining calm and kind with a somatically preoccupied parishioner may require herculean patience and deliberate empathy. When she launches into an anxiety-fueled "organ recital" or when he complains for the 100th time about why God created him with such an unsightly nose, the minister must take a deep breath and consider whether these complaints create enough life disruption for the person that a referral to a trusted MHP is indicated.

Notes

1. American Psychiatric Association. (2013). *Diagnostic and statistical manual of mental disorders* (5th ed.). Washington, DC: Author.
2. Kessler, R. C., Berglund, P., Demler, O., Jin, R., & Walters, E. E. (2005). Lifetime prevalence and age-of-onset distributions of *DSM-IV* disorders in the National Comorbidity Survey Replication. *Archives of General Psychiatry, 62*(6), 593–602.
3. Benner, D. (2003). *Strategic pastoral counseling: A short-term structured model* (2nd ed.). Grand Rapids, MI: Baker Book House.
4. Perugi, G., Frare, F., & Toni, C. (2007). Diagnosis and treatment of agoraphobia with panic disorder. *CNS Drugs, 21*(9), 741–764.
5. Beck, A. T., Emery, G., & Greenberg, R. (2005). *Anxiety disorders and phobias: A cognitive perspective*. New York, NY: Basic Books.
6. Bowlby, J. (1980). *Attachment and loss* (Vol. 3): *Loss, sadness, and depression*. New York, NY: Basic Books.
7. Barlow, D. H., & Durand, V.M. (2005). *Abnormal psychology: An integrated approach* (5th ed.). Belmont, CA: Wadsworth.
8. Howland, R. H. (2007). Managing common side effects of SSRIs. *Journal of Psychosocial Nursing and Mental Health Services, 45*(2), 15–18.
9. Dubovsky, S. L., & Dubovsky, A. N. (2002). *Concise guide to mood disorders*. Washington, DC: American Psychiatric Publishing.
10. Benner, D. (2003). *Strategic pastoral counseling: A short-term structured model* (2nd ed.). Grand Rapids, MI: Baker Book House.
11. McEvoy, J. P. (2007). The costs of schizophrenia. *Journal of Clinical Psychiatry, 68 Suppl 14*, 4–7.
12. Tseng, W.-S. (2003). *Clinician's guide to cultural psychiatry*. San Diego, CA: Academic.
13. Wood, K. M., Edwards, J. D., Clay, O. J., Wadley, V. G., Roenker, D. L., & Ball, K. K. (2005). Sensory and cognitive factors influencing functional ability in older adults. *Gerontology, 51*, 131–141.
14. Kaufer, D. I., & DeKosky, S. T. (2004). Diagnostic classifications: Relationship to the neurobiology of dementia. In D. S. Charney & E. J. Nestler (Eds.), *Neurobiology of mental illness* (2nd ed.; pp. 771–782). New York, NY: Oxford.
15. Plassman, B. L., Langa, K. M., Fisher, G. G., Heeringa, S. G., Weir, D. R., Ofstedal, M. B., . . . Wallace, R. B. (2007). Prevalence of dementia in the United States: The aging, demographics, and memory study. *Neuroepidemiology, 29*(1–2), 125–132.

16. Mace, N. L., & Rabins, P. V. (2012). *The 36-hour-day: A family guide to caring for people who have Alzheimer's Disease, related dementias, and memory loss.* Baltimore, MD: Johns Hopkins University Press.
17. Steinbrecher, N., Koerber, S., Frieser, D., & Hiller, W. (2011). The prevalence of medically unexplained symptoms in primary care. *Psychosomatics, 52*(3), 263–271.
18. Fink, P., Ørnbøl, E., Toft, T., Sparle, K. C., Frostholm, L., & Olesen, F. (2004). A new, empirically established hypochondriasis diagnosis. *American Journal of Psychiatry, 161*(9), 1680–1691.
19. Phillips, K. A., Wilhelm, S., Koran, L. M., Didie, E. R., Fallon, B. A., Feusner, J., & Stein, D. J. (2010). Body dysmorphic disorder: Some key issues for DSM-V. *Depression and Anxiety, 27*, 573–591.
20. Eastwood, S., & Bisson, J. I. (2008). Management of factitious disorders: A systematic review. *Psychotherapy and Psychosomatics, 77*(4), 209–218.

4   The Parishioner in Distress
Major Psychological Disorders, Part II

In this chapter, we continue to describe several major categories of psychiatric disturbance that ministers may encounter in their work. Although these disorders are somewhat less prevalent than depression and anxiety problems, they will occur nonetheless. In this chapter, we summarize trauma-related disorders, substance use disorders, sleep-wake disorders, and sexual disorders. As in Chapter 3, we provide subsections that address *presenting complaints, common features and symptoms, subtypes,* and *key indicators* for each disorder. A *summary and guidelines* section encapsulates the primary factors for the minister to consider when responding to a parishioner who may suffer from a particular disorder.

Trauma-Related Disorders

Presenting Complaints

Jennifer is a 17-year-old high school student who was involved in an auto accident three weeks ago. Although Jennifer sustained only minor injuries, a close friend was killed in the accident. Jennifer was trapped in the car with her deceased friend for nearly 30 minutes before help arrived. Since then, Jennifer can barely recall events surrounding the accident and she reports feeling "numb." She describes feeling as though things are no longer "real," and she avoids all reminders of the accident.

Bob has been a church member all his life. He is employed at a local service station and has held numerous jobs over the years. He has never been married and he seems to avoid relationships. He sometimes gives little attention to hygiene and others see him as "jumpy" and aloof. When Bob was in his early twenties, he was stationed aboard the USS *Iowa* when one of the main gun turrets exploded and many sailors were killed. Bob was involved in recovering bodies from the turret. Years later, Bob continues to have nightmares about the event, avoids anything having to do with ships or the ocean, and appears easily startled.

Angela is a single 28-year-old who has been actively involved in church support groups for several years. She struggles with a weight problem and poor self-esteem. Angela has disclosed a history of having been severely sexually abused as a young girl. While describing her abuse in a counseling session, she begins speaking with a young girl's voice. She also curls up in her chair and takes on the mannerisms of a child. She seems to be a different person and she refers to herself as Bonnie. The counselor learns that although Bonnie is aware of Angela, Angela does not seem to know about Bonnie.

Common Features and Symptoms

In each of these cases, a common theme is the experience of a very painful life event (or series of events) that can be considered traumatic. Traumatic events are unusual and often catastrophic events that most people never experience.[1] In traumatic situations, people believe that death or serious injury to themselves or others is imminent; they feel entirely out of control. During the trauma, the person responds with understandable fear, helplessness, or horror. Most important, the victim will typically experience the event over and over again in the form of flashbacks and nightmares—thereby hardening new neural pathways in the brain that are quite easy to "trigger" later on. Trauma can occasionally occur vicariously upon hearing that a family member or close associate has been unexpectedly killed or harmed, or perhaps even seeing a traumatic event on video. Traumatic events may include auto accidents, military combat, rape, domestic abuse, and natural disasters such as hurricanes and earthquakes. In this section, we describe the two most common categories of traumatic event–induced disorder. *Posttraumatic stress disorder* and *acute stress disorder* frequently occur following a traumatic and life-threatening experience. We further cover two dissociative disorders, *dissociative amnesia* and *dissociative identity disorder (DID)*. Whereas DID is nearly always the result of trauma experienced in childhood (most often, the trauma relates to severe child abuse of some sort), dissociative amnesia may follow trauma that occurs anytime in life.

Subtypes

Postttraumatic Stress Disorder

Posttraumatic stress disorder (PTSD) may follow exposure to a specific traumatic life event (e.g., auto accident, sexual assault, combat, tornado). The trauma typically involves the threat of death or serious injury to oneself or to others. It appears that the more severe the trauma and the longer the symptoms have persisted, the more chronic the PTSD will be. In the hours and days following the traumatic event, the person may fluctuate between re-experiencing the trauma and making efforts to avoid thinking about it altogether. During the avoidance phase, the person may feel numb, minimize the importance of the event, and report amnesia for the time surrounding the event. During the re-experiencing episodes, the person is unable to stop thinking about the trauma; these thoughts may be experienced as "intrusive" and beyond the person's control.[1] He or she is likely to have sleep problems, be easily startled, and be somewhat "paranoid" or guarded. The person will often feel anxious and may feel as though he or she is going "crazy."

MHPs first became aware of PTSD during World War II. At that time the disorder was known as "shell shock," "battle fatigue," or "war neurosis." A substantial number of Vietnam veterans suffer from very severe cases of PTSD, and ministers are certainly likely to see trauma-related difficulties in veterans of Iraq and Afghanistan. Although the lifetime prevalence rate for PTSD is roughly 6.8 percent in the general population, rates are approximately 17 percent for Iraq war veterans.[2,3] Many Veterans Administration (VA) medical centers specialize in treating PTSD among combat veterans. Persons suffering from PTSD may avoid getting assistance and may withdraw from important relationships altogether. They may use alcohol and drugs to manage their symptoms. Children and elderly persons are more vulnerable to PTSD. Individuals with a previous history of psychiatric problems are also more likely to develop PTSD following a traumatic event.

Posttraumatic Stress Disorder: Key Indicators

- The person has experienced or witnessed a traumatic event that involved actual, or threatened, death or injury. Alternatively, the person may be exposed to details about the accidental/violent death of a loved one or friend.
- The traumatic event is persistently re-experienced via intrusive, uncontrollable recollections and dreams.

- The person avoids reminders of the trauma by avoiding persons, situations, conversations, and activities linked to the event.
- There is evidence of physical arousal related to the trauma such as sleep disturbance, irritability, poor concentration, being easily startled, and being excessively vigilant about one's surroundings.
- Negative changes in thought and mood following the trauma may include selective amnesia, feelings of detachment, anxiety, guilt, self-deprecation, and loss of interest in activities.
- The person is distressed about these symptoms; the person's work and relationships are impaired as a result.
- The symptoms must persist for at least one month.

Ideally, persons who have experienced a traumatic event will undergo supportive "debriefing" conversations in the hours and days following the event. A debriefing involves talking about the trauma—preferably with others who were also present—as a way of normalizing feelings and reactions during the traumatic event. Research suggests that those who undergo such supportive and normalizing experiences are less likely to develop PTSD. For those who do, treatment often involves individual and group therapy and medication. The pastor should make every effort to get the traumatized parishioner into treatment as soon after the appearance of symptoms as possible. Common treatment approaches involve exposure to the traumatic memories and environmental cues (e.g., specific locations and situations) in order to reduce fear responses.[4] Prolonged exposure techniques require the client to face memories or memory cues over a sustained period so that the client can lower reactivity and learn to experience greater calm, even in the face of memories he or she might have vigorously avoided prior to treatment. Therapy may also help to change the person's distorted (often self-blaming) thoughts and beliefs about the traumatic event. Medications for more severe PTSD may include both antidepressant and antianxiety drugs. These medications should be managed by a psychiatrist with experience in treating trauma-related disorders. Although PTSD can, at times, improve and even dissipate altogether without treatment, untreated PTSD more often results in chronic disturbance, substance abuse, and both work and relationship failures.

Acute Stress Disorder

In acute stress disorder, the parishioner will have been exposed to some traumatic event similar to those previously described for PTSD. That is, the person experiences or is confronted with events involving real or

threatened death, serious injury, or sexual violation in themselves or someone near to them.[1] After the event, the person experiences a number of
symptoms of anxiety or *dissociation* (feeling as though things are not real,
feeling detached from one's own body, or having difficulty recalling specific
details about the traumatic event). The difference between this disorder
and the more serious PTSD is simply symptom duration. Although PTSD
requires the presence of these symptoms for at least one month, acute stress
disorder is diagnosed immediately after the trauma (within three days). If it
persists for more than four weeks, the trauma syndrome must be diagnosed
as PTSD. It is not uncommon for a person to show signs of anxiety and
dissociation following an extreme stressor. These symptoms often decline
within several weeks, and there is no need for ongoing mental health care. If
these symptoms do not dissipate or if they become more acute, it is reasonable to suspect that the person's reaction to the trauma has progressed from
acute stress disorder to PTSD.

Acute Stress Disorder: Key Indicators

- The person is exposed to similar kinds of trauma described in
  the PTSD key indicators.
- Either during or following the traumatic event, the person
  experiences some of the following symptoms of dissociation:
  (1) emotional numbing or detachment; (2) a sense of being
  "dazed"; (3) feeling as though things are not real; (4) feeling
  detached from oneself; (5) having amnesia for some events surrounding the trauma.
- The person has flashbacks or nightmares about the event.
- He or she avoids situations or stimuli that remind him or her of
  the trauma.
- There are significant symptoms of anxiety or arousal following
  the event.
- These symptoms have lasted for at least three days, but not for
  more than four weeks.

Because many cases of acute stress disorder resolve during the month
following the trauma, and because this reaction is such a normal response
to uncommon trauma, the pastor may be most helpful to the parishioner
by simply remaining patient and understanding. Inviting the parishioner
to tell his or her story about the event and describe feelings connected to
it is usually helpful. Normalizing (without minimizing) the parishioner's

feelings of anxiety and distress is also indicated. Of course, the parishioner may also benefit from referral to an MHP, particularly if the symptoms do not dissipate quickly or if they significantly worsen.

Dissociative Amnesia

Many ministers reading this guide will recall an experience or two of feeling "not with it," detached, or "spaced out." These everyday experiences of *dissociation* offer a glimpse into the experience of parishioners with dissociative disorders. These disorders involve serious disturbances in consciousness (awareness), memory, and identity.[1] The normally intact sense of self becomes fragmented as the person loses memory for periods of time or feels disconnected from his or her own body. For obvious reasons, these experiences may leave the sufferer embarrassed, confused, and distressed.

When a parishioner is unable to recall important personal information that should be easily recalled (e.g., where one grew up, one's own wedding), typically following a traumatic event, he or she may be suffering from *dissociative amnesia*. Of course, other causes should be ruled out first (e.g., substance abuse, dementia, head injury). There are many varieties of dissociative amnesia, including *generalized amnesia* (failure to recall one's entire life); *localized amnesia* (failure to recall all events during a specific period of time); and *selective amnesia* (failure to recall only certain events during a very stressful period).

Dissociative Amnesia: Key Indicators

- The person cannot recall important personal information, usually of a traumatic or stressful nature.
- The lack of recall does not fit the pattern of ordinary forgetting and is not better explained by a medical or biological cause for amnesia.
- The amnesia causes disruption in the person's life and/or distress and embarrassment.

Dissociative Identity Disorder

Dissociative identity disorder (DID) is the new name for a severe psychiatric disorder previously known as *multiple personality disorder*. It is the most commonly known and most severe of the dissociative disorders. Nearly all persons with DID report severe physical or sexual abuse as children. The dissociative "splitting" in DID is a psychological process in which the mind splits off, or compartmentalizes, certain memories or events from conscious awareness. The hallmark of DID is the existence of two or more distinct identities or personalities within the same individual. Each of these distinct identities, or *alters,* is a complex and distinct personality with a name, gender, history, personality features, medical problems, social relations, and even distinct intelligence levels. The number of alters may vary from 2 to 50 or more. The original person is sometimes called the *host* alter and is usually not consciously aware of the other alters, although they are aware of the host and may be aware of one another. The alters often show extreme departures from the host's normal personality. For example, a shy host may have alters including a prostitute, transvestite, or devil. Alters may differ in age, gender, and race from the host.

Persons with DID are often in therapy for years before being officially diagnosed with the disorder because they often come to treatment for other reasons (such as depression), and the alters are difficult to detect.[5] Signs of DID include use of the pronoun "we" instead of "I" in conversation, receiving bills for things the person (host) does not recall buying, or hearing voices coming from inside one's head (versus outside as in the case of psychotic disorders). It is very important that a professional, with *substantial* experience, assess and diagnose DID. This disorder is occasionally faked by persons who have a significant need for the attention that DID may generate.

Dissociative Identity Disorder: Key Indicators

- Two or more distinct identities or personality states are present in one person.
- At least two of these personality states occasionally take control of the person's behavior. Friends and family members may express concern about "demon possession."
- The person shows inability to recall everyday events or important personal information that is too severe to be explained by ordinary forgetfulness.

Dissociative identity disorder has often been falsely diagnosed in persons with other trauma-related disorders, depression, psychosis, or personality disorders. When this disorder is suspected, the person should be referred to a psychiatrist, psychologist, or clinical social worker with specialized training and experience; most clinicians do not often encounter dissociated clients. Therapy for DID can be long, tedious, and only marginally successful. The goal is to integrate the person's alters into a single unified personality, which requires bringing to awareness those traumatic memories that the person's alters have successfully allowed him or her to avoid.[5] Medications are generally not helpful and hypnosis can be dangerous because these people are so suggestible (new alters may be easily and inadvertently created). Although the prognosis for full recovery is guarded, full recovery does occur and maintenance of hope is critical for both parishioners with DID and their loved ones.

Summary and Guidelines

When a minister learns that a parishioner has experienced or witnessed a traumatic life event, it is wise to review the symptoms of acute stress disorder with the expectation of encountering symptoms of dissociation, avoidance, and heightened anxiety and arousal. Parishioners may feel as though they are going "crazy," and they may be ashamed about their level of fear following the experience. Normalizing posttrauma symptoms is a first step, followed closely by an invitation to meet with the parishioner to hear his or her story. When groups of parishioners are involved, arranging a formal debriefing by a professional experienced with this procedure is recommended. Keep in mind that speedy intervention following a traumatic event is the most effective method of reducing the risk of eventual PTSD. Finally, remember that PTSD, once established, can be relatively chronic. Be sure to avoid frustration with traumatized parishioners who seem unable to quell symptoms such as flashbacks, hypervigilance, and occasional anger when startled or triggered by events around them.

Finally, when a parishioner appears to suffer inexplicable gaps in memory or to have an alter personality, or there are reports from others that this is so, we recommend rapid referral to a practitioner who is well trained and experienced in the treatment of dissociative disorders. These disorders are both rare and particularly difficult to resolve. Roughly 2 to 3 percent of the North American population shows evidence of a dissociative syndrome.[1,5] DID is often associated with severe childhood abuse and serious adult personality disturbance, which make therapy challenging for even the most skilled clinician.

Substance Use Disorders

Presenting Complaints

Alex is a 20-year-old college junior who is facing expulsion from a local university following his third alcohol-related incident on campus. During the past two years, Alex has been involved in two altercations with other students and campus police while drinking. Most recently, he was arrested at a basketball game for public drunkenness. He is also on probation for driving while intoxicated. Although Alex does not use alcohol on a daily basis, he tends to drink to intoxication on weekends in spite of his arrests and the threat of expulsion.

Sumaiya is a 47-year-old married mother of two adult children. She comes to counseling with her husband who is "fed up" with her refusal to cut down on her alcohol consumption. Although Sumaiya denies excessive drinking, her husband notes that her drinking has increased dramatically since the children left home. He also mentions that Sumaiya drinks in the morning and continues throughout the day. She appears unable to skip a day of drinking, and her husband has discovered alcohol hidden in unusual places around the home. Sumaiya admits having attempted to reduce her alcohol consumption without success.

Jeffery is an attorney for a large and competitive law firm. He began using amphetamines a year ago in an attempt to increase his alertness late at night so that he could work longer and accrue more billable hours. He is up for promotion to partner in the firm and feels tremendous pressure to succeed. Jeffery became alarmed recently when he realized he is now using four times the dosage of amphetamines to achieve the same sense of alertness. When he has attempted to reduce the amount he uses, he becomes fatigued, has unpleasant dreams, feels agitated, and has trouble sleeping.

Common Features and Symptoms

Addictive behavior may include any impairing pattern of excessive use or uncontrollable "need" for a substance or activity. By *substance,* we mean any chemical that a person might smoke, drink, inject, inhale, swallow, or snort. Substances might be illicit and legal drugs—to include both prescribed and over-the-counter medications. Addictive substance use may include excessive or harmful use of substances such as alcohol, cocaine, or marijuana. A food addiction may involve excessive intake of high-calorie food—resulting in obesity. Addictions may also be present when sexual behavior becomes so disruptive that it interferes with relationships or employment.

In this section, we focus on the most commonly abused substances or *psychoactive drugs:* alcohol, opiates, amphetamines, barbiturates/benzodiazepines, hallucinogens, and marijuana (cannabis). We describe the major characteristics of *substance use disorder;* keeping in mind that the diagnostic criteria for this disorder do not vary across types of substance (e.g., the criteria for diagnosing alcohol use disorder are nearly identical to those for marijuana and hallucinogens).[1] We then very briefly describe the distinctive elements of each type of addictive substance.

Substance Use Disorder

The key feature of *substance use disorder* is the continued use of a substance despite significant substance-related problems. Disordered use of any substance is associated with use of the substance in dangerous circumstances, persistent interpersonal problems related to the substance use, increasing tolerance for the substance, and serious risk of withdrawal if use is curtailed.[1] Although MHPs distinguished between *substance abuse* (irresponsible, dangerous use of a substance) and *substance dependence* (a pattern of escalating tolerance and withdrawal symptoms), most now talk in terms of a unified view of maladaptive substance use. Parishioners with substance use disorders may present with a broad range of severity, from mild to severe, even incapacitating.

When a parishioner (or more often, a loved one) reports problems with a substance, the minister will be well served to ask about some of the more severe symptoms of substance use disorder such as increased tolerance, withdrawal, and compulsive use. *Tolerance* for a psychoactive substance occurs when the user begins to need greatly increased amounts of the substance for intoxication (or the desired mood effect). Using the same amount becomes unsatisfying. The degree to which increasing tolerance occurs varies across substances. For example, amphetamine dependence can result in a tenfold increase in the dosage used, while hallucinogenic drugs produce comparatively little tolerance. *Withdrawal* is a physical response that occurs when blood or tissue levels of a substance decline—usually after prolonged and heavy use. This decline results in maladaptive (and possibly deadly) symptoms. Although the typical withdrawal symptoms vary with each substance type, frequently occurring withdrawal symptoms include tremors, sweating, insomnia, nausea/vomiting, anxiety, seizures, agitation, hallucinations, fatigue, restlessness, poor concentration, depressed mood, and increased or decreased appetite. Someone with a severe substance problem will typically find withdrawal symptoms so aversive that they will continue to use the substance to avoid them. This may result in a pattern of repeated use that begins in the morning and continues throughout the day.

Compulsive use of the substance may include using more of a substance than intended and failed attempts to reduce the amount used. The person may also spend a great deal of time obtaining, using, and recovering from the substance. At the same time, he or she may begin to withdraw from important family, occupational, and social activities. A final indicator of compulsive use is the continued use of the substance despite clear links between the substance and the person's psychological and physical problems.

Substance Use Disorder: Key Indicators

For at least one year, the person has a pattern of substance use leading to serious impairment in daily activities or significant distress as indicated by *at least two* of the following:

- Using more of the substance over a longer period of time than intended.
- Persistent and unsuccessful attempts to cut down on the substance.
- Considerable time spent obtaining the substance or recovering from its effects.
- Strong cravings or urge to use the substance.
- Obligations at work, school, or home go unfulfilled.
- Continued use of the substance despite social and interpersonal problems.
- Important activities (e.g., socially, occupationally) are given up because of the substance.
- Recurrent use in situations that could be physically dangerous.
- Continued use despite clear physical or psychological consequences.
- Increased tolerance to the effects of the substance.
- Withdrawal symptoms when the substance is discontinued.

Substance use disorders range from moderately impairing to thoroughly incapacitating. Not only are they among the most common and costly of all health problems in Western societies each year, substance disorders are devastating for children and families. It is very important for ministers to know the indicators of substance use disorder, regardless of the specific substance(s) of concern. They must be ready to assist family members in identifying the problem, confronting the user, and assisting with arrangements for treatment and follow-up support. Remember that withdrawal symptoms from many substances can be lethal and often require medical support. When a parishioner expresses an intention to "go cold turkey," a referral to his or her physician is essential.

Major Substances

The following section briefly identifies and describes the major psychoactive substances that parishioners may begin to use abusively. Keep in mind that the previously listed key indicators apply to each of these substances. Although the specifics for tolerance and withdrawal symptoms may change, the overall behavioral characteristics of the substance-addicted person will remain consistent across substances.

Alcohol

Alcohol is the most frequently abused of the psychoactive substances. Nearly one-quarter of Americans 12 and older admits to binge drinking, and roughly 7 percent of Americans are "heavy drinkers" (they frequently consume five or more drinks).[6] Although many use alcohol moderately, millions abuse it daily and millions more will develop an alcohol use disorder during their lifetimes. Each year, more than a 100,000 Americans die from alcohol-related causes. Genetic, biological, psychological, and social factors all play a role in determining who may become alcoholic. Alcohol is a central nervous system depressant that may eventually produce chronic health problems such as erectile dysfunction, stomach problems, memory impairment, liver cirrhosis, cancer, and even brain shrinkage. As a drug, alcohol affects the higher brain centers, impairing judgment, impulse control, and rational processes. Alcoholics are considerably more prone to suicide and mental health problems as well as family and work problems than people who consume alcohol moderately.

Opiates

Morphine and heroin are the most frequently abused of the opiate (narcotic) drugs. Narcotics are derivatives of opium, and their use dates back 5,000 years. Morphine and heroin have often been used as effective pain relievers. Unfortunately, they are extremely addictive drugs that quickly lead to increasing tolerance and serious (even life-threatening) withdrawal symptoms. When injected, opiates cause a sudden "rush" of euphoria followed by a period of drowsiness. Those who begin using heroin are most likely to state that pleasure, curiosity, and peer pressure were the primary reasons for using the drug initially. The causes of opiate addiction include brain receptivity to the substances, other psychological problems (e.g., personality or mood problems), and social/cultural influences. Those who become dependent on opiates become increasingly withdrawn, indifferent to relationships and events around them, and progressively more reliant on the effects of the drug to reduce tension and keep withdrawal symptoms at bay. Opiate withdrawal is particularly awful, often including chills, cramps, vomiting, and diarrhea.

Amphetamines

In contrast to opiates and alcohol, which slow down or depress the nervous system, amphetamines stimulate and speed up the nervous system by stimulating the cortex. This is why they are known as *stimulants.* Cocaine is the most common of the stimulant drugs. It may be ingested by sniffing, smoking, swallowing, or injecting, and it typically produces a euphoric state for four to six hours after use. During this time, the user may experience confidence and contentment. As the user becomes increasingly addicted to cocaine, symptoms such as dizziness, headache, depressed mood, and restlessness may occur between doses. In more advanced cases, those who are dependent on cocaine may experience psychotic hallucinations (much like schizophrenics) and severe depression as well as serious legal, family, job, and marital problems. Because the drug is quite expensive, criminal activity may begin as a way of supporting the dependency. Other amphetamine drugs include Dexedrine, Ritalin, and Methedrine. Persons may begin using these medications or cocaine to curb appetite, decrease fatigue, or achieve a sense of arousal with respect to attention and sexual interest. Unfortunately, amphetamines have been widely accepted by middle-class culture and youth have increasing access to amphetamines prescribed for ADHD.

Barbiturates and Benzodiazepines

Barbiturates (e.g., Amytal, Luminal, Nembutal) are powerful *sedatives* that have some important medical uses, but are extremely addictive and possibly lethal when used excessively. Much more frequently prescribed— and commonly abused—benzodiazepines (e.g., Xanax, Valium, Ativan) are a closely related group of medications used for controlling anxiety and facilitating sleep. These drugs are similar to alcohol in their effect on the central nervous system; they act as depressants, causing the person using them to experience relaxation, reduction in tension, and eventually drowsiness and sleep. Although mild doses may produce only relaxation, higher doses can produce sleep almost immediately. Overdoses can paralyze the brain's respiration center, resulting in death. Repeated use of these medications can lead to increased tolerance, compulsive use patterns, and withdrawal symptoms if discontinued. Side effects from chronic use may include sluggishness, slow speech, reduced comprehension and memory, sudden mood shifts, loss of motor coordination, and depression. Even though tolerance may increase, the amount of barbiturate or benzodiazepine needed to cause death does not increase, which makes overdose increasingly more likely as use continues. The typical abuser will be middle-aged and will use the drug to reduce anxiety or help with sleep. All of these medications are especially lethal when mixed with alcohol.

Hallucinogens

Hallucinogens or *psychedelic* drugs have the effect of distorting perceptions such that people see and hear things in unusual ways. These drugs include LSD, mescaline, psilocybin, and PCP ("angel dust"). The most potent of the hallucinogens, LSD, can cause intoxication with an amount smaller than a grain of salt. Following ingestion of LSD, the person will typically experience approximately eight hours of sensory perception distortions, mood swings, and feelings of detachment. The experience of perceiving distorted objects, intense colors, and new thoughts and images can be extremely pleasant or terrifying. Traumatic responses to hallucinogens have been described as "bad trips," which can cause people to jump from high places or set themselves on fire in response to their distorted perceptions. One interesting side effect of hallucinogen use is the flashback (i.e., the involuntary recurrence of a perceptual distortion or hallucination weeks or months after taking the drug). Although LSD and other hallucinogens were touted as therapeutic and possibly consciousness-expanding drugs in the 1960s, no research has supported their usefulness in that regard. Hallucinogens are not among the most addictive drugs, yet they may produce extremely dangerous behavior and even psychosis when used repeatedly.

Marijuana (Cannabis)

Marijuana and its derivative, hashish *(hash),* are technically hallucinogens. However, the intensity and duration of their effects make them distinct from the drugs discussed previously. Marijuana comes from the leaves and tops of the hemp plant. Both marijuana and hash are typically smoked in the form of cigarettes or in pipes. Marijuana has been used for centuries, but it became particularly popular in the United States during the 1960s. Today, the majority of young adults have experimented with this drug. Although the precise effects of marijuana vary depending on the dose, purity of the drug, social setting, and the user's experience and expectations, common effects include mild euphoria, pleasant relaxation, sensations of drifting or floating, a distorted perception of time, and interruption of short-term memory. The effects of marijuana rarely last longer than two or three hours. When marijuana is used chronically, as is often the case, symptoms may include decreased self-control, memory impairment, and problems with sexual functioning in men. There is also evidence that depression is linked to chronic marijuana use. In rare cases, cannabis use has been known to trigger psychotic episodes, particularly in adolescents and young adults with a genetic predisposition to schizophrenia.

Summary and Guidelines

Substance use disorders are among the most common and costly disorders the minister is likely to face. In fact, abuse of and dependence on alcohol or drugs may be one of the most underidentified yet widespread problems in the church today. The causes of substance misuse and dependence range from genetic predisposition (as in the case of alcohol) to social pressure and intentional experimentation (especially with marijuana and hallucinogens). The minister may first become aware of a substance disorder through family members of the addicted person. Physical abuse, neglect of family or spouse, financial distress, and occupational troubles (or actual job loss) may all be initial markers of substance-induced impairment.

Because denial of the problem is a hallmark symptom of chemical impairment, the minister may play a critical role in empowering those who love the addict or alcoholic to organize a clear confrontation with the person about his or her substance problem. Family members must focus on what the person will have to do to remain in the home and salvage his or her job and relationships. It is best if this intervention is arranged by a professional who is trained in the treatment of substance use disorders. Treatment in severe cases may begin with hospitalization to manage the most severe symptoms of physical and psychological withdrawal from the substance. This will typically be followed by outpatient treatment designed to keep the individual completely abstinent from substances while focusing on a program of counseling and social support from others recovering from dependency. Many churches host meetings of Alcoholics Anonymous and other substance-related disorder recovery groups. This is often an excellent way for the church to blend stewardship, ministry, counseling, and discipleship. Because alcoholism and other forms of substance dependence are chronic problems, and the dependent person is always at risk for a relapse, the minister and family members will need to remain vigilant for signs of continued use. The minister will also need to support and empower loved ones in their attempts at setting limits with the substance-dependent person.

Sleep-Wake Disorders

Presenting Complaints

Martin is a 27-year-old parishioner who comes to you for pastoral counseling. He looks fatigued, and you note bags under his eyes. He complains of not sleeping well in spite of exercising, getting to bed on time, and avoiding all caffeine after lunchtime. He has tried praying and talking with his wife before bed, but he still stays awake until well after one o'clock in the morning. He has a new job as chief of security at a major bank. Although he was initially anxious about performing well at work, he now feels most upset about his inability to sleep and believes work is only a minor problem in comparison.

Tanya is a 34-year-old mother of one. She comes to counseling because of an increasing problem with sleeping too much. During the last year, Tanya has slept longer and longer at night. She currently sleeps 12 hours at night and still wakes up feeling exhausted in the morning. She also reports "uncontrollable catnaps" during the day. She may fall asleep for an hour while at home or on a break at work. Her boss is growing increasingly irritated with her sleepiness. Tanya denies using drugs or medications.

Stanton is a 6-year-old whose parents bring him to you out of concern for his spiritual well-being. During the last two months, he has been startling his parents in the night with seemingly uncontrollable "fits" of terror during which he cannot be comforted. Though his parents have tried many methods of waking him during these terrifying bouts, nothing seems to rouse him from his very deep but troubled sleep. Stanton often screams, trembles, and writhes during these episodes. His parents fear he is being troubled by evil forces at night.

Common Features and Symptoms

Good sleep is often taken for granted. Unfortunately, millions of people experience the negative effects of sleep problems, which can become extremely severe at times. Research suggests that sleep serves to restore us physically and psychologically, and that it is a critical form of self-protection and energy conservation. The significance of sleep is evident in the effects on those who are deprived of it. In both experimental and natural cases of sleep loss, people lose the ability to perform physical and mental tasks, and eventually show numerous health problems including decreased immune system effectiveness and a heightened risk of heart disease. Our need for sleep declines slowly over the life span. Americans are notorious for being chronically sleep deprived. Sleep researchers have commented that our fast-paced lifestyle has meant that few Americans know what it feels like to be fully alert![7]

Human beings experience a rather predictable sleep cycle consisting of movement through five distinct stages about every 90 minutes. Starting with stage 1 (light sleep) and moving through stage 4, we become more relaxed and more deeply asleep. Electroencephalograph (EEG) readings of brain activity show that our brain waves move from high frequency *beta* waves to lower frequency *theta* and *delta* waves. Our breathing deepens, our heart rate becomes regular, and our blood pressure decreases. Eventually, we will enter the fifth stage, which is called rapid eye movement (REM) sleep. Immediately, our eyes begin rapid movement as active dreaming starts. Our heart rate and blood pressure increase and brain wave activity returns to higher frequencies. In fact, the person in REM sleep appears to be physiologically awake. Actually, they are physically paralyzed, but actively dreaming. REM sleep is critical for physical and emotional restoration. Following deprivation of REM sleep, a person will experience a "REM rebound" or an extended period of REM sleep.

In this section, we briefly cover several primary *sleep-wake disorders,* all of which involve disruptions in the normal cycle of sleeping. This may mean problems in the mechanisms that cause the onset or timing of sleep as well as odd behavior or experiences during sleep. The *DSM-5*[1] sleep-wake disorders may be divided into *dyssomnias* and *parasomnias.* Dyssomnias are disturbances in the amount, quality, or timing of sleep whereas parasomnias describe abnormal behavior or bodily events that occur during sleep—usually during specific stages of sleep or in the transition between sleep and waking.

When sleep difficulties are caused by psychiatric problems, medical problems, or substance abuse, they are referred to as *secondary sleep disorders,* but we do not address these here. When a minister learns that a parishioner is suffering from a sleep problem (most typically insomnia), several common contributors can be explored. First, stress or a significant life change often produces sleep difficulties. This may include a loss, anxiety about an upcoming event, or a recent disturbing experience. Second, the minister may inquire about substance use. Caffeine or alcohol use is often a primary cause of insomnia. Is the person using caffeinated drinks late in the day or using alcohol to become drowsy? Both can disrupt normal sleep patterns. Finally, depression and anxiety are commonly linked to sleep disturbance. A parishioner's report of insomnia may actually be the first sign that he or she is struggling with depression.

Three dyssomnias *(insomnia disorder, hypersomnolence disorder,* and *breathing-related sleep disorder)* are covered first. These problems involve difficulty falling and staying asleep or excessive sleepiness. Next, we address three parasomnia disorders *(nightmare disorder, sleep terrors,* and *sleepwalking).*

Subtypes

Insomnia Disorder

Between 40 and 50 percent of Americans suffer from several nights of difficulty sleeping each year.[8] Those diagnosed with insomnia disorder consistently struggle to fall asleep or remain asleep, or feel fatigued even after sleeping a normal amount of time. Most commonly, the parishioner with insomnia will describe difficulty falling asleep or a pattern of waking up during the night and having trouble returning to sleep. If insomnia is clearly linked to another disorder (e.g., major depression, generalized anxiety), then insomnia will not be diagnosed separately. The insomnia sufferer often develops a vicious conditioned cycle of disturbance *about* not sleeping. As the parishioner becomes increasingly preoccupied with his or her lack of normal sleep, he or she may become more upset and anxious, which further disrupts normal sleep. Paradoxically, insomniacs will often begin to sleep normally when they stop trying to make themselves sleep. That is why encouraging people with insomnia to *try* to stay awake while lying in bed, or to get up and read quietly away from the bedroom often causes them to fall asleep.

Parishioners who may be most prone to insomnia are those with personality styles characterized by worry. Those preoccupied with physical health and various medical symptoms are also likely to overreact to the first signs of difficulty sleeping. Very often, insomniacs use sedatives such as alcohol or barbiturates to get to sleep. Although these drugs may produce some initial drowsiness and even sleep, they eventually disrupt the sleep cycle even further. They also lose their effectiveness over time and can be quite addictive. Although typically a response to a life stress, caffeine use, depression, anxiety, or other factors, insomnia may also signal a physical condition that be detected only by a physician. For instance, hyperthyroidism is linked with insomnia.

Insomnia Disorder: Key Indicators

- The person complains of difficulty in falling asleep, staying asleep, or waking too early in the morning.
- Because the person feels fatigued during the day, he or she becomes upset, or experiences problems socially or at work.
- The insomnia occurs at least three times per week for at least three months and is not due primarily to a physical or psychiatric disorder.

Hypersomnolence Disorder

The parishioner with hypersomnolence will report chronic sleepiness and will in fact sleep for long periods without feeling rested and alert afterward. The individual will describe sleeping longer than he or she intended at night as well as episodes of sleeping (planned or not) during the day. Very often, this person will sleep considerably longer than nine hours at night, yet will have tremendous difficulty waking. Long naps often leave the person feeling unrefreshed or experiencing "sleep drunkenness." The person may also be prone to "dropping off" when in a low-stimulation environment, which could be embarrassing or dangerous. In cases of hypersomnolence disorder, the minister should be concerned about major depression, substance abuse, or a potentially serious medical problem such as a recent head trauma or an endocrine abnormality (e.g., severe hypothyroidism). Only about 5 to 10 percent of those with sleep disorders have hypersomnia.[1]

Hypersomnolence Disorder: Key Indicators

- The person reports excessive sleepiness despite sleeping at least seven hours at night. Examples include recurrent periods of sleep during the day, more than nine hours of unrefreshing sleep at night, and great difficulty being fully awake.
- This excessive sleepiness occurs at least three times per week for at least three months and causes the person to become upset or results in social or work-related problems.
- The sleepiness is not due primarily to a physical or another psychiatric disorder.

Breathing-Related Sleep Disorder (Sleep Apnea)

Breathing-related sleep disorders (apneas) constitute a spectrum of sleep problems related to impingement or outright obstruction of the breathing airway during sleep. In *obstructive sleep apnea*—the most common of the disorders—the person will experience repeated airway obstruction during sleep and subsequent episodes of *apnea* (total absence of airflow) and *hypopnea* (reduction in airflow). Common symptoms and warning signs of a breathing-related sleep problem include significant snoring, snorting, gasping, and pauses in breathing during the night. If married, the parishioner's spouse might report feeling alarmed when the sufferer seems to stop breathing, followed by choking or gasping for air. Of course, these problems with breathing also cause serious disruption of the sleep cycles so that the person wakes in the morning feeling quite groggy or "hung over," despite not recalling ever waking in the night. Verifying sleep apneas requires that the parishioner be referred to a sleep specialist for a sleep lab study (polysomnograph).

Breathing-Related Sleep Disorder (Sleep Apnea): Key Indicators

- Evidence from a polysomnograph (sleep lab) study of at least five obstructive apneas or hypopneas in a single hour of sleep.
- Nighttime breathing characterized by snoring, gasping, or breathing pauses.
- Daytime sleepiness, fatigue, and a feeling of being unrefreshed despite adequate sleep duration.

Nightmare Disorder

On occasion, a parishioner or a family member may describe a pattern of disturbing or terrifying nightmares. Persons with nightmare disorder often have very vivid and extremely anxiety-provoking dream experiences. The individual will often awaken from nightmares abruptly, have a clear memory of the nightmare content, and be fearful of returning to sleep. The nightmares usually involve some real physical threat (being pursued or attacked) or, less frequently, extreme failure or embarrassment. If the person has experienced a traumatic event, the content of the nightmares may reflect that experience. Because nightmares are detailed dreams, these episodes occur almost exclusively during REM sleep.[1,7] As people go through several sleep cycles each night (including several episodes of REM), the nightmares can occur almost anytime. Most often, the person wakes during the second half of the night when REM is most frequent. Typically, he or she will wake abruptly from the nightmare and experience extreme arousal in the form of palpitations, increased heart rate, and sweating. Obviously, frequent nightmares are quite distressing for the person experiencing them, but they can also be upsetting to those around them. As a result, these nightmares may lead to insomnia and job-related problems. Nightmare disorder is most common in children and adolescents (2 to 4 percent),[1] but may also persist into adulthood for some.

Nightmare Disorder: Key Indicators

- The person describes a pattern of waking suddenly from sleep with vivid recall of lengthy and extremely frightening dreams involving threats to survival or physical security.
- After waking, the person rapidly becomes alert and aware that he or she has been dreaming.
- The person is upset by the dreams, which may cause disturbance in relationships or work performance.

Sleep Terror

Sleep terror is one form of *non-REM sleep arousal disorder*. It is nearly always diagnosed in children. Like nightmare disorder, sleep terror also involves an experience of extreme terror during sleep. However, in contrast to nightmare disorder, this person does not wake up following the event and does not remember specific details of a nightmare. During a typical sleep terror episode, the person will sit up abruptly, often screaming or crying, with a frightened expression and physical signs of panic such as rapid breathing, racing heart, and sweating. Attempts to wake this person are typically futile, which can be frustrating for parents attempting to wake their terrified child. If the person does wake up, he or she will usually be disoriented and confused. The following day, the person will usually be unable to recall anything about the event. Sleep terrors occur during the deepest stages of sleep—often in the first hour or two following sleep onset. Terrors often cause distress for the people sleeping with or near the person affected and can lead to relationship problems or embarrassment in adults.

Sleep terrors can persist into adulthood. In children, the disorder is not related to any emotional disturbance and usually begins between the ages of 4 and 12 and resolves on its own by adolescence. In adults, however, sleep terror syndrome is correlated with other psychiatric problems such as posttraumatic stress disorder (PTSD). In general, it is best to simply calm the person experiencing a sleep terror, without trying to wake him or her, because the person will sometimes resist with physical force such as punching or kicking.

Sleep Terror: Key Indicators

- The person has repeated episodes of waking abruptly, usually with a scream, from deep sleep.

- The person shows symptoms such as intense fear, rapid breathing, and sweating, and resists, or does not respond to, attempts by others to calm or wake him or her.
- There is little recall of the event and the episodes may lead to some impairment in functioning—especially social functioning.

Sleepwalking (Somnambulism)

Another of the parasomnias, sleepwalking is the second form of non-REM sleep arousal disorder. Between 10 and 30 percent of all children have had at least one episode of sleepwalking, while only 2 to 3 percent sleepwalk often.[1] Sleepwalking disorder involves repeated episodes in which an individual sits up or rises from bed and engages in some motor behavior, such as walking about, before waking spontaneously or returning to bed. During sleepwalking episodes, it is not uncommon for people to walk around the bedroom, up and down stairs, and even outside. They may even engage in complex tasks (some sleepwalkers have driven cars!) and respond to questions in a vague way. They may wake on their own, be wakened by others, or simply return to sleep. (They may wake up in strange places in the morning.)

Although there is some danger that sleepwalkers may inadvertently harm themselves or others, this happens only rarely, as pain or other sudden stimuli often cause them to wake up. Sleepwalking may be disturbing for other family members or roommates and, therefore, embarrassment or other social problems may occur. Also, sleepwalking will cause a person to be discharged from military service for obvious reasons. During the sleepwalking episode, a person typically has a blank stare and is only minimally responsive (or not at all) to questions or verbal directions from others. He or she may or may not report memory of the event and does not necessarily dream during these episodes.

Sleepwalking (Somnambulism): Key Indicators

- The person routinely rises from bed and walks about (sometimes talking) during the night.
- The person has a blank expression, is relatively unresponsive, and may be difficult to wake.
- There is very little memory of the event, but these repeated episodes may cause embarrassment, distress, and social or work-related impairment.

Summary and Guidelines

Sleep disorders, especially primary insomnia, are exceptionally common. In any congregation, the pastor can reasonably assume that a significant proportion (perhaps 10 percent or more) of parishioners suffer with sleep disruptions or disorders. Although the causes of sleep problems are wide-ranging, the most common include lifestyle factors (substance use, excess caffeine use, eating before bed, lack of exercise, or intentional sleep deprivation), anxiety (regarding upcoming events or preoccupation with lack of sleep), recent trauma or loss, and mood-related factors—primarily depression—which nearly always produces insomnia or hypersomno-lence. Very often, the pastor may provide powerful reassurance to the parishioner by simply informing him or her that sleep problems are quite normal. For example, telling parents of a child with sleep terrors that this is a rather common occurrence in children, that they need not wake the child, and that sleep terrors decline with age, may be very helpful. Simi-larly, suggest to a parishioner plagued with anxiety about not being able to fall asleep that he or she should stop *trying* to sleep and instead calmly get up and read quietly in another place until drowsy. Prayer and scripture reading are excellent substitutes for lying in bed and worrying about lack of sleep. Good-natured reminders that insomnia is not fatal might also be useful.

It is also worth repeating, however, that sleep disturbance may be an initial signal of a physical illness. Suggesting that the parishioner seek out his or her physician for a physical exam is always wise. Subtle head injuries, other neurological problems (e.g., brain tumor), endo-crine changes, and other disorders may cause sleep difficulties. Also, sleep apnea and other potentially serious breathing problems may first become evident when a person reports feeling fatigued, excessively sleepy, or insomniac.

Sexual Disorders

Presenting Complaints

Hugh is a 28-year-old parishioner who comes to see you, with his wife Barbara, for pastoral counseling. Both Hugh and Barbara appear uneasy about discussing exactly why they have come to see you at this time. After some vague statements about their sexual relation-ship, Hugh states that his wife is making a "big deal" about the fact that he enjoys it when she wears shoes during sex. Barbara insists that Hugh appears most aroused by her shoes. She has discovered him masturbating with her shoes on occasion and he is unable to perform sexually unless shoes play a prominent role in the sexual scenario.

Sally and Tom also come for marital counseling. Sally appears extremely embarrassed while Tom appears both weary and angry. The two have been married only two months, but Tom notes they have had "relations" only twice. He states that Sally is the problem and insists she has no interest in sex, although Tom has gone to great lengths to create a comfortable and enjoyable experience for her. Sally hesitantly acknowledges no interest whatsoever in sex. She denies ever experiencing interest in or arousal related to sexual activity.

Stuart is a 58-year-old widower who has been active in the church for years. He has been a friend of yours for some time. Over coffee one day, he sheepishly states recent trouble "raising the flagpole." When you correctly clarify that he is referring to trouble with erections, he becomes forlorn and insists it just means he is getting old. He notes that his erection problems have happened a few times in the last year and that they have caused him extreme embarrassment with his new wife. He confides that he is considering leaving his marriage and says, "It doesn't seem fair to my new bride, you know."

Common Features and Symptoms

Sexual dysfunction refers to impairment in either the desire for sexual gratification or in the ability to achieve it. In this section, we highlight the four major types of sexual dysfunction and also discuss *paraphilias*. Parishioners suffering from sexual dysfunction experience disruption in the normal sexual response cycle, which leads to distress and, often, relational problems. The four major categories of sexual dysfunction are *disorders of sexual desire, disorders of sexual arousal, disorders of orgasm,* and *sexual pain disorders*. Each of these categories involves disruption in the normal sexual response cycle or pain with intercourse. The four phases in the human sexual response cycle are as follows:

1. *Desire:* Fantasies about and longing to have sex.
2. *Excitement:* Experience of sexual pleasure and physical changes (penile erection in men, and lubrication and vaginal swelling in women).
3. *Orgasm:* Peaking sexual pleasure and release of sexual tension (ejaculation in men and vaginal contractions in women).
4. *Resolution:* Sense of relaxation and well-being.

In contrast to sexual dysfunctions, which typically involve disturbance in this sexual response cycle, *paraphilias (para = "faulty," philia = "attraction")* are recurrent, intense sexual urges, fantasies, and behaviors that involve unusual objects, activities, or situations. Repetitive acting out of these unusual sexual behaviors leads the parishioner to significant personal distress or impairment in relationships—usually with a spouse or partner, but also on occasion with the legal system.

The paradox of sexual disorders is that, although they are among the easiest mental health problems to treat, they are often the most difficult for parishioners to discuss with one another, let alone with their minister. Unfortunately, some medical doctors and counselors are equally uncomfortable talking frankly about sexuality, which can certainly make the experience more harrowing for the individual or couple. Because of this discomfort with the topic of sexuality and sexual dysfunction, we recommend that ministers be very willing to introduce the topic of sexuality early on in counseling with couples. We also encourage an open mind regarding the wide range of sexual interests, arousal patterns, and preferences among sexually healthy couples.

A matter-of-fact statement about the normalcy of sexual concerns among couples in the church may be enough of an icebreaker so that the couple will feel comfortable enough to broach problems in this area. We have also found that some parishioners are considerably more likely than the general population to view sex as dirty or pathological. Thankfully, classic research by Masters and Johnson has largely served to dispel this thinking among most medical and mental health practitioners.[9] Nonetheless, the pastor may need to educate parishioners regarding the basics of the human sexual response and dispel myths linking sexuality, or sexual difficulty, with sin in the minds of some couples.

Subtypes

Male Hypoactive Sexual Desire Disorder

When a male suffers problems of sexual desire involving the absence of sexual fantasies as well as desire for sexual activity, *male hypoactive sexual desire disorder* may be present. Even if there is nothing medically wrong with this person, sexual motivation is somehow blocked. He will experience no (or very few) erotic thoughts/fantasies and little desire for sexual activity. Such a parishioner will rarely come to the pastor's attention on his or her own. Instead, the person's partner will complain of inadequate sexual activity. Many factors may contribute to deficits in sexual desire, including normal aging, medication side effects, endocrine system problems (e.g., low testosterone), low mood, and marital problems.

Male Hypoactive Sexual Desire Disorder: Key Indicators

- Persistent deficit or absence of sexual fantasies and/or desire for sexual activity.
- The disturbance persists for at least six months and causes the person considerable distress.

Female Sexual Interest/Arousal Disorder

Like its counterpart for men, *female sexual interest/arousal disorder* refers to absent or reduced interest in sexual activity. But it may also include nonresponsiveness to erotic stimulation both physically and emotionally (formerly known as "frigidity"). Here is a caution: it is very important not to interpret a woman's relatively lower sexual interest or initiation of sex as proof of a disorder. Discrepancies in interest, desire, and initiation of sexual activity often vary between partners. Only when sexual interest or responsiveness is so diminished that it causes *her* distress or results in significant relationship problems should the possibility of this disorder even be considered. There are many potential and interacting causes of low interest/arousal including certain medical conditions (e.g., low thyroid), medication side effects, history of sexual trauma, religious/family beliefs about sex, and dislike of or serious conflict with one's partner.[1]

In many ways, female sexual interest/arousal disorder is the female counterpart to erectile disorder. Women with this difficulty do not produce the characteristic swelling and lubrication of the vulva and vaginal tissues during sexual stimulation. This, of course, may make intercourse painful and lead to avoidance of sexual activity. In many cases, the cause of the deficit in sexual arousal is situational and may be correlated with factors such as dislike of, or disgust with, one's current sexual partner, distorted views regarding the evil nature of sex, or some experience of sexual trauma.

Female Sexual Interest/Arousal Disorder: Key Indicators

- Absent or reduced sexual interest, sexual thoughts/fantasies, and sexual activity.
- Does not initiate sexual activity and is unresponsive to partner's attempts to do so.
- Absent or reduced sexual excitement/genital pleasure during sexual stimulation or activity.
- Persists for at least six months and causes significant distress.

Erectile Disorder

Erectile disorder (ED) involves an inability to achieve or maintain an erection that is sufficient to initiate or complete sexual activity (ED was formerly called "impotence"). Only about 2 percent of men under the age of 40 have consistent erection problems, but the prevalence jumps to 40 to 50 percent in the 60–70 age range.[1,10] Keep in mind that is quite common for men of all ages to have occasional lapses in the effectiveness of erections. Often, simply conveying this fact helps relieve the anxious male parishioner. The vast majority of men who experience problems with erectile functioning have what is known as acquired erectile disorder. In these cases, the male has had satisfactory erections in the past, but now suffers complete or occasional difficulty achieving erections. As men age, medical causes for ED become more likely (e.g., vascular changes, diminished blood flow, medication side effects). In younger men, erectile problems may be linked to substance use, having intercourse with a previously unknown partner, and performance anxiety. For example, it is extremely common for men to engage in "spectatoring" following a single experience of incomplete erection. The male becomes anxious and preoccupied with the experience of not "performing" sexually. He is then so nervous about his erection that he ensures subsequent episodes of erection difficulty. Ministers should never assume that ED is psychological in nature. A referral to a competent urologist is a good first step so that physical causes can be ruled out. Remember that by the age of 70, about half of married men report having had some experiences of erectile difficulties. Although many men remain capable of sustaining normal erections to the age of 100 and beyond, it is important to expect that older male parishioners may experience increasing rates of erectile difficulty and frustration.

Erectile Disorder: Key Indicators

- Persistent difficulty obtaining or maintaining an erection during sexual activity.
- The disturbance persists for at least six months and causes the person considerable distress.

Female Orgasmic Disorder

Women struggling with this problem report an inability to achieve an orgasm either through sexual intercourse or direct manual stimulation, or if orgasms do occur, they are quite rare. Although this parishioner may enjoy sexual stimulation and be responsive sexually, she cannot achieve a satisfactory orgasm.

Of course, the range of orgasmic experience varies widely among women and it is important to rely on the woman's own report of satisfaction with her sexual responsiveness before assuming any dysfunction. Also, keep in mind that many variables can contribute to inhibited orgasm in women. These may include anxiety, stress, depression, relationship problems, medication side effects, and age-related changes such as irritation or pain with intercourse.[11]

Female Orgasmic Disorder: Key Indicators

- Persistent delay in, infrequency of, or absence of orgasm.
- The disturbance lasts at least six months and causes the person considerable distress.

Genito-Pelvic Pain/Penetration Disorder

This disorder is characterized by painful vaginal experiences during intercourse. The primary foci may be (1) difficulty having intercourse, (2) vaginal/pelvic pain, (3) fear of pain or vaginal penetration, or (4) involuntary muscle spasm at the entrance to the vagina that prevents penetration and sexual intercourse.[1] Far from uncommon, approximately 15 percent of women in North America report recurrent pain during intercourse.[10] In pastoral counseling, reports of painful or uncomfortable intercourse should result in a medical referral to a good OB/GYN physician in order to rule out a physical problem before assuming any psychological issue or referring the parishioner for sex therapy. Although there is often an underlying medical cause for painful intercourse (e.g., cysts, inadequate lubrication, infections), psychological factors can also play a role (e.g., stress, childhood messages about sex as "filthy," aversion to one's partner). Some women who experience pain with sexual activity may simultaneously struggle with low interest and arousal. Be particularly sensitive to the fact that the woman with this syndrome experiences considerable discomfort during intercourse and may therefore have avoided all sexual contact for some time. The problem is likely to be extremely distressing to both her and her partner.

Genito-Pelvic Pain/Penetration Disorder: Key Indicators

- Persistent genital pain during penetration or sexual intercourse, often accompanied by anticipatory anxiety about intercourse.
- The disturbance persists for at least six months and causes the person considerable distress.

Sexual Paraphilias

In contrast to the sexual disorders discussed previously, paraphilias typically involve what most people would consider "aberrant" or abnormal sexual behavior. The essential component of a paraphiliac disorder is that the person experiences *recurring* and *intense* sexual fantasies, sexual urges, or engages in sexual behavior involving nonhuman objects, parts of the human body or *partialism* (e.g., feet), the suffering or humiliation of oneself or one's partner, children, or other nonconsenting adults.[1] The key feature of this disorder is the person's psychological dependence on the object or scenario and the need to focus on it during sexual activity. Although many well-adjusted men and women report mild or episodic enjoyment of fantasies or behavior of a paraphiliac nature (e.g., bondage, spanking, role-playing), a disorder is indicated when the focus of sexual arousal and gratification is almost exclusively on suffering or humiliation, a nonhuman object, or a nonconsenting partner, *and* when this sexual focus leads to distress or impairment—sometimes in the form of criminal arrest or threatened divorce. Paraphiliac behavior is often quite compulsive, and it is not uncommon for such individuals to require orgasmic release as often as 4 to 10 times per day.

The *DSM-5* recognizes eight categories of paraphilia:[1]

1. *Fetishistic disorder:* Recurrent and intense sexual arousal from either the use of nonliving objects, or a highly specific focus on nongential body part(s).
2. *Transvestic disorder:* Recurrent and intense sexual arousal from cross-dressing.
3. *Voyeuristic disorder:* Achievement of sexual pleasure through secretly observing an unsuspecting person who is naked, disrobing, or engaging in sexual activity.
4. *Exhibitionistic disorder:* Recurrent and intense sexual arousal from the exposure of one's genitals to an unsuspecting person.
5. *Sexual sadism disorder:* Recurrent and intense sexual arousal from the physical or psychological suffering of another person.
6. *Sexual masochism disorder:* Recurrent and intense sexual arousal from the act of being humiliated, beaten, bound, or otherwise made to suffer.
7. *Pedophilic disorder:* Recurrent and intense sexually arousing fantasies, sexual urges, or behaviors involving sexual activity with a prepubescent child or children (typically 13 years or younger).
8. *Frotteuristic disorder:* Recurrent and intense sexual arousal from touching or rubbing against a nonconsenting person.

All paraphilias must persist for at least six months before a diagnosis is appropriate. Although the causes are unclear, it is true that the vast majority of paraphiliacs are male. The fact that men are more sexually responsive to visual stimuli may make them more vulnerable than women to developing paraphilias. Men are also more prone to developing sexual associations with nonsexual stimuli. A paraphilic focus typically begins in early adolescence when sexual response patterns are first developing. Paraphiliacs often have more than one paraphilia. Parishioners with paraphilias are unlikely to come to the attention of a minister until one of two situations occurs. Either the parishioner will be apprehended in a paraphiliac act (peeping, cross-dressing, or masturbating with a child), or his adult partner will complain about his sexual focus (she may report feeling like a mere accessory or "prop" in his sexual scenario).

Paraphilias: Key Indicators

- During a period of at least six months, the person has recurring and intense sexually arousing fantasies, sexual urges, or behaviors involving nonhuman objects, inflicting or experiencing pain or humiliation, children, other nonconsenting persons.
- The disturbance causes the person considerable distress or problems with relationships, the legal system, or employment.

Summary and Guidelines

The minister should be alert to the fact that complaints of a sexual nature may indicate a host of concerns and should lead to the possibility of a referral. Some sexual problems (e.g., erectile problems, pain with intercourse) may indicate a medical problem, which should be investigated by a physician. Substance use (especially alcohol) and certain prescription medications are also frequently implicated in sexual problems. For example, many common antidepressant medications lead to erection or lubrication difficulties and inhibition of orgasm. Sexual dysfunction may also be one of many symptoms of a pervasive personality problem (see Chapter 5). This may be most evident in the case of male parishioners with paraphilias. Finally, complaints about the sexual side of a couple's relationship may be symptomatic of a more pervasive conflict or incompatibility.

The minister will be most helpful to parishioners with sexual problems when he or she is open and receptive to discussing sexual concerns. But, unless the minister has specialized training in treating sexual dysfunctions, a referral to a specialist in this area is nearly always indicated. We recommend finding a psychologist, psychiatrist, or social worker with specific training and expertise in the treatment of sexual disorders who is willing to collaborate with the church in helping parishioners with sexual concerns. It is important to evaluate both the practitioner's expertise and his or her ability to remain respectful and supportive of the parishioner's faith.

Even minor pastoral interventions in this area may be profoundly helpful to men and women suffering from sexual disorders. For example, informing a young couple that occasional difficulties with orgasm or different levels of sexual interest are fairly common (and often quite treatable) problems for couples may produce immense relief. Helping older male parishioners to appreciate the biological (especially vascular) changes that lead to erection problems and affirming the increasing normalcy of erection problems with age may alleviate anxiety and despair. Of course, such reassurance should be followed by referral to a mental health or medical provider. Finally, reassure parishioners that the sexual problems discussed in this chapter are among the most quickly and effectively treated of all mental health problems.

Notes

1. American Psychiatric Association. (2013). *Diagnostic and statistical manual of mental disorders* (5th ed.). Washington, DC: Author.
2. Hoge, C. W., Terhakopian, A., Castro, C. A., Messer, S. C., & Engle, C. C. (2007). Association of posttraumatic stress disorder with somatic symptoms, health care visits, and absenteeism among Iraq war veterans. *American Journal of Psychiatry, 164*(1), 150–153.
3. Kessler, R. C., Berglund, P., Demler, O., Jin, R., Merikangas, K. R., & Walters, E. E. (2005). Lifetime prevalence and age-of-onset distributions of DSM-IV disorders in the National Comorbidity Survey Replication. *Archives of General Psychiatry, 62*(6), 593–602.
4. Norton, P. J., & Price, E. C. (2007). A meta-analytic review of adult cognitive-behavioral treatment outcome across the anxiety disorders. *Journal of Nervous and Mental Disease, 195*(6), 521–531.
5. Dell, P. F., & O'Neil, J. A. (2009). *Dissociation and the dissociative disorders: DSM-V and beyond*. New York, NY: Routledge.
6. Moore, A. A., Gould, R., Reuben, D. B., Greendale, G. A., Carter, M. K., Zhou, K., & Karlamangla, A. (2005). Longitudinal patterns and predictors of alcohol consumption in the United States. *American Journal of Public Health, 95*(3), 458–465.
7. Reite, M., Weissberg, M., & Ruddy, J. (2008). *Clinical manual for the evaluation and treatment of sleep disorders*. Washington, DC: American Psychiatric Publishing.
8. National Sleep Foundation. (2002). *Sleep in America poll*. Retrieved from www.sleepfoundation.org/article/sleep-america-polls/2002-adult-sleep-habits
9. Masters, W. H., & Johnson, V. E. (1966). *Human sexual response*. Boston, MA: Little, Brown.
10. Lewis, R. W., Fugl-Meyer, K. S., Corona, G., Hayes, R. D., Laumann, E. O., Moreira, E. D., . . . Segraves, T. (2010). Definitions/epidemiology/risk factors for sexual dysfunction. *Journal of Sexual Medicine, 7*(4), 1598–1607.
11. Laumann, E. O., & Waite, L. J. (2008). Sexual dysfunction among older adults: Prevalence and risk factors from a nationally representative U.S. probability sample of men and women 57–85 years of age. *Journal of Sexual Medicine, 5*(10), 2300–2311.

5   Causing Distress in Others
Maladaptive Personalities

Every human being, including each parishioner, has a unique blend of behaviors, emotions, thought patterns, and relationship styles. Together, these components make up and define a person's *personality.* Each of us has consistent patterns of perceiving, relating to, and thinking about the environment, other people, and ourselves. These patterns, or *personality traits,* are fairly consistent across a wide range of important personal and social contexts. In combination, they make up our unique personalities. If a hidden camera were to record your behavior all day, every day, it would not be long before even an untrained viewer could accurately predict your behavior in a range of personal and social situations. Your personality style would quickly become evident.

By the end of adolescence or early adulthood, a person's characteristic traits, interpersonal style, and broad coping techniques have crystallized into established patterns. These consistent and predictable patterns of behavior constitute the personality, and they rarely change much after early adulthood. Although personality is rather firmly established by adulthood, one sign of psychological health is the ability to demonstrate occasional flexibility in behavior. Although most of us can modify our characteristic behaviors to meet specific environmental demands, some people are unable to do so. During the personality formation process, these individuals developed traits that are not only rigid and inflexible, but also maladaptive because the person cannot appropriately adjust or perform in some important area of life. Persons with such inflexible personality styles have a *personality disorder.*

The *DSM-5* describes personality disorders as enduring patterns of perceiving, relating to, and thinking about the environment and oneself that are exhibited in a wide range of important social and personal contexts.[1] These patterns are distinct from ordinary personality traits in that they are deeply etched, inflexible, and maladaptive. Like all personality styles, these maladaptive patterns are present from late adolescence or early adulthood. The presence of the disorder causes the person some distress or, more often, impairment in his or her social or occupational functioning.

In this chapter, we briefly discuss the 10 major personality disorders. Each of these disorders shares some common criteria: (1) the person's inner experience and behavior deviates markedly from cultural norms and this deviation is evident in thinking, feeling, interpersonal relationships, or poor impulse control; (2) these consistent patterns are inflexible and present in a wide range of situations; (3) the disordered behavior leads to problems or distress in social or work-related functioning; (4) the pattern of behavior has been stable since late adolescence or early adulthood; and (5) the disordered behavior is not a product of one of the major psychiatric problems discussed in Chapters 3 and 4.

You may wonder why we decided to devote an entire chapter to personality disorders instead of lumping them with the other psychiatric disorders discussed in the previous chapters. We believe personality disorders are among the most problematic and vexing disorders the minister is likely to face in his or her day-to-day life in the church. Why? Because parishioners with personality disorders are among the least likely of all to seek assistance or to recognize the maladaptiveness of their own behavior.[2] In fact, they will typically come to the pastor's attention only when they are in trouble, or when others in the church are angry at or concerned about them. Not only will most parishioners with personality disorders view themselves as no different from others, but also they will have little to no insight about how their behavior affects those around them. Although individuals with major psychiatric problems (see Chapters 3 and 4) view their symptoms as foreign or "outside" of themselves, those with personality disorders experience their pathological behavior as an integral and valued part of who they are. So, instead of saying, "Yes, I see why my behavior is causing problems, and I really want to change it," this parishioner will say, "That's just the way I am." Personality-disordered parishioners are less accurate at describing their own interpersonal style than those around them.[1]

How prevalent are personality disorders? One major summary of epidemiologic studies on the topic indicated that approximately 15 percent of the U.S. population would meet criteria for a personality disorder at some point in life.[3] However, personality disorders are considerably more prevalent (perhaps as high as 40 percent) among those receiving professional mental health services—either by self-referral or (more often) referral by family members or third parties.[4] Although personality disorders develop gradually from childhood through early adulthood and become progressively more inflexible, they appear to be caused by both environmental (early experience) and genetic factors.[5]

Even though personality disorders are, by definition, distinct from other major psychiatric problems such as mood disorders, anxiety disorders, psychotic disorders, substance abuse, and sexual disorders, personality-disordered parishioners are considerably more likely to develop these psychiatric problems during their lifetimes. For example, a man with an antisocial personality disorder stands a greater risk for substance dependence or depression than a male parishioner who is not antisocial.[5]

There are 10 distinct personality disorders that can be subdivided into 3 diagnostic *clusters* based on similarities among the essential symptoms:

Cluster A: Parishioners with *paranoid, schizoid,* and *schizotypal* personality disorders generally lack relationships, have a restricted range of emotional expression, and have peculiar ideas. They are considered odd and eccentric by others. Their behavior may range from aloof and detached to suspicious and distrustful.

Cluster B: Parishioners with *histrionic, narcissistic, borderline,* and *antisocial* personality disorders tend to be dramatic, emotional, and erratic. They have little insight about their behavior and are extremely impulsive and manipulative. They tend to have chronic interpersonal problems and to use speech to influence, persuade, or threaten others. Cluster B personality-disordered people are more likely to come to the attention of legal authorities and MHPs than other people.

Cluster C: Parishioners with *avoidant, dependent,* and *obsessive-compulsive* personality disorders are generally the least disruptive and problematic of the three types. Cluster C personality-disordered persons are driven by anxiety and fearfulness. They attempt to meet all demands placed on them by passively enduring, changing themselves, or withdrawing. They are sometimes difficult to distinguish from persons with anxiety disorders. Although they are more likely to seek treatment than cluster A or B types, they may respond to pastoral suggestions with anxiety, passivity, and initial compliance without ever actually altering their fundamental personality style.

A word of warning to ministers regarding the perils of diagnosing personality disorders: We recommend that you *not* suggest to parishioners that they suffer from a specific personality disorder. Psychiatrists, psychologists, clinical social workers, and other professionals with considerable experience in diagnosing these disorders will be the first to acknowledge that accurate diagnosis of a personality disorder takes considerable time and plentiful data from multiple sources (e.g., parishioner, spouse, parents, friends, employer, various records and documents). Not only might the pastor inadvertently label a parishioner inaccurately, but also personality disorder diagnoses can also be quite stigmatizing.[2] Even MHPs may unintentionally "write-off" or discount a new client referred with a personality disorder diagnosis. We think it best for the minister to be alert to clear signs of personality disorder patterns without formally attempting to diagnose parishioners. So, instead of saying, "Your behavior indicates you may suffer from a borderline personality disorder," it would be more helpful to say, "I've noticed a pattern of erratic mood swings and even rage from you at times. Have you ever considered seeing a professional about those concerns?" It is also important to keep in mind that persons with personality disorders do not generally respond quickly to treatment. Given the chronic and permanent nature of personality development (normal and abnormal), it makes sense that personality-based behaviors would be slow to change. Referrals to professionals for treatment of personality disorders should be made with an appropriate amount of guarded optimism.

As we briefly detail each of the 10 major personality disorders, we begin with a *presenting complaint* section, which provides a fictitious case example of what the disorder might "look like" in a particular parishioner. We then discuss the *common features and symptoms* of each disorder and provide a *key indicators* box highlighting some of the primary indications for the disorder. We conclude our discussion of each disorder with a very brief *summary and guidelines* section in which we discuss why such a person may come to the minister's attention and how the minister might most effectively and lovingly manage a parishioner with this personality disorder.

As is often the case with personality-disordered people, romantic relationships, including marriages, will often be in shambles. When a parishioner begins to explore the possibility that a spouse or dating partner has a personality disorder, the book *Crazy Love: Dealing With Your Partner's Problem Personality*[6] might offer a first step in helping to him or her to better understand the problem and think carefully about how best to respond.

Paranoid Personality Disorder

Presenting Complaint

Duane is a 29-year-old who works as a laborer in a textile factory. He requests an appointment with you, but insists on "complete" confidentiality and will only agree to see you when no other church office personnel are present. Duane appears agitated and uncomfortable during your meeting, and he frequently scans the environment while speaking with you. Duane believes he is being "persecuted" by coworkers because of his Christian faith and his excellent work performance. He believes (although he has no evidence to corroborate his concerns) that coworkers are conspiring to get him fired. He frequently hears them talking and laughing and is convinced they are talking about him. He interprets maliciousness in seemingly benign comments and is certain these men are planning to "destroy" his career. He also notes being recently divorced because of his wife's infidelity. Although he admits there was never "hard evidence," he is certain she was cheating on him throughout their marriage. Duane then questions you in detail about your record-keeping practices and emphasizes again that he needs utmost confidentiality, as those who intend to harm his career may "pursue all leads."

Common Features and Symptoms

The primary feature of paranoid personality disorder is a chronic pattern of distrust and suspiciousness of others such that others' motives are interpreted as intending harm.[1] This pattern begins early in life and remains rigid and consistent. Basically, persons with this disorder are mistrustful of others, always vigilant and defensive, fearful of losing independence, and chronically fearful and hostile in response. They will nearly always resist external influence and control—assuming that others mean them harm. Persons with paranoid personality disorder assume other people will exploit, harm, or deceive them. They become preoccupied with the supposedly malevolent intentions of others and the loyalty of friends and associates. They tend to view themselves as blameless and find fault for their own mistakes and failures in others. Persons with this disorder are considered hypersensitive, and they constantly read hidden meanings or threats into the everyday conversations they hear. Paranoid personality disorder differs from paranoid schizophrenia or paranoid delusional disorder in that the person does not experience psychotic symptoms (hallucinations, delusions, or disorganization; see psychotic disorders in Chapter 3).

Paranoid Personality Disorder: Key Indicators

- Chronic and consistent mistrust and suspiciousness of others, including a tendency to interpret the motives of others as malevolent.
- Specific indications of this paranoia may include the following: (1) suspicion that others are exploiting, harming, or deceiving the person; (2) preoccupation and doubt regarding the loyalty of others; (3) fear-based refusal to confide in or disclose to others; (4) perception of demeaning or threatening messages in benign remarks by others; (5) tendency to bear grudges against others for perceived wrongs; (6) suspiciousness regarding the fidelity of spouse or sexual partner.

Summary and Guidelines

The paranoid parishioner is unlikely to approach the pastor for assistance with his or her disorder. Instead, the paranoid person will complain about other parishioners, a spouse, family members, or coworkers, and may even vent anger at the pastor. This person tends to view others as "against" him or her and will be extremely distrustful of the pastor and most others in the church. Religiously, a paranoid person may be among the most rigid and dogmatic in the church, yet his or her faith tends to be legalistic, formalized, and lacking in depth. The pastor may be shocked by this parishioner's apparent lack of insight as he or she tends to be extremely critical of others, but sees no fault in himself or herself. He or she may become angry and blame others in the church—perhaps engaging in angry outbursts that are disturbing to others. The parishioner will view his or her behavior as justified and interpret concern or correction from the pastor as evidence that he or she is also "against" the paranoid person. The religiously paranoid person is characteristically self-righteous and has tremendous difficulty with truly forgiving others for perceived wrongs or slights.

As you might surmise, the paranoid person is exceptionally difficult to manage and seemingly impossible to help. The minister should remain honest (trustworthy), consistent, and should avoid criticism as much as possible. Still, the minister should recognize that establishing a relationship with a paranoid person is extremely difficult and takes a significant amount of time. Very often, a paranoid person will terminate the relationship or leave the church altogether before the pastor senses that any real change has occurred. Referring the paranoid personality–disordered person for professional therapy must be done cautiously and with an emphasis on how the professional may be able to "help with the situation" rather than treating the parishioner's disorder. Paranoid parishioners may function best in the church if placed in roles and jobs that require minimal social interaction. As long as they can work independently, there may be fewer social exchanges for them to interpret as hostile or dangerous.

Schizoid Personality Disorder

Presenting Complaint

> Don is a 51-year-old janitor at the church. Before beginning this job a year ago, Don had been at a previous janitorial job for 30 years, until the business closed. Don is very soft-spoken and never initiates conversation with others. He works slowly but steadily and prefers to work at night when no one else is in the church. Two church secretaries approach you to express strong concern that Don is a "psycho" and "demon-possessed." They cite his cold, emotionless demeanor and his active avoidance of all interaction with others as evidence. You visit Don and find that he has very poor social skills and an apparent disinterest in conversation or relationships. He tells you he prefers to be alone and that he has "always been that way." Don has no record of mental health or legal problems and he appears to be in no distress.

Common Features and Symptoms

The primary feature of persons with a schizoid personality disorder is an inability to form attachments to other people. They lack the normal human needs for love, approval, and belonging and have very few interpersonal experiences compared with their peers. As a result of their inability to form social relationships (and their clear disinterest in relationships in general), schizoids do not have friends. They may have very few social connections except for primary relatives. Schizoid parishioners will appear apathetic, with a diminished capacity to experience emotional pleasure or pain. They do not usually experience pleasure in social activity—including sexual relations. They are often listless, distant, and socially disinterested. When it comes to relationships, they are passive observers and are usually described as "loners" with solitary occupations and interests. To observers or coworkers, the schizoid person may be "weird," lacking any social savvy, and sometimes even lacking attention to personal hygiene. Schizoid persons are no more likely to be dangerous than anyone else, though their odd behavior and extreme aloofness often create uneasiness or fear in others. When placed in a generally solitary living and employment environment, the schizoid person can be quite content and reasonably productive. Requiring social interaction of the schizoid person will be counterproductive.

Schizoid Personality Disorder: Key Indicators

- A consistent pattern of social detachment and a restricted range of emotional expression in interpersonal situations.
- Specific indications of this detachment and emotional restriction may include: (1) neither desires nor enjoys close relationships; (2) consistently chooses solitary activities; (3) little to no interest in sexual activity with another person; (4) takes pleasure in few, if any, activities; (5) lacks close friends; (6) is indifferent to praise or criticism; (7) shows emotional coldness or detachment.

Summary and Guidelines

Schizoid persons rarely seek professional or pastoral assistance. They are likely to come to the pastor's attention only if others complain about them or if they experience a major life crisis that requires some immediate assistance. In Don's case, the pastor may spend most of his or her time helping others adapt to Don. Don himself is probably oblivious to the concerns of others and would probably be disinterested even if he became aware of those concerns. Schizoid personality disorders are unlikely to change in adulthood. Psychotherapy and other interventions are not likely to be helpful. Unless the person is severely depressed (which is rare), referrals to MHPs are not indicated.

When the pastor becomes involved with schizoid parishioners, he or she should expect to be very direct and do most of the talking. Given the communication problems characteristic of schizoids, the parishioner may not have the social language necessary to communicate the primary concern or source of distress. Very often, a simple pragmatic change in the parishioner's role in the church (giving permission for him or her to miss meetings while focusing on solo tasks) or an adjustment at work, which allows the person to be free from most social demands, may work magic in reducing his or her concerns. Keep in mind that many schizoid persons would do fairly well in solitary research stations or as solo night security guards. Finding the right niche for these people—in life and in the church—is a critical challenge for the minister.

Schizotypal Personality Disorder

Presenting Complaint

Larry is a 31-year-old parishioner who rarely attends regular worship services. You notice that he occasionally comes to the less formal, and more sparsely attended, evening service. However, when he does attend, he sits near the back and appears uncomfortable. Larry's hygiene is poor and, based on your few interactions with him, you would concur with others who detect that Larry is quite uncomfortable interacting with others. Since leaving home, he has been employed only intermittently and cannot seem to keep a job. During your few conversations with him, Larry has been hard to follow. His speech rambles and he speaks in vague terms about seemingly unconnected and irrelevant things. His affect is a bit odd and he has a habit of laughing at odd times. He is preoccupied with "prophetic gifts" and thinks he may have received a "word" from God Himself. He has read everything he can find on the topic and frequently describes to you his latest prophetic experience. He is worried that others will reject him as a result.

Common Features and Symptoms

Persons with schizotypal personality disorder are among the most odd and eccentric of the personality-disordered parishioners you may encounter. This personality disorder is often considered part of the "schizophrenic spectrum" of psychotic disorders (see Chapter 3). Although schizotypal personality disorder is a developmental disorder similar to the others discussed in this chapter, these individuals are sometimes initially misdiagnosed as schizophrenic. However, for the most part, schizotypal persons are odd, eccentric, and socially detached, not psychotic.

Similar to schizoids, schizotypal persons are chronically socially detached and have serious interpersonal skill deficits. They also have odd thinking patterns and perceptual distortions, and their behavior is considered eccentric or "weird" by others. Although they typically maintain contact with reality (in contrast to a truly schizophrenic or otherwise psychotic person), they engage in extremely superstitious, odd, or "autistic" thinking. Schizotypal persons communicate by mixing irrelevant, personalized, and circumstantial ideas into their speech. They will often ruminate about a specific fear or interest and engage in magical thinking about themselves and the world. For schizotypal persons, the line between fantasy and reality is easily blurred. To others, these persons will appear confused, self-absorbed, emotionally detached, and unpleasant to interact with because of their extremely poor social skills and their very odd thought processes. Socially, schizotypal persons may indeed be anxious, often because they have experienced a great deal of ridicule and social rejection as they developed. They may be suspicious of others and have ideas of reference (the belief that others are referring to them in their conversations). About 3 percent of the general population in North America may be schizotypal.[1]

If religious, a person with this disorder may be drawn to the most extreme or frankly bizarre religious beliefs and practices.[2] They may be inclined to believe they have exceptional or rare spiritual powers, psychic powers, or even the power to heal. Because they are socially uncomfortable and sensitized to ridicule and rejection, they often avoid crowded church services. If they do attend, they may sit in the back in order to avoid interaction with others.

Schizotypal Personality Disorder: Key Indicators

- A consistent pattern of social and interpersonal skill deficits including discomfort with and little capacity for close personal relationships, as well as distortions in thinking and perceiving and a pattern of eccentric or "odd" behavior.
- Specific indications of these deficits and eccentricities may include: (1) ideas that others are referring to them; (2) odd beliefs or magical thinking not shared by others; (3) unusual perceptual experiences; (4) odd or bizarre speech; (5) suspiciousness; (6) inappropriate or restricted emotional expression; (7) odd behavior; (8) few close friends; (9) excessive distrust of others and expectation of ridicule.

Summary and Guidelines

Although we emphasized at the outset that persons with personality disorders are not especially amenable to traditional forms of counseling and therapy, schizotypal persons may indeed require mental health intervention at some point. Like many of the other personality disorder types, they rarely seek mental health services on their own. They are inherently mistrustful and wary of the motives of those who might wish to refer them for psychiatric assistance. Keep in mind that they have been ridiculed and rejected most of their lives.

In addition to his or her expectation of ridicule from others, the schizotypal person has profound difficulty relating to others. He or she will ramble and speak in vague terms, have tremendous difficulty being specific about the problem at hand, and be unable to connect interpersonally as other parishioners do. As in the case of the schizoid parishioner, the pastor must go to great lengths to establish a trust-based working relationship. Kindness, consistency, and unconditional acceptance should be demonstrated. Using a kind but matter-of-fact approach to focusing and clarifying the person's thoughts and concerns is critical because schizotypal persons are highly prone to ramble.

Schizotypal parishioners may actually become looser in both their thinking and the ability to integrate all parts of themselves—in other words, they may become psychotic. In these cases (and ideally, prior to a full-blown psychotic episode), the pastor, hopefully in concert with the parishioner's family or employer, may make a referral to a psychiatrist or to an emergency room if needed. Hospitalization and medication may be indicated until the person is stabilized and capable of independent functioning once again.

Histrionic Personality Disorder

Presenting Complaint

Marla, 26, is new to the community and the church. She is referred to the pastor by the layperson who oversees the singles ministry of the church. Although Marla has only attended the singles group for two months, she has wrought havoc in the group and created considerable tension among its members. Apparently Marla has kept the focus of the group almost exclusively on herself and her relationship problems. She has been extremely seductive with several of the male group members and has become sexually involved with two of them—creating a great deal of anger and conflict among all the members. In her session with the pastor she is tearful, yet there appears to be little depth to her grief. She fluctuates frequently from one emotional extreme to the other (usually anger to tears). Although she complains of being misunderstood and exploited, she is unable to be particularly specific about her concerns and the pastor cannot help but notice her very seductive manner of sitting and dressing. She appears desperate when their meeting time is up and pleads for another appointment. The pastor feels quite uncomfortable with Marla.

Common Features and Symptoms

Histrionic is the first of the "cluster B" personality disorders we will cover. Like the other disorders in the category, histrionic personality disorder is not easily treated and persons with the disorder typically leave a wake of chaos behind them. The essential feature of this disorder is excessive attention-seeking behavior as well as excessive and poorly regulated emotionality. Histrionic persons have a nearly insatiable need for attention and approval. When they are not the center of attention, they may become depressed or angry. Two or 3 percent of people meet the criteria for this disorder and women are diagnosed as histrionic more often than men.[1]

Although they often make positive initial impressions, appearing outgoing, friendly, talkative, and dramatic, they are gradually viewed as selfish, immature, unreliable, and demanding of attention. They are extremely superficial in their thought processes and emotional lives, which means that their relationships will tend to lack depth and be short term in nature. Quite often, histrionic persons are very seductive and relationships may begin with a primarily sexual focus. It is not unusual for these parishioners to dress very provocatively, wear excessive amounts of makeup, and become almost demandingly seductive. Relationships tend to be stormy as the histrionic person demands constant attention, and attempts to control and manipulate the partner.

Thought processes in histrionic persons can be described as "flighty." They have very little internal life and generally avoid blaming themselves for their own contributions to problems. Because of their cognitive and emotional superficiality, their involvement in religion and the church is often equally superficial, and driven primarily by social needs (attention). Once members of the church begin to lose interest in them, or become annoyed at their behavior, they often drop out.

Histrionic Personality Disorder: Key Indicators

- A consistent pattern of excessive attention-seeking behavior and emotionality in a range of contexts.
- Specific indications of attention-seeking behavior and extreme emotionality may include: (1) discomfort when not the center of attention; (2) interpersonal behavior characterized by sexual seductiveness; (3) rapidly changing and shallow emotional expression; (4) use of physical appearance to draw attention to self; (5) excessively impressionistic speech that lacks detail; (6) excessive dramatization and exaggeration in emotional expression; (7) highly suggestible; (8) considers relationships to be more intimate than they are.

Summary and Guidelines

Although the histrionic person will rarely approach the minister for authentic feedback based on a desire for change, they may seek out clergy as a potential source of attention. Their behavior may also generate enough conflict within the church that the minister is compelled to respond. Ministers should exercise caution when working with the histrionic parishioner. Not only is the prognosis for real change poor, but also the minister is at high risk for becoming manipulated or, worse, seduced by this person. It would be common for the parishioner to attempt to elicit "special" attention from and time with the pastor—for example, meeting after hours or more frequently than is common.

When interacting with the histrionic person, it is important to remain very calm and measured. Because the parishioner will both think and respond emotionally in black-and-white extremes, it is often useful to get him or her to slow down and focus on the specifics of a given situation or relationship. Careful and repeated reality testing is necessary, and the pastor must be consistently aware of not participating in the person's extreme thinking or emotional reacting. Above all, setting firm limits on meeting times, meeting parameters and appropriate behavior is critical. Although histrionic persons are not generally very amenable to therapy, they may be referred for longer term personality-focused psychotherapy. Medications are unlikely to be useful; therefore the referral could be made to any seasoned psychologist, psychiatrist, social worker or counselor with considerable experience in long-term therapy with personality-disordered clients.

Narcissistic Personality Disorder

Presenting Complaint

John is a 24-year-old seminary student who has joined the church staff as an intern for the summer. John approaches the pastor with strong "concerns" about being assigned to work with young people for the summer. Although he says that youth work is important, John wonders if the pastor has overlooked his résumé and letters of reference, and suggests they would indicate that he is "not your typical summer intern." John notes that he is considerably more advanced than most of his seminary peers and is ready to do some "serious preaching." He then subtly devalues the pastor's preaching and notes how he might have approached the previous week's message differently. He recommends that the pastor have him preach regularly and says, "I think it's safe to say you'll be impressed." He goes on to note that many of his seminary professors don't seem to understand his gifts and are probably jealous of his preaching talents. He seems oblivious to how his comments may be interpreted by the pastor.

Common Features and Symptoms

Narcissistic personality disorder has three essential features: (1) an exaggerated sense of self-importance, (2) a preoccupation with being admired, and (3) poor ability to empathize with or take the perspective of others. The term "narcissistic" comes from the Greek legend of Narcissus—a young man who fell in love with himself and pined for his own reflection in the water. Chances are, you know, or have known, a severely narcissistic person. The narcissist is so self-absorbed and preoccupied with garnering admiration from others that he or she can be an extremely unpleasant person to work with, let alone have a relationship with.

Narcissists possess a grandiose sense of their own importance and an inflated assessment of their abilities. They very frequently overestimate their abilities while devaluing and underestimating the abilities of those around them. They will often make caustic or dismissing remarks about others (this can be subtle if the person is more sophisticated) while expecting that everyone else will recognize their unique or amazing talents. Parishioners with narcissism have a sense of entitlement. That is, they simply expect special recognition and privilege, whatever the context. They compare themselves favorably to famous or high-status persons, and expect others to see them as similarly entitled to special status. Other people view them as egotistical because they usually brag and make references to themselves and their talents. As a result of their inflated view of themselves, they often believe they can only be understood by other high-status people. They seek to be idealized and will delight in special recognition.

Another important feature of narcissistic personality disorder is an inability to take the perspective of others (egocentrism). Although most children slowly develop the capacity to take another perspective and empathize with the way others might feel, narcissists are generally unable to do this effectively. In addition to this empathy deficit, narcissists often take advantage of others, envy others, believe others envy them, and appear arrogant, snobbish, and exploitive to those who know them. Because their fantasy life is consumed with thoughts of unlimited success, power, beauty, ideal love, and so forth, they are often upset when others do not recognize their specialness. They are easily "wounded" when they do not receive the accolades and recognition they believe they deserve.

This personality disorder appears to be slightly more prevalent in men than women and it occurs in roughly 1 percent of the general population.[1] Although narcissistic and histrionic personality disorders share some features in common, the narcissist tends to be less dramatic and emotional than the histrionic person. In relationships, the narcissist may simply exploit out of a sense of entitlement, whereas the histrionic person is needier. Finally, the narcissist seeks admiration while the histrionic person is desperate for attention.

In the church, narcissistic parishioners will be primarily motivated by self-aggrandizement. They will be interested only in positions and involvement that brings them notice and praise. Their internal spirituality may be dominated with expectations that God exists to meet their needs and kindly answer their prayers. When this does not appear to happen, they may quickly become disenchanted—feeling God has let them down. Narcissists in the church may view themselves as having special or unique spiritual gifts that deserve praise and recognition.

Narcissistic Personality Disorder: Key Indicators

- A consistent pattern of grandiosity, need for admiration, and lack of empathy for others.
- Specific indications of grandiosity and need for affirmation may include: (1) a strong sense of self-importance; (2) preoccupation with fantasies of unlimited success, power, brilliance, beauty, and so forth; (3) belief that one is special and unique and can be understood only by other special people; (4) requires excessive admiration; (5) has a sense of entitlement; (6) exploits others; (7) lacks empathy; (8) envies others and believes others envy him or her; (9) is arrogant and haughty.

Summary and Guidelines

The narcissistic parishioner will most likely be disliked by most people with whom he or she comes into contact. Although a favorable and even awe-inspiring first impression may be created, those who spend time with the narcissist begin to experience him or her as increasingly arrogant, obnoxiously self-focused, and egotistical. These parishioners will rarely seek treatment or pastoral counseling because they view themselves as perfect or nearly perfect. They tend to blame problems on others and view those around them as failing to understand their talents or as being jealous of them. They may come to the pastor's attention if their behavior, in some role within the church, begins to alienate others or if their spouse or supervisors require them to seek assistance.

The pastor should be wary of the narcissistic parishioner who wishes to have personal counseling. The biggest problem we see is that the pastor may intensely dislike the narcissist. Strong dislike for a parishioner may be distasteful for the pastor and may cause self-recrimination and personal distress. The narcissist may consistently devalue the pastor's credentials and performance and may suggest that the pastor really does not possess the credentials and/or experience to be maximally helpful. This parishioner may arrive late for appointments, discount the pastor's advice, and expect special treatment (for example, extra-long sessions or meeting times at odd hours). The narcissistic parishioner will be insulting and arrogant, and assume that rules that apply to others in the church do not apply to him or her.

Referrals for therapy are generally not likely to be helpful. Not only do narcissistic persons rarely follow through with treatment, there is no significant evidence that they benefit from any form of intervention. Firm limit setting, gentle but consistent feedback, and perhaps counseling for the narcissist's spouse and family may be useful.

Borderline Personality Disorder

Presenting Complaint

Tina is a 25-year-old who requests "spiritual counseling" from her pastor. In her first session, she tearfully recounts a history of brief but intense relationships with men, which have all ended abruptly and angrily. Tina admits that she gets involved with the "wrong men" and that she is self-destructive when in relationships—abusing substances and engaging in sexual relations almost immediately. She initially believes that each of these men is "perfect" and "completely different," but quickly finds herself being exploited and sometimes abused. At the end of each relationship, Tina has become very depressed and even suicidal. When depressed, she has at times made lacerations on her arm "to stop the pain . . . and make sure I'm alive." Tina tells the pastor she feels "empty" inside and that she only feels like "somebody" when she is with a man. When Tina learns that the pastor will be on vacation for the following week, she appears very anxious and asks if there is a way she can reach the pastor while she is away.

Common Features and Symptoms

Parishioners with borderline personality disorder have one of the most severe and disabling of the personality disorders. They will present with a history of unstable interpersonal relationships, an undefined self-image, chaotic emotional experiences, and notable impulsivity in more than one area. Friends or acquaintances may describe the borderline parishioner as moody, prone to extremes in emotion, and episodically depressed—sometimes even suicidal—though these episodes are interspersed with periods of anger, anxiety, or even euphoria. They are also interpersonally intense and prone to conflict with others, especially those with whom they become close. Their interests appear fickle, and their attachments are intense but brief. They typically begin relationships by idealizing the other person, only to become quickly disappointed, rejected, and wounded yet again. They are frequently dissatisfied and unhappy with themselves and their lives, and are preoccupied with obtaining affection.

Parishioners with this disorder have an extremely unstable and fragile identity. For some reason, they have failed to complete the normal process of identity development that occurs in childhood and late adolescence. They are deeply fearful of abandonment and will spend a great deal of time trying to avoid this experience (even if it is imagined). Threat of abandonment may lead to angry outbursts (even physical abuse) or suicidal gestures and self-mutilation. These parishioners may attempt to establish a relationship with the pastor (or others in the church) and then create substantial conflict when, inevitably, they find the pastor, too, is imperfect and they feel abandoned. They will report feeling chronically empty and bored and have a very low tolerance for being alone. Look for a history of intense and stormy relationships as well as a pattern of impulsive and destructive behaviors such as binges in gambling, sex, substance abuse, or reckless driving.

About 2 percent of the U.S. population may qualify for a diagnosis of borderline personality disorder,[1] and 75 percent of those diagnosed are women. Borderline personalities are markedly overrepresented in psychiatric settings (inpatient and outpatient), suggesting they are a more volatile and service-intensive group. Parishioners with borderline personality disorder will also be considerably more likely to have a major mood disorder (see Chapter 3). In general, they have an extremely poor ability to regulate themselves—both their moods and their basic identities.

Borderline Personality Disorder: Key Indicators

- A consistent pattern of unstable interpersonal relationships, self-image, and emotions as well as a pattern of impulsivity.
- Specific indications of this instability and impulsiveness are evident in: (1) frantic efforts to avoid real or imagined abandonment; (2) a pattern of unstable and intense relationships; (3) a persistently unstable sense of self; (4) impulsivity in at least two areas; (5) a pattern of self-harm or suicidal behavior; (6) chronic instability in emotions; (7) feelings of emptiness; (8) problems with intense anger.

Summary and Guidelines

Parishioners with borderline personality disorder may present the minister with one of his or her greatest management challenges. Borderlines will think in rigid black-and-white terms, forcing extreme evaluations on life events, themselves, and those around them. Therefore, they will see the church and the pastor as all good (initially) or all bad (later). They will vacillate between a desire for intimacy (including safe dependence on others) and intense fear of getting close. They will see the minister and the church community as a potentially hostile and dangerous place. They will likely arrange to be disappointed and abandoned by people in the church, including the pastor. Not only are they likely to see the world and others in all-or-nothing terms, but also their religious experience is likely to be much the same. They may be entirely active in the church or absent. They may see God as loving and kind or absent and rejecting, depending on their current emotional state.

For several reasons, we highly recommend that the pastor not attempt to do formal counseling with a parishioner who is clearly borderline in presentation. Borderline clients are among the most stressful for even seasoned clinicians to manage. They are difficult to help, minimally likely to benefit from most forms of therapy, and prone to create crisis after crisis for those treating them. In the same way, the pastor can expect to experience a good deal of chaos if he or she becomes involved in a close personal counseling relationship with a borderline parishioner. Even without a formal counseling component, the pastor should anticipate volatility, episodes of anger, and, possibly, threats of suicide. The pastor will initially be idealized and later may become the object of rage. The movie *Fatal Attraction* portrays a person with this sort of unpredictable borderline rage.

If the pastor attempts to refer the borderline parishioner for professional care, this may be experienced as yet another rejection (regardless of how it is conveyed). The parishioner may have a history of seeing multiple psychotherapists (without substantial benefit) and may also have a history of attending multiple churches. If a referral is made, we recommend that the pastor seek a seasoned professional with considerable experience in treating personality-disordered clients. Dialectical behavior therapy and other forms of cognitive-behavioral therapy show particular promise in helping these persons gain personal and interpersonal stability.

Antisocial Personality Disorder

Presenting Complaint

Oscar, 48, has begun dating a recently widowed woman in the church. He is polite and engaging in conversation and tends to make a very positive initial impression, especially on women. Oscar very quickly convinces his new female friend that she should allow him to move in with her. He is "between jobs" but insists this will not be for long. Oscar convinces the pastor to give him a "small loan" to help with food until he finds employment. Soon, the pastor learns that Oscar has secured similar loans from other parishioners. Alarmed, the pastor does some background checking and finds that Oscar has a long history of short-term relationships, usually with older women whom he exploits financially before abruptly moving on. He has never held a job for more than a few months because of his unreliability (and several instances of embezzlement). He has been in and out of jail and has a chronic history of alcohol abuse. When Oscar is confronted by the pastor, he insists he wants to change and commits to being accountable to the church. The following day, the pastor learns Oscar has disappeared.

Common Features and Symptoms

Persons with antisocial personality disorder are often initially charming and likable. However, others soon find them to be manipulative, deceitful, and willing to do almost anything to achieve their own ends. They are irresponsible and unreliable, highly impulsive, prone to illegal behavior, and sometimes vengeful regarding perceived injustices. They generally avoid attachments, and their relationships are superficial and short-lived. They are disloyal, highly exploitive of others, insensitive, and even ruthless. They chronically disregard societal rules and believe that these rules do not apply to them.

Antisocials are distinct from the other personality disorder types in that a criterion for the diagnosis is the presence of the precursors to antisocial behavior in childhood and adolescence. Antisocial parishioners (men are considerably more likely to be diagnosed as antisocial) will always have a history of *conduct disorder* in adolescence (see Chapter 6). That is, they engaged in behaviors such as shoplifting, truancy, lying, cruelty to animals, fire setting, vandalism, and frequent fighting. The more conduct problems in adolescence, the more likely the development of antisocial personality disorder in adulthood. In the church, ministers should be alert to two major manifestations of this disorder. The first type of antisocial is the smooth, personable, charming person who manipulates and exploits others subtly—often without detection—for some time. The second type is the belligerent, antagonistic, and overtly criminal antisocial type. This parishioner will have a clear criminal history, arouse fear in others, and be viewed as unpredictable and dangerous. The difference between the two may be emotional intelligence or social polish. Both smooth and belligerent antisocials can be dangerous, and they are unlikely to experience remorse following acts of harm and exploitation.

Key characteristics of parishioners with antisocial personality disorder include the following:

1. *Inadequate development of conscience:* Although his or her intelligence is often normally developed, the antisocial person appears unable to truly understand and accept ethical and moral values—even though he or she may claim to value these standards.
2. *Irresponsible and impulsive behavior:* Prone to thrill seeking and intense need for novelty, antisocials will impulsively break the law with little regard for the consequences of their behavior. They also callously disregard the needs and rights of others.

3. *Ability to impress and exploit others:* They are likable and disarming and can readily "read" the needs and vulnerabilities of those they exploit. Even when caught in a lie or criminal act, they can effectively rationalize their behavior or appear genuinely sorrowful.

4. *Rejection of authority:* Beginning in adolescence, antisocials act as though rules do not apply to them. Despite frequent contacts with authorities and various criminal convictions, they continue to act as though they are immune to the consequences.

5. *Inability to maintain good relationships:* Antisocials rarely have close friends. Instead, they have a long string of superficial acquaintances and appear incapable of truly bonding with another person. Not only are they exploitive and prone to extreme sexual promiscuity, they may additionally be violent in relationships, particularly when their immediate goals or desires are blocked.

Antisocial Personality Disorder: Key Indicators

- A consistent pattern of disregard for and violation of societal laws and the rights of others.
- This disregard and exploitation is evident in the following: (1) repeated criminal behavior; (2) deceitfulness (lying or conning others); (3) impulsivity; (4) irritability or aggressiveness; (5) disregard for the safety of self or others; (6) irresponsibility in work and relationships; (7) lack of remorse after harming or violating another.

Summary and Guidelines

If we can recommend only one thing to pastors when it comes to the antisocial personality, it is *be careful.* Although children of God, these men (and less frequently, women) have developed without a conscience; they have a tendency to exploit without remorse. It is not unreasonable to assume that the faith of antisocial people will be limited in its overall impact on their lives. They will typically fail to practice what they say they believe, and they may relate to God as they relate to other people—in a superficial and pragmatic manner.[2]

The pastor must appreciate the significance of this parishioner's underdeveloped conscience. Because such people are really unable to grasp essential moral principles on an emotional level (though there may be some intellectual understanding), they will not be amenable to interventions focusing on the "wrongness" of their behavior. They will not experience guilt or remorse in a genuine way. The pastor can expect that they will only seek assistance to get something they want, such as money or assistance with convincing a spouse that they have changed this time, or when a temporary crisis ensues because of criminal behavior.

Referrals for treatment are not indicated, as no single approach is likely to be helpful. True antisocial personality-disordered parishioners do not follow through or benefit much from mental health intervention. In the church, management of antisocial behavior should center on firm limit setting and clear, nonnegotiable consequences for inappropriate, exploitive, or illegal behavior. Good communication among ministerial staff can be crucial as the antisocial may attempt to manipulate several persons at once. Recognizing that this person has little capacity for conscience may help the pastor avoid anger and hostility toward the parishioner (which is often a natural reaction to the parishioner's exploitive behavior). Instead, the pastor can matter-of-factly confront the antisocial behavior, point out choices made, and the consequences that will follow.

Avoidant Personality Disorder

Presenting Complaint

Glenna is an attractive and intelligent 27-year-old college administrator. She holds two master's degrees, one of which is in theology. Although she has attended the church for nearly three years, she has not become involved in any of the groups or forms of ministry. In fact, she appears aloof and avoids relationships. When the pastor tells Glenna she would like to meet with her to talk about her potential coleadership of the college-age ministry, Glenna appears startled and anxious. During their meeting, Glenna insists she has "nothing to offer" others and that she does not believe college students would enjoy having her lead the group. She also says she "hates being up in front" of others and that it takes her quite a long time to feel comfortable with a group. She insists she would like to get to know some others in the church, but she says, "It always takes a long time with me."

Common Features and Symptoms

Unlike "cluster B" personality disorders, those in "cluster C" rarely become disruptive and thus often go unnoticed. Avoidant personality disorder is the first of the cluster C disorder types. Initially, the avoidant parishioner may appear schizoid because he or she is aloof, avoids interpersonal interaction, and has few friendships. However, in contrast to the schizoid who prefers his or her solitude, the avoidant person wants relationships but is too fearful of rejection to pursue them. While the schizoid is indifferent to criticism and interpersonally cold, the avoidant is shy, insecure, and hypersensitive to criticism. He or she usually has a lifelong pattern of avoiding social relationships and a reluctance to enter social situations. When it comes to relationships, avoidant parishioners are cautious, mistrustful, and fully expectant of ridicule or rejection. They experience anxiety symptoms in social situations and therefore work to reduce this discomfort through the well-learned mechanism of avoidance. They feel deeply inadequate and tend to read criticism into the behavior of others even when it is not present. Although they actively avoid others out of fear, they are often lonely, bored, and desire affection. Because they cannot face even the slightest risk of embarrassment or criticism, they will avoid social activities unless guaranteed acceptance. Thus, if the avoidant person has friends, they tend to be few and he or she may rely excessively on these limited friendships.

The avoidant parishioner will have recurring thoughts such as, "I am inadequate and have nothing to offer others," "There is nothing much about me to like," and "I am defective or obviously lacking." Their self-esteem is extremely poor. The irony is that, like Glenna in the case study, the avoidant person may actually have many desirable traits and be quite likeable. Finally, there is a strong correlation between avoidant personality disorder and social anxiety disorder (see Chapter 3). Whereas the avoidant person has a long-term personality style characterized in part by fear of humiliation and social rejection, the socially phobic person experiences extreme fear only in social situations in which he or she may be scrutinized. The socially anxious person may have little problem entering and enjoying relationships. Nonetheless, expect many of the symptoms of social anxiety disorder to be present in avoidant parishioners.

Avoidant Personality Disorder: Key Indicators

- A long-term pattern of social avoidance, feelings of inadequacy, and hypersensitivity to negative evaluation.
- This pattern of avoidance, inadequacy, and fear of evaluation is evident in the following: (1) avoids jobs that require significant interpersonal contact; (2) is unwilling to get involved with others unless certain of being liked; (3) avoids relationships because of fear of shame and ridicule; (4) is preoccupied with being socially rejected or ridiculed; (5) feels inadequate and therefore avoids social situations; (6) views self as inferior and unappealing socially; (7) is reluctant to explore new activities because of fear of embarrassment.

Summary and Guidelines

Of all the personality disorders we cover in this section, the avoidant type is among those with the best prognosis for change. Although these parishioners will respond to the pastor in much the same way they respond to others—with fear and avoidance—they desire connection and are quite lonely. The minister and the church can offer and encourage gradually increasing social involvement. In fact, the church is perhaps the "ideal" location for the avoidant person to decrease his or her avoidance and develop some close friendships. When the minister and other church members present a consistent, unconditionally accepting relational environment, the avoidant person stands the best chance of expanding his or her social risk taking.

Avoidant persons may see God in much the same way they see other people—as potentially threatening and rejecting. They may have difficulty accepting that God loves them without condition, and they may expect God to be critical of them. They will expect the same thing from their pastors and may be shocked and distrusting if the pastor expresses interest or finds value in them. Avoidant parishioners will require the pastor to take a long-term incremental approach to establishing a relationship with them. They may avoid admitting even normal shortcomings for fear of disapproval. Modeling self-disclosure, admission of human weaknesses, and social connectedness may be very helpful.

Avoidant persons may benefit from counseling to address their avoidance and perhaps symptoms of social anxiety as well. As long as making a referral does not communicate to these parishioners that the pastor finds fault with them, the pastor could consider referring to MHP with experience in treating avoidant people in long-term therapy relationships. Medications are unlikely to be useful unless the parishioner is disabled by anxiety or depression connected to his or her personality disorder.

Dependent Personality Disorder

Presenting Complaint

Jenna, 40, has attended church all her life. Although she has never been a leader in the church, she has routinely served "behind the scenes," always saying "yes" to setting up for and cleaning up after church activities. In fact, the pastor has never known Jenna to say "no" to any request or to be anything but pleasant and accommodating. On many occasions, Jenna has apparently been exploited by others who know she will never object to being put out. At the same time, those who have worked with Jenna have sometimes expressed frustration at her lack of initiative because she requires specific direction and ample reassurance that she is doing things correctly. Recently, Jenna's physically and emotionally abusive husband, Tom, left her and her two children. Even though Tom had been very cruel to Jenna, she comes to the pastor in crisis and insists she simply "can't make it" without Tom "telling me what to do." She says she can't make decisions without him and that she is "not the kind of person who can just decide what to do or be all alone."

Common Features and Symptoms

Parishioners with dependent personality disorder are extremely dependent on others and have strong needs to be taken care of by others—resulting in clinging and submissive behavior. These behaviors are designed to get others to care for them and arise from a core belief that they cannot adequately function alone. Dependent people have tremendous difficulty making even everyday decisions (e.g., what to wear, how to spend free time) without reassurance and advice from others. Adults with this disorder typically rely on a spouse while adolescents may rely on parents to determine most aspects of their daily routines.

Parishioners with dependent personality disorder will show discomfort and even panic at possibly having to be separated or alone for a time. They typically build their lives around another person (spouse or parent) and then work hard to keep them present by subordinating their own needs. Because they are fearful of being alone, they often fail to get appropriately angry when they are harmed or exploited. They will squelch their own reactions and rights rather than risk losing the person on whom they depend for guidance. They are markedly lacking in self-confidence and therefore do not initiate activities or projects without ample direction and reassurance from others. Because they are convinced they are incompetent, they present themselves to others as inept and requiring guidance. Dependent persons are preoccupied with fear of being alone and having to care for themselves. Therefore, when one relationship ends, they will often seek out a new one as quickly as possible and with great urgency. The few friends of the dependent person will describe him or her as bland, passive, needy, deferential, cooperative, and willing to do anything to help another—the primary motivation for this behavior is to maintain affection. The movie *What About Bob?* offers a fine example of this sort of clingy dependence.

Dependent Personality Disorder: Key Indicators

- A chronic and excessive need to be taken care of that leads to submissive and clinging behaviors as well as fear of separation.
- This pattern of submissiveness and fear of separation is evident in the following: (1) difficulty making everyday decisions without advice and reassurance; (2) need for others to assume responsibility for this person; (3) difficulty expressing disagreement or anger for fear of losing approval and support; (4) difficulty initiating projects on own; (5) feels uncomfortable and helpless when alone; (6) goes to excessive lengths to obtain nurturance—even volunteering for demeaning tasks; (7) urgently seeks another relationship as a source of care when a close relationship ends.

Summary and Guidelines

Parishioners with dependent personality disorders rarely pose a "problem" for the pastor or the church in the same way that other personality disorders often do. They are not disruptive, demanding, or disturbing to others. In fact, they are often among the most quiet and service-focused members of a congregation. They may only come to the pastor's attention when a relationship ends and they are anxiety ridden about the possibility of being alone. Or they may be referred to the pastor by a friend or spouse upon whom they have been dependent for years. This person may be exasperated or preparing to terminate the relationship.

The dependent parishioner sees himself or herself as unable to handle the trials of life and, therefore, must attach to a stronger person in order to survive. He or she is essentially in search of a protecting nurturer to direct him or her in every area. The problem, of course, is that the pastor will be seen by the dependent parishioner as a particularly gifted expert with great potential for telling him or her precisely how to live— religiously and otherwise. These parishioners will be prone to become dependent on the pastor in the same way that they have depended upon others. They may praise the pastor profusely and follow each shred of the pastor's advice simply to please (not because they internalize the importance of changing their behavior). Additionally, they may see God as a great protector and rescuer who must take care of their every need.[2] However, when prayers are not answered, they may feel that God has abandoned them.

There are some specific risks for the pastor in caring for the dependent parishioner. First, some pastors are inclined to want to rescue dependent parishioners, particularly when the pastor is male and the parishioner female (more women than men are diagnosed with this disorder).[1] In this case, the pastor may be at risk for romantic involvement, which the dependent parishioner may foster as a means of securing caretaking. Another potential problem occurs when the pastor assumes an authoritative-directive stance, thus promoting a dependent stance on the part of the parishioner. In this case, the pastor will simply become the object of dependency. Instead, a peer relationship is recommended in which the pastor gradually gives less and less advice and pushes the parishioner to articulate his or her own feelings, needs, and agenda. Finally, ministers may naturally respond with annoyance and irritation to the dependent person. Obviously, this is unlikely to be helpful. Instead, a kind but firm approach to encouragement mixed with limits on advice and direction giving is indicated.

Although dependent parishioners may benefit from a healthy counseling relationship, and such a referral may be indicated, be aware that the therapist will have to avoid the same dependent relational dynamics. Once again, we recommend finding a seasoned MHP with excellent personal boundaries and experience in treating persons with personality problems.

Obsessive-Compulsive Personality Disorder

Presenting Complaint

> Norman is a single, 34-year-old technical writer for a publishing company and a parishioner in the church for several years. Since his appointment as the director of the Sunday school program two months ago, the other teachers have become increasingly unhappy and annoyed at what they consider "micromanagement" and "anal retentiveness." Norman has instituted many new regulations and tasks, including mandatory weekly meetings with lengthy agendas, weekly inventories of all supplies, and step-by-step teacher guides for each lesson. Norman has gone to the pastor on several occasions asking about "denominational regulations" or "church bylaws" that might relate to Sunday school. He appears uptight and controlled, and rarely laughs. He seems driven to control the education process, yet shows little enjoyment of his new role. Finally, the high school class leader goes to the pastor in exasperation when Norman rejects his idea for taking the high schoolers to a water slide park. Norman

insisted that such a trip was not part of the "accepted curriculum," and that any such deviation would need to be considered by the education committee, church board, and, possibly, the denomination headquarters.

Common Features and Symptoms

People with obsessive-compulsive personality disorder (OCPD) are excessively concerned with maintaining order and are extremely perfectionistic.[1] Although most successful people are well organized and attentive to detail, persons with OCPD are dysfunctionally preoccupied with maintaining personal and interpersonal control via excessive attention to rules and schedules. They will be known for painstaking development and use of rules, procedures, and lists. They get so wrapped up in trivial details that they often lose sight of the ultimate goal or purpose for the activity. They may spend so much time on details that time is used poorly and they end up finishing projects late or at the last minute. They often have a poor sense of how annoyed others become about their obsessive perfectionism.

It is common for obsessive-compulsive parishioners to have trouble relaxing or enjoying leisure activities. They tend to focus on work-related activity to the exclusion of recreation and friendships. Obsessive-compulsive persons will believe they do not have time to "waste" on such activities, and they may take work along on vacations. They may also be excessively rigid and scrupulous when it comes to matters of ethics or values and may be highly inflexible with scriptural interpretation, changes to worship, and so forth. They adhere powerfully to dogma and have a low tolerance for deviation. Obsessive-compulsive individuals may also have difficulty getting rid of old and worn-out household items and may be quite miserly and stingy. Interpersonally, they are likely to be experienced as rigid and stubborn. They have great difficulty delegating tasks to others and are most comfortable having direct control over things. Other members of the community may experience them as rigid, stiff, and interpersonally cold.

Although certain jobs and situations are well suited to someone with a few obsessive-compulsive characteristics (e.g., airline pilot, accountant, nuclear power plant supervisor), those with the full-blown disorder are so excessively perfectionistic and detail oriented that they actually become dysfunctional and less able to successfully get the job done. A pastor with obsessive-compulsive personality disorder may languish for days on end with the original Greek and Hebrew translations of biblical texts for an upcoming sermon—spending so much time agonizing over precise definitions and textual meanings that he or she fails to actually write the sermon until late the night before.

Obsessive-Compulsive Personality Disorder: Key Indicators

- A consistent pattern of preoccupation with orderliness, perfectionism, and control at the expense of flexibility, openness, and efficiency.
- Specific indications of this perfectionism and rigidity are evident in: (1) preoccupation with details, rules, lists, order, and schedules so that the major point of the activity is lost; (2) perfectionism that interferes with task completion; (3) excessive devotion to work and productivity and neglect of leisure activity and friendships; (4) unable to discard worn-out or worthless objects; (5) reluctance to delegate tasks; (6) adopts a miserly spending style toward both self and others; (7) demonstrates rigidity and stubbornness.

Summary and Guidelines

As is the case with all the personality disorders, it is not realistic to expect that the obsessive-compulsive parishioner will make marked changes in his or her basic personality style. Rather than asking an obsessive-compulsive person to give up his or her perfectionistic behaviors, it may be most productive to emphasize those behavioral aspects that are positive and helpful, while showing the person how some flexibility may actually increase and enhance productivity and effectiveness in accomplishing tasks.

In the church, it is recommended that obsessive-compulsive parishioners not be placed in direct supervisory positions—particularly if their preoccupation with rules and order has negative effects on the performance of others. Instead, they may be given jobs that are fairly independent and routine. For example, organizing and keeping track of church supplies or membership rolls may be an ideal match. It is also recommended that the assignments of obsessive-compulsive people seldom be changed, as they tend to have tremendous difficulty with change and readjustment to new tasks, new policies, and novel situations.

The obsessive-compulsive parishioner's faith may be based primarily on dogma, principles, and rules rather than an emotional connection with God. He or she is likely to show little spontaneous expression of faith and is likely to prefer more structured prayer and ritual. On occasion, the parishioner will be consumed with fear of committing or preoccupation with avoiding a grievous sin. He or she may be rigid in making moral judgments about himself or herself and others. It is often difficult for the pastor to develop much of a relationship with these parishioners, and they may only seek the pastor out when looking for correct or certain solutions to theological or task-focused questions. They may be very disappointed or even agitated if certainty is not offered. If a relationship can be established, the pastor might help the parishioner to slowly begin to appreciate the fact that perfection is not a realistic goal and that the obsessive-compulsive person's constricted way of navigating life is actually lessening the probability that he or she will efficiently and successfully "get the job done." Psychotherapy and counseling are not typically sought out or continued by the person with obsessive-compulsive personality, and prognosis for change is guarded at best. However, as is the case with obsessive-compulsive disorder (OCD; see Chapter 3), cognitive-behavioral treatments may be helpful for challenging at least some of the obsessive-compulsive person's erroneous beliefs and decreasing some compulsive behaviors.

Notes

1. American Psychiatric Association. (2013). *Diagnostic and statistical manual of mental disorders* (5th ed.). Washington, DC: Author.
2. Vaughan, R. P. (1994). *Pastoral counseling and personality disorders.* Kansas City, MO: Sheed & Ward.
3. Grant, B. F., Hasin, D. S., Stinson, F. S., Dawson, D. A., Chou, S. P., Ruan, W. J., & Pickering, R. P. (2004). Prevalence, correlates, and disability of personality disorders in the United States: Results from the National Epidemiologic Survey on Alcohol and Related Conditions. *Journal of Clinical Psychiatry, 65*(7), 948–958.
4. Zimmerman, M., Rothschild, L., & Chelminski, I. (2005). The prevalence of DSM-IV personality disorders in psychiatric outpatients. *American Journal of Psychiatry, 162*(10), 1911–1918.
5. Millon, T., Millon, C. M., Meagher, S., Grossman, S., & Ramnath, R. (2004). *Personality disorders in modern life.* New York, NY: Wiley.
6. Johnson, W. B., & Murray, K. (2007). *Crazy love: Dealing with your partner's problem personality.* Atascadero, CA: Impact.

6   The Family in Distress
Childhood and Relationship Problems

Roughly one-quarter of American children will suffer from a psychological disorder at some point in childhood or adolescence.[1,2] Anxiety disorders are the most frequent conditions in children, followed by behavior disorders (including ADHD), mood disorders, and substance use disorders. Throughout childhood and adolescence, boys are diagnosed with psychological disorders at higher rates than girls for all of the established *DSM-5* disorders except eating disorders.[3] In this chapter, we present the essential features of the most common disorders of childhood and adolescence. We have selected disorders that are most likely to impact children and families in the church.

In contrast to psychological problems in adults, many problems in children are short-lived and some resolve rather easily in the course of normal development. Because normal development in childhood and adolescence is rapid (and sometimes tumultuous), episodes of mood disturbance, anxiety, and even some behavioral acting out are considered somewhat normal—as long as they do not persist or begin to interfere with academic performance or social relationships. When youth become "stuck" in some area of development or when mood, anxiety, or behavior problems become serious, then parents, families, schools, and communities may begin to show distress. It is good to remember that children have a less stable and secure sense of identity and are therefore more vulnerable to the impact of immediate change or perceived threats. This normal vulnerability leaves them more exposed than adults to experiences of rejection, failure, and disappointment. Treatment focused on serious childhood disorders is crucial because effective intervention early in the process can effectively reshape the child's or adolescent's future.

In this chapter, we highlight *autism spectrum disorder, attention-deficit/ hyperactivity disorder (ADHD), oppositional defiant disorder, conduct disorder, separation anxiety disorder,* and *eating disorders.* We also cover *child and spouse abuse* as a pervasive problem that may impact families with or without children. Although depression and psychosis are problems affecting both children and adolescents, we refer the reader to Chapter 3 for descriptions of those disorders. It is worth noting that depression in children and adolescents can be quite serious; a referral to an MHP is strongly recommended when depression appears to be consistent or severe.

You may wonder why we have chosen to include abuse in this chapter. With over 3.5 million cases of child abuse or neglect reported annually in the United States,[4] and many more cases not reported, it is clear that ministers in all sectors of society are likely to encounter evidence of abuse or neglect at some point. Abused children are at increased risk for a number of the childhood and adult disorders discussed in this book, as well as permanent physical and social impairment. Similarly, violence aimed at adult women in families is a significant societal problem. Violence against women is primarily intimate partner violence: 64 percent of the women who are raped, physically assaulted, and/or stalked are victimized by a current or former husband, cohabiting partner, boyfriend, or date.[5] We hope that the information on child and spouse abuse will be useful to ministers who may be among the first in their communities to become aware of abusive relationships.

As in the previous two chapters, we include a *presenting complaint* section that offers a look at each disorder in a fictitious case. We then cover the *common features and symptoms, subtypes* (when applicable), *key indicators,* and conclude with a *summary and guidelines* section that offers the minister a brief recap and some recommendations regarding referrals and pastoral management.

Autism Spectrum Disorder

Presenting Complaint

The Johnson family is new to the church. Over the past several months, you notice that only one of the parents attends worship services each week—you have never seen the couple together on Sunday morning. During a staff meeting, the Director of Sunday school reports that the teacher for the third graders is "about to quit." A new girl in the Sunday school class, Shawna Johnson, has great difficulty communicating and interacting with the other children—often appearing overwhelmed by the social demands of the classroom and frequently having small tantrums or trying to bolt from the room. When she is calm, she tends to stand alone by one of the felt boards and rub the felt biblical figures. This appears to calm her. Although one of Shawna's parents is always present to assist and calm Shawna, it is a real struggle on some Sundays. When you reach out to Mrs. Johnson following the next worship service and ask her how things are going, she instantly tears up. You notice she appears exhausted. She immediately asks if you want them to stop bringing Shawna to church. She tells you that two previous churches asked them to "make other arrangements" for their daughter. She then bursts into tears.

Common Features and Symptoms

Autism spectrum disorder is a syndrome involving multiple problems such as difficulty with communication and social interaction and very restricted interests and rigid patterns of behavior. These problems are evident early in a child's development—often by 1 year of age. Children with autism have difficulty in all contexts (e.g., home, playground, school). Although a few people with autism spectrum disorder will have unusual intellectual talents—*savant* skills—in isolated areas (e.g., memory, math computation), more will have an intellectual disability (mental retardation). The term "autism spectrum disorder" accounts for a range of autistic disturbances that had previously been diagnosed separately, such as childhood autism, Asperger's disorder, and childhood disintegrative disorder. The prevalence of autism spectrum disorder in the North American population is approximately 1 percent.[3] In the 1950s, it was common to blame parents—especially mothers—for their children's autism (the term "refrigerator mother" was used by some mental health experts at that time, indicating that a perceived lack of maternal warmth was to blame), it is now clear that this disorder is almost exclusively genetic in origin.

It is often the case that parents will notice persistent deficits in in their autistic child's interactions and communication very early. For example, autistic infants or toddlers may scream, arch their backs, and push away when a parent tries to hug or provide comfort. Language will be slow to develop or may not develop at all; the child may communicate through grunts and gestures. In many cases, these children will demonstrate *echolalia,* merely repeating what they hear over and over. Games that lead to delight in many infants or toddlers (e.g., peekaboo) may be experienced as aversive to an autistic child. Don't be surprised to find that the child or adult with autism spectrum disorder is hyperreactive to sensory input such as sound and touch, and be prepared for a powerful fixation on one or two interests and activities (e.g., cars, animals). They often want everything to be the "same" each day and may not be flexible when it comes to meeting new people or changing their routine. Finally, stereotyped or repetitive motor movements are common. For example, rocking may be persistent or the child may even be consistently self-injurious, perhaps repetitively banging his or her head against a wall.[6]

Autism Spectrum Disorder: Key Indicators

- Persistent problems communicating and interacting socially in most situations as demonstrated by very poor communication skills, great difficulty interacting with other people, and chronic problems developing, maintaining, and even understanding relationships.
- Very limited and repetitive interests and behaviors as demonstrated by repetitive movements, repeating words or phrases, inflexibility in routines and rituals, fixation or preoccupation with very narrow interests, and either hyperreactivity or complete lack of response to sensory input.
- These symptoms are evident early in development and cause serious problems in nearly all areas of functioning.

Summary and Guidelines

It is nearly certain that a minister will encounter autistic children or adults in the course of his or her work. Just as it is important to create a welcoming space for the person with autistic spectrum disorder, it is just as crucial to create a supportive environment for their parents and family members. Parents of autistic children are often quite distressed and may feel depressed, alone, and ostracized by other parents whose withering looks may communicate judgment and disdain when an autistic child is reacting to the environment. In addition to specially designed education programs for autism spectrum children, parent support groups may be invaluable in creating a caring and supportive "home" for parents. The minister should also be mindful that early intervention in the form of intensive training to build skills in language, socialization, self-care, and academic skills can often go a long way toward mitigating the impact of autism on a child's long-term success in life and relationships.[7] In pastoral counseling with parents, emphasize the biological nature of the disorder and be sure to address false beliefs about the cause of autism (e.g., poor parenting, childhood immunizations). Moreover, provide referrals to excellent programs in the community (intensive day programs for treatment, family/parent support programs), or work with other local ministries and churches to create your own!

Attention-Deficit/Hyperactivity Disorder

Presenting Complaint

Alfred is a 9-year-old Sunday school student who is causing havoc in his class. His Sunday school teacher describes him as "out of control" and "completely hyper." He has been a problem for the teacher and the other students because of his impulsiveness and inability to control his motor behavior. You learn that, in his regular fourth-grade classroom and at Sunday school, Alfred will impulsively hit other children, knock things off their desks, erase material on the blackboard, and damage books and other school property. Alfred's regular teacher believes he is bright, but says she is "worn out" and that Alfred is the closest thing she has seen to the "Tasmanian Devil" cartoon character. Alfred's impulsivity and inattention require an excessive amount of attention from both his teachers and parents. In the classroom, he is in perpetual motion, darting about, talking excessively, and unable to focus on the task at hand. In spite of his behavior problems and poor self-esteem, Alfred is very intelligent. Nonetheless, he feels "stupid." A recent physical exam shows him to be healthy. His parents are "at wits' end" and wonder what to do.

Common Features and Symptoms

The essential features of *attention-deficit/hyperactivity disorder* (ADHD) are hyperactivity, short attention span, and developmentally inappropriate impulsiveness.[3] ADHD is typically diagnosed prior to or during early elementary school, as the symptoms tend to be present and problematic by early childhood. In the church, these children will be recognized by their physical overactivity, inattention, impulsiveness, and seemingly constant distractedness. They are often the bane of Sunday school teachers and, in the worship service, they tend to fidget, fuss, and fall off chairs far more than is common of other children. They are unable to wait their turn, interrupt conversations, and constantly talk or physically provoke others. When they burst into a room, they are noticed.[8]

Many ADHD children are socially very immature. They are often of normal intelligence, but may have impaired math and reading skills. They hear well but listen poorly. They are generally physically healthy but very difficult to manage behaviorally. When ADHD symptoms are present in infancy, they most often include overreactivity to stimuli such as noise, light, and temperature, as well as agitation, constant crying, and sleeplessness. Roughly 50 percent of those diagnosed with ADHD present some clear symptoms by the age of 4; clear symptoms must be evident before the age of 12 in order to diagnose ADHD. In the United States, the incidence of

ADHD is estimated to be about 5 percent of the child population, and boys are diagnosed with the disorder four times more often than girls.[3] Firstborn boys are at higher risk for ADHD and about 50 percent of those with this disorder will also have problems with conduct disorder.

Although the specific causes of ADHD are still unclear, most MHPs see the disorder as having a strong biological component. Genetic influences are supported by the finding that ADHD children are three times more likely to have a sibling with the disorder. Also, when parents exhibited ADHD as children, there is a much higher chance that their own children will as well. What is going on in the brain of an ADHD child? There is consistent evidence that the frontal lobes of ADHD sufferers have less blood flow and are simply less active.[9] Of course, the frontal portion of the cortex is essential for judgment, impulse control, and the ability to focus attention.

ADHD: Key Indicators

- Consistent signs of inattention and/or hyperactivity-impulsiveness, which have persisted for at least six months, and are present by the age of 12.
- Symptoms may include the following:
  - *inattention* (a) fails to pay attention or makes careless mistakes in schoolwork; (b) has difficulty sustaining attention to tasks or play; (c) does not listen when spoken to directly; (d) does not follow through on instructions and fails to finish tasks; (e) has difficulty organizing tasks or activities; (f) avoids or dislikes tasks that require mental effort; (g) loses necessary items (e.g., pencils, paper); (h) is forgetful of daily activities.
  - *hyperactivity-impulsivity* (a) fools with hands or feet or squirms in seat; (b) leaves seat when staying in seat is expected; (c) runs or climbs in situations where it is inappropriate; (d) has difficulty playing quietly; (e) constantly "on the go"; (f) talks excessively; (g) blurts out answers before questions are completed; (h) has difficulty waiting turn; (i) interrupts or intrudes on others.
- The symptoms are present in at least two different settings (e.g., home, school, social activities), and there is clear evidence that the symptoms reduce the quality of academic, social, or occupational functioning.

Summary and Guidelines

Children with ADHD are not uncommon in the church. They may range from the severely hyperactive and hard to manage child to the more reserved but extremely inattentive child. When parents have concerns about their children's behavior, or the minister or other professionals (e.g., experienced teachers) believe a child may have ADHD, it is important make a referral to a qualified MHP with expertise in childhood disorders. At the same time, it is critical not to label normal overactivity and intensity in children as pathologic. The minister should look for signs of actual relational and educational impairment before assuming that a child may have ADHD. It is also important to distinguish between ADHD and conduct disorder (covered in this chapter). In the case of conduct disorder, the child will engage in criminal behavior.

The primary medical treatment of choice for ADHD is stimulant medication. The most commonly used medications are methylphenidate (Ritalin and Concerta) and dextroamphetamine (Adderall). Stimulant medications appear to effectively diminish ADHD symptoms while increasing attentiveness, vigilance, and appropriate social interaction in 70 percent of children and adults with ADHD. Stimulant medications do not facilitate learning, but make the child more capable of paying attention and therefore more likely to learn. Although most pediatricians and family physicians will prescribe medications for ADHD, a psychiatrist or pediatrician with considerable experience in managing stimulants for ADHD children is preferred. If a pediatrician or family doctor provides medication, the family may benefit from an additional referral to an MHP who can provide behavioral and family-oriented strategies for helping the child. For example, family counseling, group therapy, social skills training, and parent behavior coaching have been shown to be very helpful in treating ADHD.[10] While on medications, children must be monitored routinely by the prescribing doctor as the medications nearly always come with side effects. These include difficulty sleeping and low appetite. We now know that many adolescents with ADHD continue to struggle with the inattentive aspects of the disorder into adulthood, although the hyperactivity-impulsivity dimensions often diminish with age. Adult ADHD—often called ADD—is also typically managed with low doses of stimulant medication.

Parental guilt may be one of the major issues the minister will have to address when dealing with ADHD, and it is one of the barriers to effective treatment. By providing support and accurate information to parents of ADHD children, the pastor will increase the probability that these children will be effectively treated and will become more adaptive in behavior. In larger churches, support groups for parents of ADHD children may be helpful.

Oppositional Defiant Disorder

Presenting Complaint

Ten-year-old Jose's parents come to you and begin to describe Jose's behavioral problems, which are so severe, you find it hard to believe that he is the same 10-year-old you see at the church. Jose begins each day arguing with his mother about what to wear and what to eat. He typically has a tantrum at least once before school. He is banned from riding the bus because of his retaliations against children who tease him and his episodes of cursing at the bus driver. During the school day, Jose may curse at his teacher if she asks him to stop doing something. He may overturn his desk and stomp out of the room if not allowed to use the bathroom on demand. When not in conflict with his teacher or principal, Jose usually plays alone. After school, he battles his mother over homework, often breaking pencils and refusing to work altogether. When his mother restricts him to his room until he completes his homework, Jose screams, slams his door, and turns up his music as loud as he can. Although Jose calms down somewhat when his father comes home, he usually has a few more tantrums before bedtime. His parents appear desperate. They seem to try to mollify Jose and have a hard time following through with consequences.

Common Features and Symptoms

Children with *oppositional defiant disorder* (ODD) are chronically aggressive, argumentative, volatile, spiteful, and vindictive. They openly defy rules and requests and often go out of their way to annoy others (especially those they know well); this is usually the reason they are brought to the attention of a pastor or MHP. Irritability is a way of life for these children, and getting a reaction from others is a primary objective. They are rarely sorry for their defiant behavior and believe that fault lies with others (usually parents). Children with ODD are distinct from ADHD children in that they are chronically defiant and argumentative but not hyperactive or inattentive (although some children have both ODD and ADHD, which certainly makes them more difficult to manage). Oppositional defiant disorder is among the most common of all childhood psychiatric disorders, occurring in about 3 percent of all children.[3] Although ODD is more common in boys than girls prior to puberty, the rates are about the same following puberty. Symptoms of ODD typically become evident between the ages of 1 and 3, and are nearly always present by age 6.

Oppositional defiant disorder, characterized by negative, disobedient, and defiant behavior toward authority figures, may be a prelude to a much more serious disorder—conduct disorder. Conduct disorder involves violations of the rights of others (e.g., stealing, destroying property, coercing others). While ODD is typically present by age 6, conduct disorder is not usually evident until slightly later. Research has shown that ODD is nearly always present in children and adolescents who develop conduct disorder.[11] However, only about 25 percent of all children with ODD will go on to develop conduct disorder.

Oppositional Defiant Disorder: Key Indicators

- A consistent pattern of angry/irritable, argumentative, and defiant behavior which is indicated by several of the following: (1) often loses temper; (2) often argues with adults; (3) often actively defies or refuses to comply with adult's requests or rules; (4) often deliberately annoys people; (5) often blames others for his or her mistakes or misbehavior; (6) often "touchy" or easily annoyed by others; (7) often angry and resentful; (8) often spiteful and vindictive.
- These symptoms persist for at least six months and cause distress in the person or others in his or her immediate environment.

Summary and Guidelines

Parents with ODD children could benefit from a high level of ministerial support. This may be difficult for two reasons. First, because ODD children usually reserve their obnoxious and overtly defiant behavior for their parents (and others they feel especially close to), and because they often display better behavior in front of people they see less often, the minister may have difficulty believing that they are as difficult to manage as the parents report. Second, the pastor may view the ODD behavior exclusively as the result of poor or inadequate parenting. Although poor parenting skills or inconsistent delivery of discipline may contribute to ODD behavior in children, parenting style may not always be the primary problem; a few children appear to be inherently oppositional and defiant in their behavior—even in the face of competent parenting.

For these reasons, it is recommended that the minister offer the parents encouragement and, if the parents are willing, refer them to an MHP with expertise in treating child behavior disorders. Because ODD children may be masters at creating conflict between caretaking adults—sometimes creating conflict among parents, teachers, and relatives—it is important that a neutral party with expertise in managing ODD behavior be consulted. There is an excellent resource for parents when children have trouble with this syndrome. *Parenting with Love and Logic*[12] is an exceptionally clear manual for using effective limit-setting and firm consequences in the context of unconditional love. We find it to be a terrific resource for parents of ODD children. The prognosis is usually guarded; some ODD children will go on to demonstrate conduct disorder in adolescence and antisocial behavior in adulthood. Among the available treatments, systematic training of parents in the use of behavioral techniques (consequences and reinforcements) with their children is generally more effective than other kinds of therapy, including family therapy.

Conduct Disorder

Presenting Complaint

Adam is an 11-year-old who seems "headed for trouble." His mother, who is a single parent, approaches you and appears anxious and overwhelmed by her son's incorrigible behavior. Adam has been stealing money from his mother and has been constantly fist fighting with his two brothers and peers at school. Although he is supposed to go directly home from school, he refuses to comply with his mother's rules and routinely wanders the streets alone, breaking windows, vandalizing property, and smoking cigarettes. He has been arrested once for shoplifting and has been expelled from school for stealing and fighting. Adam appears to have little regard for authority and pays almost no attention to his mother's attempts to discipline him. He lies frequently and shows little remorse for his behavior. Adam's father has almost no contact with the family. His mother works long hours and is rarely effective in monitoring, let alone controlling, Adam's behavior or whereabouts.

Common Features and Symptoms

The key features of conduct disorder are a persistent, repetitive violation of rules and a disregard for the rights of others. It is as though the conduct-disordered child or adolescent specializes in "bad" behavior. These behaviors are often *criminal* in nature, violate social norms, and often violate or exploit other people. The prevalence of conduct disorder ranges from 3 to 4 percent and is considerably more prevalent in boys; and it is often the precursor to adult antisocial personality disorder (see Chapter 5).[11,13] Children who develop conduct disorder by age 10 are considerably more likely to become antisocial adults than children who develop this disorder in adolescence. Characteristic conduct-disordered behaviors include lying, stealing, truancy, physical aggression, cruelty to animals and other people, and destruction of property. These children often run away from home, abuse substances, and engage in sexual activity. They may also be irritable, impulsive, and prone to angry outbursts. They typically come to the attention of the church and various MHPs via their distraught parents or the juvenile court system.

Risk factors for conduct disorder include a family history of antisocial personality disorder, substance abuse, child abuse (physical, emotional, or sexual), and learning disabilities that interfere with school success. Evidence for a genetic predisposition comes from the finding that adopted children whose biological fathers have criminal records have higher rates of conduct disorder.[11] Conduct disorder is considerably more common in families where there is marital conflict, divorce, father absence, and authoritarian parenting. Although many conduct-disordered children are quite manipulative and socially savvy ("street smart"), they tend to be delayed with respect to verbal intelligence and academic achievement—often because they have been unable to learn (learning disability) or unavailable for education because of their behavior and home situation.

Conduct Disorder: Key Indicators

- A persistent and repetitive behavior pattern that violate the rights of others and major societal norms, as indicated by symptoms in several categories:

  - *Aggression toward people and animals:* (1) bullies, threatens, intimidates others; (2) initiates fights; (3) has used a weapon that can seriously harm others; (4) has been physically cruel to animals; (5) has been physically cruel to people; (6) has stolen while confronting a victim; (6) has forced someone into sexual activity.
  - *Destruction of property:* (1) has deliberately set fires with the intention of causing damage; (2) has deliberately destroyed others' property.
  - *Deceitfulness or theft:* (1) has broken into a house, car, or building; (2) often lies to obtain goods/favors or avoid obligations; (3) has stolen items without confronting a victim (e.g., shoplifting).
  - *Serious violations of rules:* (1) often stays out at night past parents' curfew—begins before age 13; (2) runs away from home for lengthy periods; (3) is often truant from school.

- These symptoms persist for at least six months and cause significant impairment in social, academic, or occupational functioning.

Summary and Guidelines

The conduct-disordered child or adolescent presents a troubling picture to the minister. These children are often quite resistant to rebuke or correction. Their lack of remorse or regard for authority, or the suffering of others, makes most interventions ineffective. When there are clear signs of conduct disorder, it is important for the minister to encourage parents to have the child evaluated by a professional with expertise in this disorder. Although no specific treatment is likely to be consistently effective (as in the case of stimulant medication for ADHD), most professionals agree that one key to a positive prognosis in treating conduct disorder is early intervention.

A psychologist who treats childhood disorders may be an especially good referral, as commonly coexisting disorders such as learning disabilities, mood problems, ADHD, and substance abuse will require careful assessment and, if present, simultaneous treatment. In some cases, medications that reduce arousal, impulsivity, and aggression have been helpful. Other common interventions include removing children from abusive homes, parent coaching to both reduce the frequency of authoritarian parenting behaviors and increase effective behavior management, and teaching limit-setting skills. Most often, parents of conduct-disordered children are too permissive or too authoritarian. The church may be especially helpful by providing parenting resources, educational materials, and peer support. Because many conduct-disordered children have learning/academic problems, the church may also consider tutorial help as an outreach of the deacon's or children's ministry. Finally, the pastor can be a source of hope to both parents and children by conveying God's promise that if they "train up the child in the way that he should go, and when he is old, he won't depart from it" (Proverbs 22:6, RSV).

Separation Anxiety Disorder

Presenting Complaint

At an evening adults-only meeting at the church, you are surprised to see Mary's 11-year-old daughter, Diana, sitting in the hallway outside the church meeting room. When you ask Mary if everything is OK, she rolls her eyes in exasperation and explains that Diana refuses to allow Mary to go out without her. In fact, Diana will have a tantrum, scream, and have what appears to be a full-blown panic attack if her mother attempts to leave her with a babysitter, or alone for any period of time. Mary says she has had to home school Diana, not because Mary values home schooling, but because Diana refused to attend school if it meant being away from her mother. Diana is obsessed with concerns that her mother will be killed if the two are apart or that Diana will be kidnapped and unable to see her mother again. You are particularly surprised to learn that Diana refuses to go to sleep without Mary in the room and that as a result, Mary now sleeps in the same room with her daughter.

Common Features and Symptoms

Children with separation anxiety disorder live in constant fear of separation from their major "attachment figure" (usually a parent). They fear that their caregiver will die or that they (the child) will be lost, kidnapped, or otherwise permanently separated from the parent. They continually cling to or shadow their caregiver and are miserable, anxious, and depressed when separated from them. Going to a friend's house or staying with a babysitter may be a substantial ordeal, and these children often refuse to attend school. If they are forced to attend school, they may attempt to sneak away or may remain sullen, withdrawn, and refuse to complete work. Children with this disorder often have a number of other fears—especially fear of the dark. Although they may have some legitimate physical symptoms of anxiety when threatened with separation from their parents (e.g., nausea, headaches, vomiting), they may also learn to manufacture these as a means of keeping their caregiver from leaving.

While children may be truly afraid of being separated from their primary parent, their clinging behaviors are often inadvertently strengthened by parents who habitually "give in" and remain with or rescue these children. Parents of children with separation anxiety disorder are frequently called out of church services by Sunday school teachers to retrieve their children who are having extreme anxiety reactions or are sobbing uncontrollably. Very often, parents of these children will seek professional help or approach their ministers about the problem only when the children reach school age and refuse to attend.

Although most children go through a time of anxiety about separation from their parents in early childhood and again around the time school starts, children with separation anxiety disorder do not outgrow this transitional phase. Instead, their anxiety can become overwhelming and prevent them from learning, developing relationships, and enjoying any independence. Boys and girls are equally likely to have this disorder, and it is present in about 4 percent of children and adolescents.[3] If unresolved, separation disorder can persist into adulthood. The initial symptoms of this disorder often emerge following a significant stressor (e.g., loss of a family member, serious illness, a family move), and they almost always appear before adolescence. The symptoms may fluctuate for years, and children who struggle with this anxiety problem are considerably more likely to develop anxiety disorders, particularly panic disorder (see Chapter 3), in adulthood.

Separation Anxiety Disorder: Key Indicators

- Age-inappropriate and excessive anxiety about separation from one's primary caregiver (usually a parent) for at least six months.
- Signs of this inappropriate and excessive anxiety include (1) consistent excessive distress when the child anticipates being separated from home or parent; (2) ongoing worry about losing, or possible harm befalling, major caregiver; (3) ongoing worry that a major event (kidnapping or getting lost) will separate him or her from the caregiver; (4) persistent reluctance to attend school because of fear of separation; (5) excessive fear about being alone; (6) refusal to go to sleep without being nearby a caregiver; (7) repeated nightmares involving separation; (8) repeated physical complaints (e.g., headaches, stomachaches, nausea, vomiting) when separation occurs or is anticipated.

Summary and Guidelines

A general rule of thumb among professionals working with children diagnosed with separation anxiety disorder is that both the child and the primary caregiver contribute to the anxiety. Although the child often comes from a family that seems very close-knit and caring, closer examination will often reveal a parent with profound difficulty letting go of the child and who—internally at least—experiences great distress at leaving the child. The minister may have to balance sensitivity to the parent's well-intentioned zeal about caretaking with gentle suggestions that perhaps the parent contributes to the child's anxiety and avoidance behavior by not allowing him or her to experience the normal distress that comes with separation and healthy individuation. In other words, these parents can be viewed as giving their child "too much of a good thing." Of course, many parents of children with this disorder will be quite defensive regarding their role in perpetuating their children's behavior. The minister would be wise to make an appropriate mental health service referral if this is the case.

Although a number of different treatment approaches have proven helpful with separation anxiety disorder, all of them require full parental compliance to be effective. *Transitional objects* such as blankets, stuffed animals, and pictures of family members can be helpful for the child learning to tolerate parental absence. Helping a parent to reduce his or her own anxiety about a child's distress is also helpful because a child often becomes most upset when he or she senses a parent's anxiety. Finally, grief work may be necessary for children whose separation anxiety is the result of the death or loss of a major attachment figure. Again, we recommend an MHP experienced in working with children and who understands normal and abnormal child development.

Eating Disorders

Presenting Complaint

The church youth pastor phones you and reports "a little problem" at the church summer camp. One of the counselors, a 19-year-old college sophomore named Tammy, has been discovered forcing herself to vomit on several occasions after meals and at least two times late at night. This has been a problem because several junior high school girls in Tammy's cabin are aware of Tammy's behavior and have made worried comments to other counselors. When confronted, Tammy "broke down" and admitted that she began binging and purging during her freshman year in college. Tammy comes to see you the following week and describes the onset of bouts of excessive eating followed by forced vomiting. These bouts began during the previous fall when her first serious college boyfriend ended their brief but intense relationship. Tammy describes becoming very depressed and anxious about whether she is attractive. She describes binges late at night that can include an entire pizza and a two-pound bag of cookies. Although she has felt quite depressed after her purging, she admits, "I just can't seem to stop."

Common Features and Symptoms

Anorexia nervosa and *bulimia nervosa* are the two most prevalent eating disorders. Both involve a preoccupation with weight, body image, and unhealthy (potentially lethal) approaches to restricting intake or using food to self-soothe (binging). The prevalence of these disorders combined is approximately 2 percent in the population. Adolescent girls and young adult women account for the largest group of sufferers and both disorders are more common in women than men by about 10 to 1. These disorders are among the most distressing to parents because of the helplessness they can engender. The minister may be called upon to provide support as well as referrals for assistance. It is important to be aware that anorexia can quickly become life threatening if not actively treated, and both anorexia and bulimia can cause chronic health problems.

Subtypes

Anorexia Nervosa

First documented in 1689 and labeled in 1874, anorexia is characterized by an irrational fear of becoming fat, an obsessive pursuit of thinness, excessive weight loss, perceptual distortions regarding one's body, and the erroneous belief that one is fat. Between 1950 and 1980, the incidence of anorexia among adolescent girls increased more than 300 percent. The average age at which anorexia begins is 17, although it can begin even before adolescence. Less than 1 percent of women meet criteria for this disorder. Among those diagnosed with the disorder, about 5 percent can be expected to die as a direct result.

More serious cases of anorexia are usually easy to spot. Anorectic persons may appear cheerful and energetic, yet very emaciated, and even skeleton-like in appearance. Anorectic men and women often begin as model children who subsequently begin dieting because of concern that they are slightly overweight. The initial diet often begins after the anorectic has experienced a life stressor (e.g., parents' divorce, a failed romantic relationship). After losing some weight, the person will often decide to continue weight reduction until she or he nearly stops eating altogether. Except for the most advanced cases, anorectic persons think about food almost constantly. They enjoy cooking for others, memorize their caloric intake, hoard food (but eat very little), and often eat alone. To accelerate weight loss, they may exercise excessively, abstain from fats or carbohydrates, use laxatives, or induce vomiting (although this is more common in bulimia).

Anorexia is a very serious disorder that can last for years. It can be cyclical, with periods of remission, or it can be persistent and uninterrupted. Although nutritional recovery may occur within a few years of appropriate eating, abnormal eating patterns and preoccupation with weight and body shape may last much longer. About 40 percent of anorectics recover fully. Another 30 percent show significant improvement, and 30 percent remain severely impaired by the disorder. Chronic anorexia results in life-threatening health changes such as bones, muscles, and hair that become weak and brittle, reduced blood pressure and breathing, and lethargy. Unfortunately, 5 percent of those with the disorder will eventually die from it.[14] The typical anorectic person is a teenage or young adult female from the middle to upper class. In the last several years, there has been a slight increase in the risk of anorexia and bulimia among young men. Often, these are athletes in sports that require "making weight," often leading to patterns of extreme weight loss punctuated by normal or even overeating.

Anorexia Nervosa: Key Indicators

- Restriction in food intake relative to requirements resulting in significantly low body weight in light of one's age, sex, and developmental trajectory.
- Intense fear of gaining weight or becoming fat (even though the person is underweight), and persistent interference with weight gain.

- Distorted perception of one's own body weight or shape (sees himself or herself as overweight or fat when this is not the case, or denies the seriousness of his or her low body weight).
- These behaviors place the person at significant risk for serious health problems.

Bulimia Nervosa

First recognized in the 1950s, this disorder is characterized by periods of binge eating followed by self-induced vomiting or other compensatory behaviors. The term "bulimia" means "hunger of an ox," and aptly describes the prodigious quantities of food consumed (as many as 12,000 calories or more) during a single binge episode. Bulimic persons describe being driven to consume huge amounts of unhealthy food (binge) and have been known to do so as many as nine times per day. The binge may last for an hour and the bulimic will typically "devour," instead of chew, a substantial volume of high-caloric foods. The person may spend $100 or more on food binges in a day. They may also steal food for binges, and they almost always engage in binge eating while alone. The binge will end when the person is discovered, falls asleep, develops stomach pain, or forces him or herself to vomit (approximately 88 percent of bulimics self-induce vomiting). After vomiting, the bulimic may or may not continue to binge. A hallmark symptom is the experience of feeling entirely out of control once a binge begins. It is important to recognize that although purging is the most common *compensatory behavior* following a binge, many bulimics employ other strategies—especially if they are in a context in which throwing up is not possible. These may include laxatives, diuretics, fasting, or excessive exercise.

Prevalence rates for bulimia are about 2 percent for the general population and as high as 4 percent for the college student population. Like the anorectic, the bulimic will most often be a white, middle-to upper-class female (90 to 95 percent of those with bulimia are women) high school or college student. She is likely to view her binge eating as abnormal and may despise and fear her inability to control it. She is likely to be unhappy, self-deprecating, and preoccupied with appearance, body image, and sexual attractiveness (in contrast to the anorectic, who has less concern about sex appeal). A period of mild to serious depression often precedes a binge. Although the binge may provide temporary mood relief, postbinge experiences of depression are also common—thus creating a vicious mood-related cycle. Bulimic persons often have impulse control problems in other areas. Approximately one-third have abused alcohol or drugs, engaged in shopping sprees, or been promiscuous.

Bulimia usually begins later than anorexia, but it too may follow some difficult loss or life event. It is often a chronic disorder with alternating periods of normal and binge eating. Most bulimics improve and recover completely. Although death related to this disorder is relatively rare (usually linked to deficiencies in potassium because of frequent vomiting), many bulimic persons suffer from electrolyte imbalance, dehydration, cardiac problems, intestinal damage, and dental problems. Many individuals with bulimia have other psychiatric disorders such as depression (75 percent), anxiety disorders (43 percent), substance disorders (49 percent), and personality disorders (50 percent).

Bulimia Nervosa: Key Indicators

- Consistent episodes of binge eating (eating, in a discrete period of time, an amount of food larger than most people would eat during a similar time period and under similar circumstances) and a sense of lack of control over the binge eating.
- Recurrent inappropriate compensatory behavior following a binge such as (1) self-induced vomiting; (2) laxative use; (3) diet pill use; (4) diuretics; (5) fasting; (6) excessive exercise to prevent weight gain.
- The binging and compensatory behavior both occur at least once a week for at least three months.
- The person's evaluation of himself or herself is unduly based on body shape or weight.

Summary and Guidelines

The minister's role in assisting parishioners (and their family members) who suffer with eating disorders can be very significant. In most cases, stress on the family as a result of this unremitting condition is enormous. Few things are as distressing to a family as a child who begins to systematically starve him or herself, or one who engages in repeated episodes of dangerous compensatory behavior (e.g., vomiting). The church pastor may provide a critically important listening ear. He or she may also be the first to recognize the signs of an eating disorder and may provide the vital function of recommending immediate intervention with a qualified professional. Among parishioners with eating disorders, it is wise to expect a high degree of denial that any problem exists. The first red flags for an eating disorder might be a dentist's observation of serious enamel decay on the back of the teeth (bulimia) or a physician or gym teacher's discovery that a teenager has lost considerable weight (anorexia). The minister may be called to participate, with the family or others, in a loving but tough confrontation of the sufferer in order to break through denial and leverage him or her into treatment. Given the severity of these disorders, it would be unwise for the minister to attempt an intervention on his or her own.

Psychologists, social workers, or counselors with expertise in treating eating disorders are highly recommended in nearly every case. In the most severe cases, merely getting the person transported to a hospital may be critical. Considering the potentially fatal consequences of anorexia, the initial treatment goal is always to simply keep the person alive and stabilize him or her medically (stop weight loss and balance internal systems). When weight loss has made the parishioner medically unstable, he or she may be involuntarily hospitalized. Once stabilization has been achieved, treatment typically focuses on treating medical complications, modifying unhealthy eating habits, improving family relationship patterns, enhancing self-control and self-concept, and correcting distorted thoughts, which often precipitate self-starvation.

Most bulimic parishioners can be treated as outpatients. Exceptions include those who have medical complications, a severe binge-purge cycle, sudden weight loss, or a family crisis (leading to a psychiatric admission). Cognitive-behavioral therapies, interpersonal therapy, and antidepressant medications have all been used with success in helping bulimic persons. Treatment typically includes two phases: (1) breaking the binge-purge cycle with behavioral techniques, and (2) modifying disturbed attitudes and beliefs about body shape, weight, and dieting using cognitive-behavioral interventions.

Child and Spouse Abuse

Presenting Complaint

The Jenkins family has attended your church for several years. Tom is a night security guard at a local college, and Jennifer works as a teaching assistant in the elementary school. Another parishioner comes to you and expresses concern that Tom may be abusing his wife. She notes that Jennifer sometimes has marks around her face that she refuses to discuss or insists are related to a recent fall or other accident. You have known Tom to be very short-tempered and "uptight." He has also been threatened with unemployment lately, and the family is under a good deal of stress. At church, you notice that the couple's two young children appear sullen and frightened around their father. You wonder how to respond to this situation and if it is really possible that Tom could be abusing his wife or perhaps even his children.

Common Features and Symptoms

Child and spouse abuse affect millions of families each year. Both forms of domestic violence are almost certain to occur within some families in most congregations. The minister should anticipate that a percentage of his or her congregation will be impacted by the effects of violence or neglect. In this section, we highlight the essential characteristics of both child abuse and spouse abuse with an emphasis on characteristics of abusers, causes of abuse, and effects or outcomes. We also offer some recommendations for ways the church might work to reduce violence in the home. We do not provide a key indicators box because abuse and neglect can vary widely, and the specific impact on a child or spouse may depend on a host of factors. Our primary recommendation is that clergy accept the fact that abuse of children and spouses is probably occurring in some church members' homes. It is imperative to know that in approximately half of U.S. states and territories, clergy working in any denomination or context have a legal obligation to report evidence of child abuse.[15] Even in states without mandatory reporting laws, we encourage ministers to take seriously the moral obligation to prevent harm and promote the best interests of children and other vulnerable people whenever possible.

Subtypes

Child Abuse

Although child abuse and neglect can be defined in a multitude of ways, Public Law 104–235 defines child abuse and neglect as, at a minimum, any recent act or failure to act on the part of a parent or caretaker resulting in death, serious physical or emotional harm, sexual abuse or exploitation, or an act or failure to act which presents an imminent risk of serious harm. A child is anyone under the age of 18. The National Clearinghouse on Child Abuse and Neglect has identified four primary types of child maltreatment: emotional abuse, neglect, physical abuse, and sexual abuse.[15]

Emotional abuse. Emotional abuse includes acts or failures to act that cause or could cause serious distress or disorder in children. This may include a range of behaviors including bizarre forms of punishment (e.g., confinement to a closet), rejecting or belittling treatment, use of derogatory terms, and habitual scapegoating or blaming. Emotional abuse is sometimes referred to as verbal abuse and mental abuse.

Neglect. Neglect is the failure to provide for a child's basic needs. Neglect can be physical, educational, or emotional. Examples include failing to provide adequate food, clothing, or medical attention, allowing children to be consistently truant from school, or withholding emotional support or attention from a child.

Physical abuse. Physical abuse is most simply the infliction of physical injury upon a child. Physical abuse may include burning, hitting, punching, shaking, kicking, beating, or otherwise harming a child. Although the parent may not have intended to harm the child, the injury is not an accident. Parents who harm their children during the course of "discipline" are also guilty of physical abuse.

Sexual abuse. Sexual abuse may be defined as any inappropriate sexual behavior with a child. It includes fondling a child's genitals, making the child fondle the adult's genitals, intercourse, rape, sodomy, exhibitionism, and sexual exploitation. To be considered child abuse, these acts must be committed by a person responsible for the child's care or a person related to the child. If a stranger commits these acts, it would be considered sexual assault and handled solely by the police or criminal courts.

In the United States in 2011, there were an estimated 3.7 million cases of child abuse reported to child protective agencies as victims of abuse or neglect.[4] Ample data suggest that child maltreatment is pervasive enough to be an issue at the local church level. Ministers and education staff should be vigilant for signs of abuse and neglect among children in the congregation.

Although boys are more often physically abused than girls, girls are three times more likely to become victims of sexual abuse. Research has consistently demonstrated that children who are abused and neglected are at increased risk for a host of childhood and adult psychological problems. These include impaired intellectual functioning and memory difficulties, problems with relationships, depression, antisocial personality traits, and self-destructive behaviors. Children who are sexually abused can be expected to have poorer social adjustment, relationship and sexual problems, guilt and shame regarding the abuse, and a range of psychiatric problems as adults (mood disorders are particularly common).

What kinds of parents are likely to abuse? Overall, abusive parents tend to be younger (under 30), lower in socioeconomic status, prone to psychological problems of their own, and suffering from a range of stressors (e.g., marital discord, unemployment). The minister should remain watchful for these risk factors as well as impulse control problems, anger management difficulties, alcohol or drug abuse, and obvious signs of abuse or trauma in children. The vast majority of child abuse perpetrators are the parents of the children. It is important to keep in mind that any parent can abuse a child under certain circumstances or in a stressful situation. Belsky noted, "There is no one pathway to these disturbances in parenting; rather, maltreatment seems to arise when stressors outweigh supports and risks are greater than protective factors."[16]

Although no single behavior or behavior pattern reliably identifies children who are being abused, there are some common physical and behavioral signs for which MHPs remain vigilant when assessing children. These include external marks (bruises and scars), depressed mood, anger problems, poor self-esteem, sexual acting out or sexually laden speech, interpersonal detachment or interpersonal "clinging," and an exaggerated startle response (flinches or cowers). Of course, children may simply disclose abuse to the pastor or Sunday school teacher. Because children rarely fabricate stories of abuse, their comments should be taken very seriously.

In many states, clergy and other professionals are required to report cases of known or reasonably suspected child abuse.[15] This means that ministers may at times be required to do something that precipitates a substantial crisis in the lives of some parishioners. Informing these parishioners of this obligation prior to any sort of formal pastoral counseling is wise. Beyond reporting cases of abuse and attempting to support children and families in the wake of the ensuing intervention by authorities, the church might be proactive in preventing child abuse and supporting parents at risk. Specifically, the church might consider educationally focused programs that increase awareness of abuse—both for parents and youth workers. Parent preparation training for soon-to-be-married couples or couples preparing to have their first child might also incorporate training in risk factors for abuse and strategies for reducing this risk. Support groups for parents who have had trouble with abuse or anger control might also be useful, and could focus on development of adaptive and effective parenting skills.

Spouse Abuse

Violence within marriage is now recognized as a considerable social problem in the United States. According to various surveys, about 1.3 million women are assaulted by male partners each year.[5,17] If about 1 in 8 husbands is physically violent with his spouse each year, it is reasonable to assume that some of these couples will be involved with the church. Yet admission of violence in the home can be quite stigmatizing and shaming for both partners. It will be a challenge for most churches to create an environment in which admission of a range of problems—including violence—is acceptable.

The most obvious concern related to domestic violence is the risk of serious injury or death. Up to 25 percent of all homicides committed in the United States each year are committed by a husband or wife. Violence from husbands to wives is the primary pattern in over 90 percent of cases of domestic violence. Marital violence is also strongly linked to psychological problems and major disorders, including depression, alcohol abuse, and

PTSD (see Chapters 3 and 4). We know that violence between adult partners is linked to higher rates of child abuse as well. Even when children are not physically abused, they tend to be traumatized and disturbed by watching violence between parents.

Why do marriage partners batter one another? Although many factors help explain the problem of battering in marriage, most violent men have learned this approach to handling stress, anger, or conflict—typically from their own fathers or other male models. Violent men are quite likely to have come from violent homes as children. They often have a restricted range of appropriate responses when it comes to managing their own anger or negotiating disagreement with their partners. Very often, they have impulsive personality features, personal rigidity, and poor communication skills. These men are also more likely to believe strongly that they should have control over their wives and that their wives should submit without condition. The minister may need to be particularly vigilant for male parishioners' selective use of scripture to support highly controlling and violent behavior. For example, some men may focus exclusively on verses such as "Wives, be subject to your husbands as you are to the Lord" (Ephesians 5:22, RSV), while ignoring related versus such as "Be subject to one another out of reverence for Christ" (Ephesians 5:21, RSV).

It is critically important that congregational pastors be vigilant regarding the possibility of marital violence among parishioners—particularly those who seek counseling from the pastor. One reason is that, among couples seeking counseling, studies show that as many as half have experienced marital violence (most often perpetrated by the husband). Although most abused women will not spontaneously offer this information, research suggests that when specifically asked about violence, over 50 percent will acknowledge it.[18] Therefore, the pastor should remain aware of the potential for violence in all marriages and not hesitate to matter-of-factly inquire as to whether this has been a problem for any couple that he or she is counseling.

As in the case of child abuse, a church congregation that offers support to couples and individual victims of violence is likely to be most helpful. Beyond support groups, however, the minister must be willing to intervene in cases where violence appears serious and likely to be repeated. Although states do not generally mandate reporting of partner abuse (as is nearly always the case with child abuse), victims of domestic violence are sometimes murdered or permanently injured by spouses when they attempt to leave an abusive marriage. Ministers and church bodies are encouraged to have a clear plan for responding to these cases. This may involve contact with the police and immediate referral to a shelter for battered women in the community, or an equivalent service offered via the church.

Notes

1. Merikangas, K. P., Nakamura, E. F., & Kessler, R. C. (2009). Epidemiology of mental disorders in children and adolescents. *Dialogues in Clinical Neuroscience, 11*(1), 7–20.
2. Merikangas K. R., He, J. P., Burstein, M., Swanson, S. A., Avenevoli, S., Cui, L., . . . Swendsen, J. (2010). Lifetime prevalence of mental disorders in U.S. adolescents: Results from the National Comorbidity Survey Replication—Adolescent Supplement (NCS-A). *Journal of the American Academy of Child and Adolescent Psychiatry, 49*(10), 980–989.
3. American Psychiatric Association. (2013). *Diagnostic and statistical manual of mental disorders* (5th ed.). Washington, DC: Author.
4. U.S. Department of Health and Human Services, Administration for Children and Families, Administration on Children, Youth and Families, Children's Bureau. (2012). *Child Maltreatment 2011*. Retrieved from www.acf.hhs.gov/programs/cb/research-data-technology/statistics-research/child-maltreatment
5. Tjaden, P., & Thoennes, N. (2000). *Full report of the prevalence, incidence, and consequences of violence against women: Findings from the National Violence Against Women Survey.* Washington, DC: U.S. Department of Justice.
6. Klinger, L. G., Dawson, G., & Renner, P. (2003). Autistic disorder. In E. J. Mash & R. A. Barkley (Eds.), *Child psychopathology* (2nd ed.; pp. 409–454). New York, NY: Guilford.
7. Sicile-Kira, C. (2004). *Autism spectrum disorders: The complete guide.* New York, NY: Perigee.
8. Barkley, R. A. (2003). Issues in the diagnosis of attention-deficit/hyperactivity disorder in children. *Brain and Development, 25*(2), 77–83.
9. Bush, G., Valera, E. M., & Seidman, L. J. (2005). Functional neuroimaging of attention-deficit/hyperactivity disorder: A review and suggested future directions. *Biological Psychiatry, 57*(11), 1273–1284.
10. Barkley, R. A. (2005). *Attention-deficit hyperactivity disorder: A handbook for diagnosis and treatment* (3rd ed.). New York, NY: Guilford.
11. Quay, H. C., & Hogan, A. E. (1999). *Handbook of disruptive behavior disorders.* New York, NY: Kluwer Academic.
12. Cline, F., & Fay, J. (2006). *Parenting with love and logic* (Updated and expanded ed.). Colorado Springs, CO: NavPress.
13. Burke, J. D., Loeber, R., & Birmaher, B. (2004). Oppositional defiant disorder and conduct disorder: A review of the past 10 years, part II. *Focus, 2*(4), 558–576.
14. Millar, H. R., Wardell, F., Vyvyan, J. P., Naji, S. A., Prescott, G. J., & Eagles, J. M. (2005). Anorexia nervosa mortality in northeast Scotland, 1965–1999. *American Journal of Psychiatry, 162*(4), 753–757.
15. Child Welfare Information Gateway. (2012). *Clergy as mandatory reporters of child abuse and neglect.* Washington, DC: U.S. Department of Health and Human Services, Children's Bureau.
16. Belsky, J. (1993). Etiology of child maltreatment: A developmental-ecological analysis. *Psychological Bulletin, 114*(3), 413–434.
17. Tjaden, P., & Thoennes, N. (2000). *Full report of the prevalence, incidence, and consequences of violence against women: Findings from the National Violence Against Women Survey.* Washington, DC: U.S. Department of Justice.
18. Holtzworth-Munroe, A. (1995, August). Marital violence. *The Harvard Mental Health Letter, 12*(2), 4.

7   Ministerial Triage

Pastoral Care and the Art of Referral

Howard Clinebell, a luminary in the field of pastoral care, reflected that, "whenever you look at a group of people, remember that many of them have heavy hearts and that they are walking through shadowed valleys . . . such burdened people often trust the entire fabric of their lives to the caregiving skills of religious leaders."[1] Ministers are frequently the first professionals that suffering parishioners will allow into their private lives.

With more than a quarter of a million religious congregations in the United States alone, clergy will inevitably become de facto providers of mental health counseling in the context of pastoral care.[2] Both clergy and religious communities provide a sense of context, support, and continuity for psychologically disordered parishioners before, during, and after professional mental health care. Ministers must be attuned to the mental health of parishioners and willing to engage, listen, and provide support and direction when problems arise. With appropriate education and supervision in basic helping skills, parish clergy, institutional chaplains, and well-trained laity might prove eminently important, even instrumental, in providing first-line care to parishioners emotionally overwhelmed by the vicissitudes of life or swamped by a serious mental disorder. As frontline professionals, ministers must evidence basic helping competencies such as active listening, eliciting essential problems and symptoms, communicating empathy and positive regard, facilitating expression of feelings, respecting confidentiality, collaboratively evaluating and strategizing, and most important for the purposes of this chapter, making appropriate referrals to mental health professionals (MHPs) when this is indicated.[1]

Ministerial Triage and the Art of Referring

Wayne Oates once reflected on a key reason why so many pastors become burned out and why so many parishioners may not get the mental health care they require: "One of the reasons that pastors do not have time to do their pastoral ministry is that they insist on doing it all themselves . . . They have failed to build a detailed knowledge of their community as to the agencies, professional and private practitioners, etc., who could help them in their task."[3] Because seminaries have only recently started to consistently teach professional pastoral skills, and because there may be only one or two courses in the curriculum bearing on pastoral counseling,[4] it is imperative that ministers honor the real limits imposed by their time, training, and competence in the arena of mental health care. Because a wise and well-timed referral may be one of the most significant caregiving services a minister can offer suffering persons and their families,[1] we encourage readers of this guide to both give themselves permission to refer and to practice the art of working collaboratively with several trusted MHPs in the community.

Because the church and various ministries will often be the "point of entry" to mental health services, we encourage ministers to consider their first encounters with suffering parishioners as a form of *triage,* a process of assessing and categorizing the urgency of mental health problems. We hope that the chapters in this guide on common psychological disorders and treatments might prove useful in making these initial and informal assessments. Here are some key questions to consider in the context of your interactions with a parishioner who appears to be struggling with a mental health issue:

- What is the nature of the problem and how severe does it appear to be?
- Is the person an immediate risk to themselves or others?
- Is the person able to reasonably engage in self-care and make good decisions?
- What sort of mental health care—if any—would best meet the needs of the parishioner?
- How urgent is the need for a referral to an MHP?

Answers to these questions will be useful in determining whether pastoral care alone might be adequate or whether the problem severity, the parishioner's impairment, and the time constraints on the part of the minister suggest that a referral is indicated.

Selecting a Mental Health Professional

In Chapter 2, we encouraged ministers to intentionally develop a list of reliable and collaborative MHPs to whom they might refer parishioners for a variety of psychological issues (e.g., depression, anxiety, relationship conflict, substance abuse) and treatment needs (e.g., individual psychotherapy, family counseling, marital therapy, psychiatric medication). Collaborative engagement between clergy and MHPs is defined by the following qualities:[5]

- *Relationship:* They take time to get to know each other, developing a relationship over time.
- *Common goals:* They have similar goals for the person(s) they are serving.
- *Communication:* They keep each other informed about the parishioner within the bounds of confidentiality.
- *Trust:* They are careful not to undermine the other.
- *Respect:* They demonstrate genuine respect for each other.
- *Complementary expertise:* They appreciate the services the other person was trained to offer.
- *Common values:* They hold similar values and respect differences when these are evident.
- *Awareness of spirituality:* The MHP is aware of spiritual and religious dimensions of life and affirm these in the context of mental health care.

Finding a few competent MHPs who are both respectful and good at communicating with a client's referral source—when a parishioner welcomes such communication—is an important first step to building a constellation or network of collaborative MHP working relationships.

For many ministers, especially those with limited training in counseling, the task of selecting a MHP for parishioners can be daunting. In cities of even modest size, the phone books are often filled with a range of individuals advertising themselves as people helpers of one kind or another. A wide range of titles, credentials, and specialties are typically highlighted. Sometimes, the ads strongly imply guarantees of help for nearly any psychological problem. How do you choose MHPs who are right for your parishioners? It is customary for MHPs of every sort to grant 30-minute complementary sessions to prospective referral sources. These sessions will allow you to gather important information about each provider's background (personal and professional), experience, qualifications, and specialization. It will also allow you to get a "sense" of providers, how skilled they seem to be, and how sensitive they appear regarding issues of faith. We believe getting to know MHPs on this more personal level is critical in helping you determine whether you would feel confident referring your church members to them. If a prospective MHP refuses such a complementary session, we recommend against including that provider on your referral list.

Types of Mental Health Professionals

In this section, we describe the different kinds of MHPs, including their training, general areas of expertise, and credentialing.

Clinical or Counseling Psychologist (PhD, PsyD)

Clinical and Counseling Psychologists are trained in psychology doctoral programs, which involve four to six years of education at the graduate level. The final year is devoted to a full-time supervised internship, preferably at a site approved by the American Psychological Association (APA). Psychologists receive extensive academic training in human development, personality, pathology, assessment, and treatment interventions. They also undergo a great deal of practical training with a range of clients and problems. Psychologists have expertise in assessment and treatment of disorders ranging from mild adjustment problems to very severe organic and psychotic disorders. Psychologists often work with severe behavioral and emotional problems and typically use a change-oriented approach in which behavior change is the primary goal.[6] They are qualified to administer psychological tests as part of their assessment of clients and use a range of behavioral strategies and counseling or psychotherapy approaches to resolve problems. They are considered expert witnesses in court.

Psychologists are required to be licensed in all 50 states and in most provinces and territories, and usually undergo written and oral examinations to become licensed. They are required to adhere to the APA ethics code and are subject to disciplinary procedures for unethical conduct. Maintenance of licensure typically requires ongoing education in the field. Psychologists do not prescribe medications in most states, and only licensed clinical and counseling psychologists are qualified to provide assessment and treatment services.

Psychiatrist (MD, DO)

Psychiatrists complete medical school to become physicians prior to completing a three-to-four-year residency in psychiatry. Following the residency, psychiatrists may become board certified in this specialty, and board certification is an important indication of competence to practice. Psychiatrists have extensive medical training and expertise in biologically and psychologically based disorders. They are able to prescribe psychiatric medications and, in fact, are known for frequently prescribing medication such as antidepressants to treat serious depression or antianxiety medications to treat severe anxiety. Psychiatrists often have admitting privileges at local hospitals and may facilitate a parishioner's inpatient hospitalization, if necessary, in the case of a serious psychiatric disorder. Also, some psychiatrists practice electroconvulsive therapy (ECT) for severe depression.

Psychiatrists may employ a great variety of interventions. Many psychiatrists rely rather exclusively on medications and may only meet with patients briefly to check on the success of certain medications and dosages. A smaller number of psychiatrists also practice talking therapies with clients and, in fact, may be quite skilled at this. It is imperative to know in advance whether a psychiatrist has much training in psychotherapy and, if so, whether he or she actually uses this training in practice. Psychiatrists may be designated as expert witnesses in court and are typically the most expensive mental health providers.

Social Worker (MSW)

Social workers complete a two-year master's degree in social work followed by a year of full-time postgraduate supervised experience. These practitioners receive training in the diagnosis and treatment of individual and family problems, social work techniques, and focused skills in linking people with community resources. Many states allow social workers to become licensed clinical social workers (LCSW), and this should be an important selection criterion in those states. LCSW may collect third-party reimbursement similar to psychologists and psychiatrists. About 50 percent of social workers have been admitted to the Academy of Clinical Social Workers (ACSW). Social workers have clear expertise at troubleshooting complex system problems and linking clients to services in the community. Many of them are also quite skilled in the practice of therapy for various problems.

Counselors and Marriage and Family Therapists (MA, MEd, MFCC)

Counselors and Marriage and Family Therapists typically have a BA and two to three years of graduate training in counseling, psychology, marriage and family therapy, or pastoral counseling. These degrees may be offered in secular universities or religious colleges and seminaries. The academic requirements of such degree programs vary widely, and it is possible that such practitioners have a great deal of supervised clinical experience or nearly none at all. Counselors are generally trained to help with areas such as careers, adjustment issues, relationships, or general mental health difficulties. Marriage and family therapists are especially well trained for management of relationship problems. They neither have extensive training in diagnosis and treatment of more serious disorders, nor are they qualified to administer or interpret psychological tests, or prescribe medications. The primary concern with this category of MHPs is the wide variability in training and expertise.

Most states and provinces allow for registration or licensure of *professional counselors* or *mental health counselors*. Certification indicates that, in addition to an appropriate graduate degree, the counselor has accumulated a specified number of hours of supervised practice and has passed a written state board exam. Licensed professional counselors (LPCs), and sometimes marriage and family therapists (MFTs), can receive direct third-party reimbursement for services rendered; however, this varies widely across states. Most counselors belong to national organizations such as the American Counseling Association (ACA), the American Association for Marriage and Family Therapy (AAMFT), the National Board for Certified Counselors (NBCC), and the American Association of Pastoral Counselors (AAPC).

Values and Faith Commitment

In the same way that you would be cautious about placing a parishioner with emotional problems in the hands of someone who is inexperienced or ineffective, it is unlikely that you would send him or her to a therapist who is openly or subtly antagonistic toward the parishioner's religious faith and values. Although licensure or certification indicate that the MHP has passed certain educational and training milestones, and (probably) does not have obvious character defects, it does not ensure that the therapist will be either effective or respectful of the client's faith and values. In fact, many MHPs have been historically antireligious in their practices and some of them work to convince clients that religious beliefs are highly correlated with mental illness. Because the process of therapeutic change is often painful and threatening to a client, it is essential that the pastor match the parishioner with an MHP who will be both effective and respectful of the client's faith. There is evidence that if a client has very different values from his or her therapist, then therapy may not be productive.[7]

Research shows that, during the course of counseling, a client's personal values (including those related to faith) are likely to change in the direction of the counselor's. This means that effective therapy often involves some adoption or acceptance of the counselor's values. For this reason, we recommend considerable care in selecting MHPs who will at least be very sensitive to and respectful of Christian beliefs and values. Better yet, you may find MHPs who are explicitly Christian in their own lives and who will not only honor but actively promote a client's faith-based lifestyle and find ways to use the client's faith to overcome difficulties. During your interview with a prospective MHP, we highly recommend asking some very direct questions about the practitioner's own religious beliefs, the extent to which he or she feels comfortable working with religious clients, and the manner in which he or she might respond to a few common problems that may have clear connections to the client's beliefs. For example, how would he or she typically respond to crises of faith or marital difficulties?

Experience and Specialties

As previously noted, having a graduate degree does not ensure that a particular provider will be competent to treat a specific mental health disorder or problem. For example, a psychiatrist may have tremendous expertise when it comes to managing serious psychotic and depressive disorders with elaborate combinations of psychotropic medication, yet know almost nothing about how to help couples with marital problems. A psychologist may have remarkable experience in treating adults with a range of problems, yet may never have worked with a child client. A newly minted counseling program graduate may have far less experience than you, the pastor, in providing counseling for the specific problem that you may want to refer to him or her.

The point here is that, as a referral source, it is important for you to glean information about each MHP's actual experience in the field. How much practical training has each had? To what degree is he or she competent to work with adults, children, couples, and families? Would he or she prefer not to work with specific groups of people or types of problems? Does he or she have focused expertise in working with certain problems or kinds of clients? If so, is this expertise recognized by others in the field or other pastors who routinely refer parishioners to him or her? In our experience, MHPs who are the most "expert" and competent are those who are open and clear about areas in which they are not competent to practice. They frequently set limits and recommend other providers when asked to practice outside their areas of competence. Furthermore, when asked about these relative weaknesses in preparation or preference, they are nondefensive. Be wary if an MHP suggests to you that he or she can work equally well with almost any kind of client and any sort of difficulty.

Personal Traits

Is this person kind, competent, and fun to be around? This may sound like an odd question, but we take it seriously when it comes to evaluating individuals who are likely to be helpful or "therapeutic" to those they serve. MHPs can have remarkable IQs, top-notch academic credentials, and advanced specialties in several areas, yet be utterly unhelpful. If they lack excellent interpersonal skills, be suspicious. In our experience, the best therapists are those with great training, extensive experience, and a "knack" for knowing how to convey warmth, unconditional regard, and kindness to clients. Excellent therapists are personable. They often have a wonderful sense of humor, yet know when to use this without offending their clients. They are gentle, yet willing to set boundaries and clearly confront clients when needed. Their clients look forward to seeing them, and feel genuinely cared for and respected by them regardless of the problem(s) with which they present. In essence, we are recommending that you seek out men and women who are interpersonally gifted and obviously healthy. How *you* feel when you interact with them may be a strong indicator of how your parishioners will feel.

Other Details

It is important, in your assessment of a prospective MHP, to inquire about his or her fee structure and approach to handling finances with clients. For instance, it is helpful to know if insurance is accepted, what the provider's standard hourly fee is, and whether the provider employs a sliding scale to assist clients with few financial resources. Additionally, it would be helpful to know if the provider ever sees clients "pro bono" (without charge). Psychologists, for example, are encouraged by their ethical code to provide some service without charge to those in need.

Another important issue concerns the extent to which an MHP is comfortable working with you, the minister, in helping parishioners. Specifically, if your parishioner signs an appropriate release of information and prefers to have you speak to his or her MHP, is the provider open to this sort of liaison work? Of course, it is important that both you and the MHP minimize unnecessary violations of the parishioner's privacy, but sometimes coordinating counseling or other services will substantially benefit the parishioner. For example, following an inpatient period of treatment for alcohol dependency, a parishioner may continue in outpatient substance abuse therapy and come to see you to address spiritual and/or marital concerns. If requested by the parishioner, is the provider willing to discuss the treatment with you and recommend certain topics or approaches? We think a good provider should be willing to do this.

Although it is important to respect the MHP's right to privacy, it may be important in some cases to ask more detailed questions about his or her beliefs or practices related to certain kinds of clients or client problems. For example, how does the professional typically work with issues such as marital discord, parent–child conflict, and sexual relationships outside of marriage?

Notes

1. Clinebell, H. (2011). *Basic types of pastoral care and counseling* (Rev. ed.). Nashville, TN: Abingdon Press.
2. Milstein, G., Manierre, A., Susman, V. L., & Bruce, M. L. (2008). Implementation of a program to improve the continuity of mental health care through clergy outreach and professional engagement (C.O.P.E.). *Professional Psychology: Research and Practice, 39*(2), 218–228.
3. Oates, W. E. (1974). *Protestant pastoral counseling.* Philadelphia, PA: Westminster Press.
4. Roberts, S. B. (Ed.). (2012). *Professional spiritual and pastoral care: A practical clergy and chaplain's handbook.* Woodstock, VT: SkyLight Paths Publishing.
5. McMinn, M. R., Aikins, D. C., & Lish, R. A. (2003). Basic and advanced competence in collaborating with clergy. *Professional Psychology: Research and Practice, 34*(2), 197–202.
6. Barlow, D. H. (2007). *Clinical handbook of psychological disorders: A step-by-step treatment manual* (4th ed.). New York, NY: Guilford.
7. Smith, E. W. L. (2003). *The person of the therapist.* Jefferson, NC: McFarland.

8   Ethical Guidelines: What to Expect From Mental Health Professionals

What should I expect from the mental health professionals (MHPs) to whom I refer parishioners? Should they tell me anything I want to know about the case? Is it normal for a professional to insist that he or she can treat any mental health problem with 100 percent success? Should I be concerned to hear that a parishioner has been seeing her therapist "socially"? Is it OK for a counselor to recommend that his or her clients use Benadryl to help them sleep at night? Each of these questions raises important issues regarding professional behavior and adherence to ethical principles. As a minister who refers parishioners to MHPs, you have a vested interest in ensuring that the MHPs with whom you do business are personally healthy and adhere to the highest standards of their profession—including the code of ethics relevant to their professional group. Although it is also ideal to find a practitioner who is theologically competent and spiritually mature, this may not be feasible in many small communities.

In this chapter, we briefly outline the major ethical guidelines common to all major mental health practitioner groups. These groups include psychiatrists, psychologists, social workers, counselors, and pastoral counselors; each professional association adheres to a clearly articulated set of ethical guidelines or standards.[1-7] We first discuss the basics of ethics and differentiate moral from ethical standards. We then describe six essential ethical standards, which you should be aware of when your parishioners are referred to an MHP.

For each standard, we give both an unethical and ethical version of the same case example. We then describe the standards and discuss indicators that an MHP is not practicing within the ethical standard. Finally, we recommend an approach you may use in responding to concerns of unethical conduct on the part of MHPs. Although we hope this will be a rare occurrence, we provide contact information for the ethics boards of all the major MHP organizations, should it become necessary for you or a parishioner to file an ethics complaint.

An Ethics Primer

Most ministers will not, and some would say *should* not, devote a great deal of their time to pastoral counseling.[8] Unless counseling is the minister's specific assignment and the minister has specific professional training in mental health and counseling skills, most would be wise to set firm limits on the frequency and intensity of formal counseling relationships with parishioners—particularly those with indications of serious psychiatric symptoms (see Chapters 3 through 6). Most pastors will want to refer their parishioners to MHPs who can provide specialized and effective treatments and who will (we hope) collaborate effectively with clergy. In Chapter 7, we suggested that pastors should be accountable for referring their troubled parishioners to other professionals and be knowledgeable about when, and to whom, a parishioner should be referred. This requires some effort on the part of the pastor or pastoral staff to become familiar with local MHPs and assess the extent to which these professionals appear competent, caring, respectful of parishioners' faith concerns, and willing to work in tandem with the pastor, particularly when this is the parishioner's wish.

Once a referral to an MHP has been made, the minister can usually assume that the practitioner will care for the parishioner competently and ethically. However, MHPs, like other human beings, will make errors or simply not be competent to provide the needed service. In this section, we briefly describe the notion of professional ethical codes and why they exist. This provides the foundation for our discussion of the major ethical principles shared by all mental health professions.

Ethics codes for MHPs exist for one primary reason—to protect the welfare of the clients these practitioners serve. When it appears that a parishioner has been harmed by an MHP, it is reasonable to ask the question, "Was the professional's decision or behavior really in the parishioner's best interest?" Ethics codes are rooted in moral principles and adapted by groups as rules for right or "correct" conduct. While moral principles provide a broader standard or context than ethics, they are often hard to translate to specific situations or professional dilemmas.

Most ethical codes have several fundamental moral principles. Kitchener identified four essential moral principles, which she believes provide the backdrop for nearly all ethics codes and a reasonable starting place in making ethical/moral decisions about how best to care for clients.[9] These principles are (1) *autonomy*—the promotion of self-determination or the freedom of clients to choose their own direction, (2) *beneficence*—promoting the good of others, (3) *nonmaleficence*—avoiding doing harm, including refraining from actions that risk hurting clients, and (4) *justice*—fairness, or providing equal treatment to all people. These attitudes are fundamental to appropriate and sound ethical decisions in clinical practice.

It is reasonable to think of ethics codes as *necessary, but not sufficient* guidelines for ethical practice, for the reason that ethical codes are not explicit enough to deal with every situation the practitioner might face. Further, it is often difficult to interpret ethical codes, and people differ over how to apply them in specific cases.[10] For example, psychiatrists and psychologists in the state of Oregon may struggle with how to ethically respond to the *Death with Dignity Act* passed by Oregon voters in 1994, that requires mental health evaluations of terminally-ill patients who legally elect to terminate their own lives. As you might expect, there is tremendous disagreement among professionals regarding the "most" ethical and moral response to this new law.

Although ethical standards are clearly needed, they are also often reactive—responding to violations that have occurred instead of seeking to prevent or anticipate future difficulties. Also, ethical standards may at times conflict with legal requirements or other regulations. For example, MHPs working with military personnel may be required to violate the client's confidentiality if the commanding officer believes there is a "need to know" about the service member's treatment.

Even though the better training programs carefully screen those who graduate at both the application and training stages, other programs do very little screening—resulting in a steady stream of poorly suited or personally troubled practitioners into the marketplace. Also, some MHPs may have excellent intentions and strong moral convictions, yet at times might be exhausted, burned out, or poorly suited for clinical work. MHPs may themselves lead unhealthy lives, have very disturbed relationships, and have no intention of following the very advice they deliver daily to their clients. Others may become burned out or overwhelmed as a direct result of their work. If they do not have the self-awareness and support needed to address these problems, the problems may worsen and negatively impact their professionalism. For all of these reasons, it is essential that the minister get to know the practitioners to whom he or she refers parishioners. What have other parishioners and clergy said about their professional and personal conduct? Are they involved in continuing education, consultation, and professional organizations? We raise these concerns to alert clergy to the fact that practitioners are human, and that there is often a wide range of competence and professional conduct among MHPs.

It is important for the pastor to keep in mind that the vast majority of MHPs to whom he or she might refer parishioners will be highly responsible and ethical. When ethical violations do occur, it is often because the specific situation was novel or unexpected, because of competing demands between ethical guidelines and other requirements, or because of a simple lack of awareness or experience on the part of the practitioner. Yet even if the root of the problem is benign or innocent, these practitioners are still responsible for the outcome of their services and the extent to which their behavior is in the best interest of their clients. Thankfully, malignant and irresponsible MHPs are clearly the small minority.

Ethical Standards

Multiple Relationships (Boundaries)

Unethical. Helen is a 49-year-old parishioner who has become increasingly depressed and "aimless" over the past several months. Aware of her depressive symptoms, you refer her to a psychiatrist who begins seeing her in weekly therapy sessions. Three months later, Helen reports back to you that she is "not sure what to do about my psychiatrist." You learn that they are now meeting twice a week and that the majority of each session is devoted to "sharing our problems with each other." She describes in great detail her psychiatrist's struggles with his own midlife depression, his job, and even his marriage. Although there is no physical side to their relationship, it is clear Helen has been placed in the role of a therapist, or at least a friend, to her therapist. Although she likes him, she is worried she "can't really help him."

Ethical. Dr. Jensen has been struggling with some symptoms of depression and some midlife concerns for about a year. Aware of these developments, he has been careful to monitor his feelings about clients and his standard of practice, particularly with clients he finds especially warm and nurturing. When he begins seeing Helen, he quickly becomes aware that she is bright, kind, and even "mothering" in some ways. He is tempted to disclose more to her than would be typical of his practice in general. He therefore consults with a colleague and describes the problem in detail. He decides he will be most helpful to Helen if he continues to monitor her antidepressant medication every other week while referring her to an excellent social worker colleague for ongoing counseling. He carefully explains to Helen that he believes this will be most helpful for her.

What to Expect

Good therapists have good boundaries. Specifically, they place careful boundaries around their professional roles with clients, recognizing that this is ultimately best for their clients. Ethics boards are asked to investigate countless cases of negative outcomes related to MHPs allowing their professional roles with clients to become blurred or mixed with social or business roles. The problem with engaging in more than one kind of relationship (role) with a client is that the client (and MHP) can become confused about the nature of the relationship, and the primary focus on helping the client with a specific problem almost always gets blurred. In general, MHPs know to avoid combining roles (e.g., therapist/teacher, therapist/relative, therapist/ social acquaintance, therapist/romantic partner, therapist/business partner). Imagine the potential damage to the client, and the therapy relationship, when he or she feels exploited by a therapist in a sexual or business relationship, or when a grade in a course taught by the therapist seems either too high or too low. In general, MHPs should avoid entering into any kind of relationship with a client, other than the therapy relationship.[11]

MHPs who attend the same church as the parishioner are at risk for unintended multiple relationships that can potentially harm the client. Although it may be impossible to avoid all multiple roles with clients, especially in small communities, keep in mind that parishioners usually feel most "safe" and that their concerns are most confidential when they have no contact with their therapists outside of the therapy hour. In the church, there is danger of inadvertent violation of the parishioner's confidence or of being placed in a situation (committee or social gathering) with a parishioner that makes him or her uncomfortable. Therefore, we almost always recommend that ministers have a list of good MHPs who do not attend their churches.

It is important to offer a few words about sexual involvement with clients. It is *always* wrong. In no case will sexual involvement with a client ever be acceptable professional behavior, and such relationships nearly always lead to harmful outcomes for clients (e.g., depression, substance abuse, other forms of emotional disturbance).[11–12] Sexual relationships with therapy clients are the leading cause of malpractice suits against MHPs, and most insurance companies now limit the coverage for this class of ethical violation. In addition to malpractice suits, therapists engaging in these relationships are likely to lose their professional licenses, their jobs, and their insurance coverage, and in some states, they may be convicted of a felony.

Although sexual involvement with clients is always wrong, sexual attraction to clients is likely to occur at times. Good MHPs are aware of their responses to clients and are careful to guard against becoming romantically and sexually involved. They seek consultation from peers in the field and refer clients to other providers when this appears wise. Good MHPs also avoid even subtle forms of sexual harassment or exploitation. For example, they do not request or encourage disclosure of material in therapy that is not directly related to the problem at hand.

As a minister, you should be alert to reports from parishioners of blurred boundaries and inappropriate roles with their MHPs. Although a client may occasionally hug his or her therapist, especially during a final session, physical contact should not be a frequent component of a therapy relationship. Social and business relationships are nearly always wrong. In general, be suspicious of any MHP who attempts to engage the parishioner in anything but a professional relationship focused on the parishioner's primary symptom or complaint.

Competence

Unethical. You learn that a member of your congregation, Tim, has been having considerable back pain lately (probably because of his construction job). He says he has already been to a doctor and that he has only been given "pain killers." You decide to refer Tim to a local psychologist who may be able to help with pain management. Six months later, Tim is dead as a result of a large tumor on his spine (the source of his pain). Unfortunately, the psychologist had very little experience or training in pain management and had attempted to treat the pain symptoms without recognizing the potential signs of a tumor. He had not ensured that Tim had a complete physical exam. It turns out that Tim had never seen his physician, but had received some prescriptions over the phone.

Ethical. Dr. Phillips receives a "pain management" referral from a local pastor. He recognizes immediately that he has not had either the training or practice experience necessary to treat pain patients without supervision. He informs the pastor that he would prefer to have the parishioner see a colleague of his with expertise in pain management and whom he trusts to do excellent work. Dr. Phillips provides the referral information to the pastor and then calls his colleague and explains the nature of the referral—emphasizing that the parishioner is devout in his faith and may find treatments that integrates his faith with pain reduction (e.g., contemplative meditation) techniques to be especially useful.

What to Expect

State boards and professional organizations offer licensure and certification of MHPs. This assures the public that practitioners have completed the minimum number of hours of supervised training and have gone through evaluation or screening to ensure minimum competence.[10] However, these bodies do not ensure that MHPs will competently *do* what their credentials permit them to do.

Ministers typically refer parishioners to various MHPs precisely because they recognize the boundaries of their own competence to treat mental disorders. In a similar fashion, they will want to refer to MHPs who recognize the limits of their own competence and are ready to refer if they lack the expertise to help particular parishioners or those with specific kinds of problems. Ideally, MHPs provide the services and use techniques *only* for which they are qualified by training and experience.[11] Not only are they cognizant of their limitations, but they pursue additional education, experience, professional consultation, and spiritual growth in order to improve their effectiveness in serving people in need.[13]

As a minister, we recommend that you look for MHPs who sometimes respond to your referrals by saying, "I'm not prepared to treat that sort of problem, but let me give you a couple of names of people I'd recommend." Truly competent professionals accept client populations and problem types only for which they are qualified. Before practicing in a new treatment area, they seek additional training and experience. Competent MHPs do not imply that they have qualifications, experiences, or capabilities that they do not.[12] When it seems to you that a professional suggests that he or she is equally "expert" in treating a wide variety of problems, be cautious. Finally, competent MHPs routinely seek peer support and peer review. This means that they have a strong professional network (much like wise pastors who network and seek support from their colleagues); they are willing to remain accountable and seek consultation from other experts when this is indicated.

Confidentiality

Unethical. Concerned that Rashad, a parishioner whom you referred to a pastoral counselor, is looking increasingly sad and withdrawn, you call the counselor to report this change and ask if there is anything else you could do to help. The counselor thanks you for calling and then immediately begins telling you that Rashad has good reason to be "down," as he has been dealing with concerns about his sexual orientation in his counseling sessions. The counselor notes that she thinks Rashad may in fact be gay, but that she needs more time to discern this. You feel startled that this information was disclosed by the counselor so quickly, given that Rashad is a very private person. It is unlikely that Rashad would have signed a release allowing his therapist to discuss his case with you.

Ethical. Nina Brown, a certified pastoral counselor, receives a phone call from the pastor who recently referred a new client to her. He notes that the client has appeared more depressed lately, and he is concerned. Ms. Brown thanks the pastor for calling and for referring Rashad to her. She acknowledges that ongoing support from the pastor is likely to be very helpful to Rashad. She kindly thanks him for the referral, but also informs the pastor she is unable to discuss any client information unless that client is willing to sign a formal release of information allowing her to legally and ethically do so. She promises to mention this to Rashad when he comes to see her and reminds the pastor that he can also discuss this with Rashad.

What to Expect

Client *confidentiality* may be the closest thing to "sacred" among all types of MHPs. Confidentiality refers to an ethical—and usually legal— responsibility of MHPs to safeguard clients from unauthorized disclosure of information provided in the therapy relationship. With a few exceptions (discussed later), information revealed by clients in the context of treatment must not be disclosed. In general, there will rarely be cause for the MHP working with one of your parishioners to violate the principle of confidentiality and disclose private information. If an MHP does violate a client's confidence (and the reason is not one of those covered in the following list), you should avoid referring your parishioners to that person in the future.

Confidentiality is closely linked to two additional terms that are distinct, but related.[10,12] *Privileged communication* is a legal concept referring to a client's right to prevent legal testimony (on the part of the MHP) in court proceedings. Most state statutes clearly identify communication between a therapist and client as privileged, and this communication is therefore protected from disclosure in legal settings. *Privacy* is a basic freedom (constitutionally protected) that allows clients to decide when and where they wish to have their beliefs, behavior, and opinions shared or withheld from others. In general, MHPs should work hard to protect the privacy of their clients by making sure that privileged communication protections and the ethical mandate for confidentiality are both honored. In addition, MHPs protect privacy by requesting only that information from the client that is germane to the problem and by documenting only that information that is relevant to treatment. For example, disclosures made by a client about his or her love life should probably not be included in the client record unless they are directly related to the client's disorder and treatment.

When may an MHP violate a client's confidentiality? Ethical guidelines and state laws usually require or allow MHPs to violate a client's confidence by disclosing information obtained during treatment under the following circumstances:

1. When the client is a clear risk to himself or herself (acutely suicidal) or clearly a risk to others (homicidal).
2. When the client is so disturbed that he or she cannot care for himself or herself—such as in the case of psychosis or head injury.
3. When the client has abused a child or elderly person, or if a minor or elderly client has been abused.
4. When the client takes legal or ethical action against the therapist, the record may be disclosed as part of the therapist's defense.
5. When a legitimate court order compels the MHP to release the record.

All exceptions to confidentiality must be fully disclosed to clients before they begin treatment. This is known as *informed consent* and is discussed in the next section. Keep in mind that these circumstances are relatively rare and that in the vast majority of cases, an MHP would violate a client's confidence only in order to keep him or her alive or to protect the immediate well-being and safety of others who could be harmed by the client.

We highly recommend that you seek out MHPs who are extremely cautious when it comes to protecting the confidentiality of their clients. If an MHP discusses a client before obtaining a signed release from the client, or e-mails you copies of the client's evaluations or record, you have reason to be concerned. Although it is admittedly difficult to maintain confidentiality in small communities, including churches, we believe confidentiality is the cornerstone of good mental health treatment. It is true that the minister can often serve as an important part of the overall treatment plan for parishioners undergoing therapy; however, it is not appropriate for a pastor to hound his or her clients into signing releases to speak with MHPs. We recommend simply letting parishioners know, preferably at the time of referral, that you will be available to assist in any way—including talking with parishioners' therapists if they feel that would be useful. Parishioners can then decide whether to involve the pastor in this way.

Informed Consent

Unethical. A 25-year-old parishioner whom you have referred to a psychiatrist for assistance with severe anxiety symptoms approaches you following Sunday services with a bewildered and concerned look on her face. She notes that she was able to see the psychiatrist only for 15 minutes because of his busy schedule. She pulls a bottle of antianxiety medication from her purse and states that the pills have helped her feel less anxious, but that they make her very drowsy. She is alarmed by some physical sensations that have occurred since starting the medicine. She is not even sure what the medicine is, how it works, or what the side effects are. When you ask what else the treatment might entail, how long it might last, or whether she can contact her psychiatrist on an emergency basis to report the side effects, she is unsure and states that none of these things were addressed in the short first session.

Ethical. Dr. Reed Smith has a busy psychiatry practice and particularly enjoys consulting with clergy. He receives a call from a woman who has been referred for assistance with worsening anxiety symptoms. Given that he has only a 15-minute time slot available in the next two days, he offers to refer her to another provider. She insists she is "OK" waiting and schedules a regular 50-minute intake appointment for three days from now. During the initial session, Dr. Smith does a careful assessment of her physical and psychological functioning. He also provides her with an informed consent form that lists all the parameters of treatment, emergency procedures, limits on confidentiality, and financial information. He discusses each of these issues with her and then describes the treatment options available for her anxiety disorder, including medication. He describes the pros and cons of talking therapy and medication, and the client agrees to try both. He recommends an antianxiety medication and carefully reviews all of the possible side effects with her.

What to Expect

Informed consent refers to a client's right to be informed about the therapy that he or she is to receive and to make independent decisions about it.[10] In order to become active participants in their own mental health treatments, it is critical that parishioners are treated by competent professionals who recognize and honor clients' needs for information about therapy and therapy options. At the most basic level, clients have a right to decide whether to even enter treatment. To make this decision, they must be clearly informed about the treatment options including risks and benefits. When MHPs fail to adequately inform clients about the services they provide, there are two possible legal complications: (1) breach of contract, and (2) negligence or malpractice.

When a minister refers a parishioner to an MHP, it is reasonable to expect that person to come away from the very first session with a basic understanding of the following:

1. Treatment alternatives for his or her specific problem or disorder.
2. Risks and benefits associated with each of the treatment options.
3. The MHP's qualifications.

4. Financial issues (including billing, bill collection agencies, and fees).
5. Emergency procedures and any anticipated treatment interruptions.
6. Limits on confidentiality.
7. What services the MHP will provide, and what is expected of the client.
8. The anticipated length of treatment.
9. Willingness of the MHP to collaborate with clergy if this is requested by the client.

Informed consent is a critical component of competent mental health treatment. Look for MHPs who are careful about providing parishioners with all the information they need to make good decisions about their own treatments without overwhelming them with irrelevant details. It is imperative that parishioners have the capacity to fully understand what MHPs are conveying to them about treatments. In cases where the client is a child or an adult who is psychotic, a legal guardian is often able to provide the informed consent required for mental health care. In the same way that one would want to carefully understand an elective surgery, a parishioner is often most comfortable (and successful) in mental health treatment when he or she actively participates in making decisions about the type and direction of treatment.

Advertising

Unethical. You receive a flyer from Todd Noonan, a new social worker in town. The flyer is a large multicolored advertisement for this man's private practice, which states in emphatic tones that Mr. Noonan has a specialty in treating codependence. In fact, he has developed a biblically based "anticodependence therapy," which he claims is guaranteed to help the 50 to 75 percent of American people who are codependent. His brochure offers several testimonials from actual clients (one of whom attends your church) who claim their lives were radically changed for the better thanks to therapy with Mr. Noonan. The flyer also hints that failing to have this therapy is all but certain to lead to suffering and discontent compared with the "abundant happiness" available after anticodependence therapy. Mr. Noonan phones you later in the week and asks if he can announce his new services from the pulpit the following Sunday.

Ethical. A new social worker in the community contacts you to let you know that he is beginning a practice and that he prefers to work with Christian clients when possible. He is interested in meeting with you sometime to discuss his background, special interests, and to explore any specific needs the church might have that he might be able to address. He notes having a special interest in working with dependent clients and clarifies that he means those stuck in unhealthy relational patterns.

What to Expect

Good MHPs are careful to avoid any public statement or advertisement that contains false or deceptive statements.[12] They are very concerned about not misleading or misinforming their clients or the public. Any advertisement or promotion of their practice is tasteful and appropriate. It may include brief information about their credentials, training backgrounds, institutional affiliations, and the kinds of services they are competent to render. They may describe the kinds of clients or disorders with which they have particular expertise. Appropriate and professional advertising is not flashy or otherwise outlandish.

When you see evidence of the following in the promotional materials of MHPs, we recommend that you exercise caution about referring parishioners to them:

1. Promises of dramatic, though unsubstantiated, positive personal change.
2. Suggestions of "one of a kind" or unique therapeutic techniques or abilities.
3. Personal aggrandizement.
4. Overdiagnosis of problems (e.g., "Nearly everyone is at least a little codependent").
5. Creating fear as a way of generating business (e.g., "If you care about your adolescent, you'll call us today").
6. Use of client testimonials.

All of these techniques involve some misrepresentation or exploitation, and they raise concerns about the integrity and competence of the provider. Finally, we recommend that you watch out for MHPs who attempt to solicit potential clients in person. This is unethical according to most professional organizations[10–11,13] and, again, is a possible indicator that these MHPs are attempting to exploit vulnerable populations. In our experience, excellent MHPs are often the subdued and cautious in their efforts to promote their practices. They do not claim unique abilities, and they are clear about the limits of their competence.

Respect for Differences

Unethical. You have met with a couple regarding some marital problems. The husband, Daniel, is Jewish and occasionally attends services at a local synagogue, while his Christian spouse attends your church. During their meeting with you, Daniel acknowledges a considerable history of pornography use and compulsive sexual activity which, at times, interferes with his job and responsiveness to his wife. You refer him to a Christian psychologist who happens to specialize in sexual disorders. Two weeks later, Daniel comes to see you in a state of anger. He reports being very offended by the psychologist who, in the first session, insisted on praying with him and attempted to "convert" him to Christianity instead of focusing on his sexual problem. Daniel notes, "He read scriptures from the New Testament and suggested that placing myself under Christ's rule was probably 'just the medicine I needed.'"

Ethical. Dr. Hugh Lucas receives a referral from a local pastor. Dr. Lucas determines in the initial session that the client's primary objective is to curtail and eliminate his use of pornography. Dr. Lucas is a Christian and sensitive to the manner in which the client's religious background and belief may both contribute to his problem and serve as a potential aid to treatment. He asks the client to help him understand sexual concerns of this kind from the perspective of the Jewish faith and whether the rabbi or others connected with the synagogue might offer support. When the client expresses hesitancy to explore this further, Dr. Lucas reminds him that religious resources are simply one source of support. He moves on to outline a cognitive-behavioral approach to reducing the undesirable sexual behaviors and is careful to secure the client's full consent before proceeding.

What to Expect

Every MHP to whom you may refer parishioners will hold important personal values. Most professional organizations now recognize that it is neither possible nor desirable for MHPs to be "neutral" with respect to values. Instead, therapists should be aware of and clear about their own values and how these values influence their work with clients. Practitioners should be honest about their own value positions without attempting to coerce clients into modifying their own perspectives.

Although it would be ideal for ministers to find a range of MHPs who hold religious and moral values similar to their own and those of the majority of parishioners, this may be difficult in some communities with limited numbers of MHPs. When the minister cannot find same-faith practitioners in his or her community, we recommend looking for MHPs who are congruent and honest about what they believe, evidence sincere respect for clients' religious values, and express concern about minimizing the influence of their own values on clients. Excellent MHPs, whether religious, are interested in using the client's own values and beliefs to enhance the counseling process and strengthen the client's faith.

When an MHP holds moral or religious values that differ from a client's, he or she should be willing to refer when the value differences lead to any of the following conditions: (1) the MHP is uncomfortable working with the client, (2) the boundaries of the MHP's competence are reached in addressing moral/religious issues, (3) the MHP is unable to remain objective, or (4) the MHP has grave concerns about imposing his or her values on the client.[14] In a nutshell, competent MHPs need not have experienced everything their clients have experienced, or believe or value all that the client does. It is essential, however, that MHPs be cognizant of their own values, sensitive to the differences between themselves and their clients, and willing to refer them to MHPs with more congruent values when this both feasible and likely to be helpful.

A Strategy for Responding to Unethical MHP Behavior

As a minister, you may be among the first to learn of problematic or clearly unethical behavior on the part of an MHP in the community. We recommend two distinct strategies for responding to this information—depending on how you become aware of it. Unethical MHP behavior described to you by a parishioner/client calls for a very different response than unethical behavior that comes to your attention via other avenues, including your direct experience with the MHP.

Most commonly, a minister will hear directly from a parishioner that he or she has concerns or questions about a particular MHP's professionalism or conduct. The minister must remember that respecting the parishioner's right to privacy and confidentiality are paramount concerns and that, in these cases, it is critical to explore the parishioner's concerns while refraining from taking any action independent of the parishioner. In most cases, licensing boards and ethics committees refuse to pursue complaints regarding client care that are not filed directly by the client. When a parishioner discloses ethical concerns about an MHP to you, we recommend the following strategy for responding:

1. Assure the parishioner that you will not violate his or her confidence.
2. Listen carefully to the concerns or questions about the MHP's behavior.
3. Inform the parishioner of your concerns and the nature of any apparent ethical violations. For example, "It sounds like your therapist has had trouble keeping your relationship strictly professional and that she has allowed a multiple relationship to develop. Let me tell you why multiple relationships are a concern . . ."

4. Describe the range of possible responses available to the parishioner. These include no response, discussion of the concerns with the MHP, termination of the relationship, and, in more serious cases, making a formal complaint to a licensing or ethics board.
5. Provide support and any necessary assistance as the parishioner pursues one or more of these options. This may include providing organizational contact information listed at the end of this chapter.
6. If you have good reason to believe that the concerns expressed are valid, you may elect to cease referring parishioners to this MHP. In cases where the parishioner gives you permission to do so, you may also explain to the MHP directly that you have reservations about making additional referrals. This seems to us to be the most Christ-like response to the MHP.

For those cases in which you, the minister, become aware of dubious or troubling MHP behavior without any disclosure by a parishioner or client of the MHP, we recommend a somewhat different approach. Essentially, the pastor has at least three options in such cases and they are not mutually exclusive because one or all of these options may be appropriate in a specific situation. First, you may simply elect to discontinue making referrals to the MHP. For example, a minister may learn from a colleague that a certain MHP often ridicules devout religious beliefs and practices. In such cases, it may simply be prudent not to make any referrals to this person. Second, you may elect to inform the MHP of your concerns in hopes of correcting or clarifying the initial impression or information regarding the MHP's behavior. In this case, the MHP may provide information that allays your concerns or may appear genuinely surprised by and concerned about his or her oversight or error, and express a clear willingness to correct it at once. Finally, there may be cases in which you elect to file a complaint against an MHP directly. In these cases, you may have attempted to discuss the issue collaboratively with the MHP with no receptivity on his or her part, or the nature of the unethical behavior may be so severe that the pastor feels the MHP's clients may be at significant risk. For example, when a pastor becomes aware that a local MHP routinely requires clients to stop attending church and describes all pastors as "psychotic," or when an MHP refuses to cease outlandish and unethical advertising to Christian clients in the community, the pastor may elect to file a formal ethics complaint with the MHP's state licensing board or primary professional organization.

The addresses and contact numbers listed at the conclusion of this chapter correspond to each of the major professional organizations covering the majority of MHPs. Although most of these organizations will have a formal ethics panel that reviews and investigates complaints, contacting the state licensing board may be more expeditious. Although we do not have space to list the various licensing boards for each state, these are generally available from the state's professional licensing division webpage. In cases where the state does not license a certain kind of MHP (e.g., some states do not license master's level counselors), then referring the complaint directly to the national organization is recommended. If a state or national board takes action against an MHP, this information will be shared with other professional boards and licensing agencies—meaning that the minister need not worry about making complaints to multiple bodies.

Contact Information for National Professional Organizations

American Association for Marriage and Family Therapy

112 South Alfred Street, Alexandria, VA 22314-3061 (703) 838-9808

American Association of Pastoral Counselors

9504-A Lee Highway, Fairfax, VA 22031-2303 (703) 385-6967

American Counseling Association

5999 Stevenson Avenue, Alexandria, VA 22304-3300 (800) 347-6647

American Psychiatric Association

1000 Wilson Boulevard, Suite 1825, Arlington, VA 22209-3901 (703) 907-7300

American Psychological Association

750 First Street NE, Washington, DC 20002-4242 (202) 336-5500

National Association of Social Workers

750 First Street NE, Suite 700, Washington, DC 20002-4241 (202) 408-8600

National Board of Certified Counselors

3 Terrace Way, Greensboro, NC 27403 (336) 547-0607

Notes

1. American Association for Counseling and Development. (1988). Ethical standards of the American Association for Counseling and Development (3rd rev.). *Journal of Counseling & Development, 67,* 4–8.
2. American Counseling Association. (2005). *ACA code of ethics.* Alexandria, VA: Author.
3. American Association for Marriage and Family Therapy. (2012). *AAMFT code of ethics.* Alexandria, VA: Author.
4. American Association of Pastoral Counselors. (2012). *AAPC code of ethics.* Fairfax, VA: Author.
5. American Psychological Association. (2010). *Ethical principles of psychologists and code of conduct.* Washington, DC: Author.
6. National Association of Social Workers. (2008). *Code of ethics of the National Association of Social Workers.* Washington, DC: Author.
7. American Psychiatric Association. (2013). *The principles of medical ethics with annotations especially applicable to psychiatry.* Arlington, VA: Author.
8. Blackburn, B. (2013). Pastors who counsel. In R. K. Sanders (Ed.), *Christian counseling ethics: A handbook for therapists, pastors and counselors* (2nd ed.; pp. 368–381). Downers Grove, IL: InterVarsity Press.
9. Kitchener, K. S. (1984). Intuition, critical evaluation and ethical principles: The foundation for ethical decisions in counseling psychology. *The Counseling Psychologist, 12*(3), 43–55.
10. Corey, G., Corey, M. S., & Callanan, P. (2010). *Issues and ethics in the helping professions* (8th ed.). Pacific Grove, CA: Cengage Learning.
11. Barnett, J. E., & Johnson, W. B. (2008). *Ethics desk reference for psychologists.* Washington, DC: American Psychological Association.
12. Johnson, W. B., & Ridley, C. R. (2008). *The elements of ethics for professionals.* New York, NY: Palgrave Macmillan.
13. Christian Association for Psychological Studies. (2005). *Statement of ethical guidelines.* New Braunfels, TX: Author.
14. Tjeltveit, A. C. (1986). The ethics of value conversion in psychotherapy: Appropriate and inappropriate therapist influence on client values. *Clinical Psychology Review, 6,* 515–537.

Index